T0192601

Oracle WebLogic Server 12c Administration I Exam 1Z0-133

A Comprehensive Certification Guide

Gustavo Garnica

Apress®

Oracle WebLogic Server 12c Administration I Exam 1Z0-133: A Comprehensive Certification Guide

Gustavo Garnica
San Jose, California, USA

ISBN-13 (pbk): 978-1-4842-2561-5
https://doi.org/10.1007/978-1-4842-2562-2

ISBN-13 (electronic): 978-1-4842-2562-2

Library of Congress Control Number: 2017962906

Cover image by Freepik (www.freepik.com)

Managing Director: Welmoed Spahr
Editorial Director: Todd Green
Acquisitions Editor: Susan McDermott
Development Editor: Laura Berendson
Technical Reviewer: Julian Ortiz Iregui
Coordinating Editor: Rita Fernando
Copy Editor: Karen Jameson

To my sweet wife Lety . . .
I love you, thank you for our awesome family.

Table of Contents

About the Author

Gustavo Garnica is an experienced Technical Architect and Consultant with over 15 years of international experience implementing and supporting IT infrastructure and operations processes in financial and telecommunications environments. He is a former BEA Systems and Oracle employee, and holds several cloud and enterprise software certifications, including Oracle WebLogic Server certified system administrator. He started developing software back in the Netscape days, and currently architects and operates enterprise software environments on cloud infrastructure.

About the Author

About the Technical Reviewer

 **Julian Ortiz Iregui** is a Cloud Solutions Architect at Oracle's Development Organization. He has extensive technical architecture experience in enterprise organizations running Oracle Fusion Middleware for mission-critical systems. Today, he currently focuses on cloud computing and infrastructure.

Acknowledgments

I think I may have made life a little harder for several people while authoring this book. First my family's. Sorry about keeping you waiting for so long; your love and patience will always be an unequivocal reminder that a book is not the product of authors alone.

I extend the same heartfelt gratitude to my editors Susan McDermott and Rita Fernando, to my technical reviewer Julian Ortiz, and also to those who I did not personally meet, but whose work for this book was essential nonetheless.

I wish I could also properly thank so many people with whom I worked over the years, and who I look up to. I sincerely expect you will not be disappointed in this work.

Lastly, to those in the same category but outside of the technical realm, you have influenced my life so much. Thank you.

Foreword

WebLogic is one the most successful and powerful enterprise application development platforms ever. Thousands of mission-critical applications serving some of the most demanding business computing workloads in the world depend on WebLogic. That is a fact that is unlikely to change any time soon.

Such a computing platform almost inevitably comes with complexities. The complexity in part comes from the wide number of deployments, rich history, and longevity that WebLogic boasts. The WebLogic team does what it can to manage these complexities – principally by making sure that the official WebLogic documentation is both comprehensive and up to date. As good as the official WebLogic documentation is, it has always lacked a certain personal touch and approachability. After all, what better way to learn WebLogic than from your own personal mentor, patiently showing you the ropes and sharing years of hard-earned personal experience in the field? This is equally true whether you are beginning to use WebLogic on the job or are seeking to certify yourself on WebLogic. If you have such a personal mentor around you, consider yourself very lucky. Chances are, however, that most of us that need to work with WebLogic in the real world do not have ready access to such a person. That is where this book and Gustavo Garnica come in.

Gustavo has years of in-depth knowledge and hands-on experience with WebLogic. Much of this knowledge and experience comes from being a part of the WebLogic field team at Oracle and working with some of the most daunting WebLogic deployments in the world. It should not surprise you that Gustavo has worked with almost every feature he has written about in this book in real life. In addition, Gustavo is a friendly, approachable, and patient person by nature. You would be very hard pressed to find a better person to mentor you on WebLogic than Gustavo. He has synthesized all these valuable personal characteristics beautifully into the book. Each complex WebLogic topic is explained in the simplest and most approachable way – covering the basics whenever possible. Gustavo also shares unique knowledge that can only be gained through years of real-world experience working inside the WebLogic team throughout the book. While the book is comprehensive enough, it leaves out just enough detail to keep the book from becoming overwhelming in the way the WebLogic official documentation can be. There are ample diagrams, screenshots, and code examples wherever helpful.

The book covers a range of topics including basic installation, configuration, administration, monitoring, logging, clustering, networking, data access, and security. The coverage of domains, the node manager, the console, JMX, and WLST shine particularly bright. The content should definitely be good enough for the purposes of WebLogic certification. Particularly helpful are the sample certification questions and exercises included at the end of each chapter. The sequence of topics covered is very sensible throughout. In fact, beyond the goals of certification, the book is a valuable reference on the bookshelf of anyone working with WebLogic in the real world.

Your decision to make a personal investment in WebLogic and using this book as a tool to do so is undeniably sound. I hope you enjoy the book and learn as much from it as I did!

Reza Rahman
Senior Manager/Architect, CapTech Ventures Inc.
Former Java EEE/GlassFish/WebLogic Evangelist, Oracle

Introduction

Some time ago as an Oracle employee, and while on a consulting assignment with some very nice IT folks in Caracas, Venezuela, I spoke with someone in a product management team in Oracle regarding the configuration of the environment I was working on. He also happened to be an Apress author. I do not think he remembers our brief conversation but I do. He shared with me that it was his point of view that basically anyone could achieve anything in technology given the right time and resources.

Becoming a certified Oracle WebLogic Server System Administrator is certainly a task where this true notion can be validated.

For experienced WebLogic Server administrators, passing the exam will require almost no effort as they will most likely already have spent enough time and resources around WebLogic Server so that they will have gained the breadth and depth of knowledge required by exam 1Z0-133.

For anybody else interested in passing the exam, the effort will require a varying investment of time and resources, depending on their previous exposure to Java EE and Java application servers in general, and to WebLogic Server in particular.

The Certification Process and Requirements

As published on the Oracle University website, the 1Z0-133 exam is a proctored exam delivered at PearsonVue centers around the world. Passing the exam earns the designation of Oracle Certified Associate, Oracle WebLogic Server 12c Administrator certification.

At the time of writing this book, the exam has a duration of 120 minutes and is comprised of 77 multiple choice questions with a minimum passing score of 64%, and is validated against Oracle WebLogic Server version 12.1.2 (released in June 2013). Figure 1 shows these details as published in the Oracle University website.

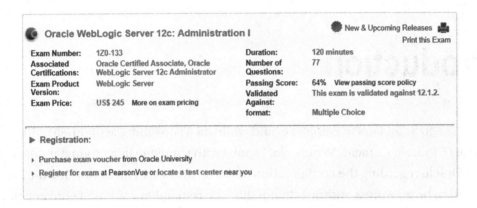

Figure 1. *Details of Oracle University exam 1Z0-133*

In order to register and schedule the exam, candidates must have active accounts with both Oracle and PearsonVue. The Oracle account can be created at `www.oracle.com` and the PearsonVue account can be created at `www.pearsonvue.com/oracle`. Creating a PearsonVue account will also create an Oracle Testing ID. This ID must then be entered at Oracle University's certification website at *certview.oracle.com,* thus linking the Oracle and PearsonVue accounts. There is a one-hour delay between the time that the Oracle Testing ID has been created by PearsonVue and the time that it will be recognized by the CertView website.

Once the candidate profile has been completed, the exam can be purchased and scheduled directly from PearsonVue. The Oracle account can then be used to access exam history, scores, and other details regarding the certification efforts at the CertView website.

The exam experience is simple and standardized across test centers. Candidates are required to present a photo ID at the selected test center and are not allowed to introduce any objects into the test room. The exam terminal presents a simple user interface displaying one question and its possible answers per each screen. The questions can be marked for later review.

Once all questions have been answered, the exam may be submitted to Oracle for grading. After a short period of time, usually under 30 minutes, a notification of the exam result will be emailed to the candidate. There is a delay of around 24 hours between the time that the notification of exam results is received and the time that the results will also appear in the CertView website.

The two possible exam results are pass or fail. Regardless of the exam results, feedback will be provided to help identify any questions that were answered incorrectly. Users with a failing score should return to this feedback in preparing for future attempts.

Once Oracle has notified a candidate of a passing score, he or she has officially become a certified Oracle WebLogic Server 12c Administrator. PearsonVue and Oracle also offer badges for certain certifications. These badges are useful to publish certification credentials to third parties and on social networks such as LinkedIn.

At the time of writing this book, there are no hard requirements enforced by Oracle or by PearsonVue for a candidate to meet before attempting the exam, other than a policy that specifies that a candidate who fails must wait 14 days before attempting the same exam again, with a maximum of 4 attempts in a 12-month period. Candidates should consult the Oracle certification website though, in order to ensure that the requirements have not changed.

The only soft requirement for passing the exam is being conversant with the 16 topics covered. These topics range from a very basic introduction to WebLogic Server, the product installation and basic configuration, and a review of the components and features that most administrators use in their day-to-day work.

The following is the complete list of topics covered by the exam:

- Overview of WebLogic Server

- Installing and patching WebLogic Server

- Creating domains

- Starting servers

- Using the Administration Console

- Configuring JDBC

- Monitoring a domain

- Node Manager

- Deploying applications

- Network channels and virtual hosts

- Creating and configuring clusters

- Cluster proxies and sessions

- Cluster communication, planning, and troubleshooting

- Transactions

- WebLogic Server security

- Backing up and upgrading WebLogic Server

The depth of the exam questions covering these topics is such that a person with limited experience administering WebLogic Server could probably find it hard to tackle.

Unfortunately, there is probably no way to objectively define a certain period of time of actual work experience with WebLogic Server that will qualify a candidate to pass the exam. Candidates should aim to gain experience working with the product, either on the job, supporting real business applications on real production environments, or at least performing guided exercises in a laboratory for a reasonable amount of time.

Practical experience will directly impact their ability to answer the questions correctly. To illustrate this, consider the following question:

1. Which is the correct set of options available when configuring feature X:

   a. A, B, and C

   b. C, D, and E

   c. B, D, and F

   d. All of the above

I remember a question like this from when I first became an Oracle WebLogic Server certified administrator. I had recently worked with that particular feature in more than a few environments, I knew how to use it correctly and I thought I had it right but I did not.

I knew very well what the options were individually, and I was able to quickly recognize which one of the choices included an invalid option, but, to my surprise, it was the first time that I had to think of these as sets of options rather than individual options that could be used separately.

As exemplified by this, experience administering WebLogic Server should be considered a first-class requirement for passing the exam, as opposed to simply having an understanding of the concepts involved.

Approach to Presenting the Content

The topics that the Oracle WebLogic Server 12c: Administration I certification exam indeed covers can be classified in two groups:

- Topics that review how to configure and use the implementation of a portion of the Java EE 6 specification[1] in WebLogic Server, such as Java Database Connectivity.

- Topics that review how to configure and use the features through which Oracle differentiates its product from other Java application servers, such as with the WebLogic Administration Console or WebLogic Scripting Tool.

Note   Not all elements of the Java EE 6 specification implemented in Oracle WebLogic Server are covered in exam 1Z0-133. The outstanding subset is covered in exam 1Z0-134.

Each chapter in this book will present the content using the following structure:

- Brief description of the topic

- Step-by-step descriptions of well-known procedures to configure and use WebLogic Server features

- List of recommended exercises to perform

- List of sample certification questions related to the topic covered

The topic description may include introductory information regarding the relevant element of the Java EE specification. When included, this information will be brief and provided solely as a general contextual reference to the topic at hand.

Often, there may be more than one way to perform a single administration task in WebLogic Server, such as configuring a feature using a CLI interface, writing and invoking a script to automate the configuration, or using the Administration Console

---

[1]The Java EE compatibility page in the Oracle website at URL: `http://www.oracle.com/technetwork/java/javaee/overview/compatibility-jsp-136984.html` includes links to the Java EE 7 specification version, as well as links to our target Java EE 6 version.

to achieve the same goal. Each topic will cover the as many ways to perform the administration procedures as the logical sequence of chapters allows.

As stated before, seasoned WebLogic Server administrators may have enough of a refresher in preparing for the certification exam by simply challenging themselves to respond correctly to all of the sample questions, whereas new administrators may find that the recommended exercises will provide good practice for the concepts presented in each chapter. Answering the sample questions will then be a good way to assert whether or not they are making the required progress in their preparation.

Recommended Exercises and Sample Questions

The recommended exercises will be listed by a simple statement describing a requirement, such as:

- Configure A by using B.

No specific steps required to complete the exercises will be specified. It is expected that the candidate will have gained enough understanding and context to the exercise statement in order to resolve it. Candidates should be able to infer the specific procedure to perform from the content presented in the corresponding chapter.

A laboratory or development environment upon which to complete the exercises will be required. Completing the practices listed in Chapter 3 will result in such an environment, which can then be cloned or otherwise enabled to complete all practices in subsequent chapters.

Even though clustering and other high availability features will be addressed in the topics, the CPU and RAM requirements of the laboratory will be minimal so that these can be accomplished on any fairly recent laptop geared for geeks.

The sample questions in the book have been formulated to resemble the type and depth of questions found in the certification exam and will test the understanding of the topic covered but should not be considered a comprehensive reference. The answers to these sets of questions can be found in Appendix A.

CHAPTER 1

Overview

Java technology was created by a group of brilliant engineers from Sun Microsystems headed by Dr. James Gosling. It could probably be fair to state that nearly all technologists around the world have at least heard about, if not used, Java. This chapter provides both, a brief of Java technology and an overview of the Java EE 6 features implemented in WebLogic Server 12c.

Today the Java ecosystem appears more alive than ever. Java became 20 years old in 2015 and was also named TIOBE[1] programming language of the year. Some would say that there has never been a better time to work with Java technology, and I believe there is truth in that statement, considering the recent evolution of the language and the platform.

Java is run truly just about everywhere. It can be found in places ranging from homes to scientific laboratories, from gaming consoles and Blu-ray players to the computers in the control room of NASA's Jet Propulsion Laboratory.

In enterprise computing around the globe, a very large number of applications with extreme requirements of availability and performance, in the most demanding industries such as finance and telecommunications, are powered by Java application servers such as WebLogic Server.

Nowadays, it is possible to launch a Java application server instance, deploy upon it a modern application, and have it up and running, listening for requests, in just a few seconds. It is possible to run enterprise Java technology on all sorts of infrastructure, from high-end appliances to commodity hardware, from virtual machines to cloud servers and containers.

---

[1]The TIOBE Programming Community index is described as an indicator of the popularity of programming languages whose ratings are based on several factors including the number of skilled engineers worldwide.

© Gustavo Garnica 2018
G. Garnica, *Oracle WebLogic Server 12c Administration I Exam 1Z0-133*,
https://doi.org/10.1007/978-1-4842-2562-2_1

For New Administrators

Java technology includes among other elements a programming language and a platform. At a high level, the Java platform can be described as the environment in which applications written in the Java programming language can be run. In this book, we touch on two of such Java platforms, namely, Java Standard Edition or Java SE, and Java Enterprise Edition or Java EE.

The Java SE platform is comprised of the basic elements required to run Java applications, including a Java Virtual Machine, the core API, as well as development and deployment tools. The Java EE platform provides its own API and a runtime environment for developing and running enterprise applications. Java EE sits on top of Java SE.

The evolution of the Java EE platform is guided by the Java Community Process through expert groups that are comprised of individuals and organizations interested in the development of the Java technology. These expert groups work on Java Specification Requests that later become part of the Java EE Platform Specification. The Java EE specification can then be implemented by product vendors.

WebLogic Server administrators are expected to be able to perform installation, configuration, maintenance, and other operations on the full Java EE technology stack. This includes having a proper understanding of the JVM, the Java SE and EE APIs, and related tools and components, as well as the runtime environment and the enterprise applications deployed on it. Typically, WebLogic Server administrators are also skilled at working with related software products, from operating systems and file systems to networking tools, from load balancers and proxies to databases and so forth.

Enterprise Applications

Enterprise applications are named so because they exist to resolve the requirements of information systems in large enterprises. For applications, enterprise requirements include but are not limited to persistence, distribution, transactionality, security, ubiquity, etc. For infrastructure, enterprise requirements include scalability, availability, fault tolerance, performance, etc.

In order to tackle these requirements, enterprise applications are commonly designed to separate functionality into tiers. Typically, at least three tiers can be easily identified: a front tier, a middle tier, and a data tier. Depending on the application requirements, these tiers can be further subdivided by isolating even more specific functionality into additional tiers. Java EE defines the technologies that once implemented support to each of these tiers.

Enterprise applications are developed as self-contained components that reside in one of these tiers. Before execution, an application component must be assembled into a Java EE module and deployed into the right container for its type. The assembly process specifies container configuration settings for each component in the Java EE module and for the Java EE application at large. Most of the configuration is defined through annotations in the application code rather than on XML deployment descriptors, some of which have now become optional.

Java Application Servers

A Java application server, such as Oracle WebLogic Server, implements the Java EE APIs and provides the required standard infrastructure services in the form of runtime environments or containers. Examples of these containers include the web container for front tier components and the EJB container for business logic components residing in the middle tier.

Enterprise applications are developed, deployed, and run on a container that supports the specific services required by it. Application components are meant to interact with one another, but they will only do so indirectly, through the platform services available in the container where they have been deployed. Figure 1-1 depicts the logical Java EE architecture described in the preceding paragraphs at a very basic level.

Java EE Architecture

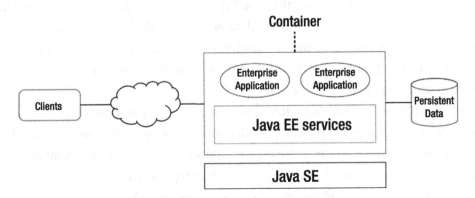

Figure 1-1. *Logical view of the Java EE architecture*

In this logical view the Java platforms are represented by the larger rectangles. These two platforms, Java SE and Java EE, will work in unison everywhere a Java enterprise application is run. The same architectural elements may be seen running application components in any tier of the Java enterprise architecture as described before.

Java EE Services

A partial list of the standard services supported by Java EE containers include the following:

- *Hyper Text Transfer Protocol (HTTP)* – Web clients are commonly processed and transferred for display on a client browser using the HTTP protocol, including over SSL or TLS. Relevant Java EE APIs include Servlet, JSP, JSF, and Web Services.

- *Java Transaction API (JTA)* – used by the container and the application components to demarcate transaction boundaries.

- *Java Database Connectivity (JDBC)* – enables connectivity with relational database systems. The JDBC API is included in the Java SE platform but has additional requirements specified by the Java EE platform.

- *Java Persistence API (JPA)* – manages persistence and object/relational mapping used in Java domain models.

- *Java Message Service (JMS)* – used for messaging and supports point-to-point as well as publish-subscribe models whereby messages are delivered to individual consumers or to multiple subscribers, respectively.

- *Java Naming and Directory Interface (JNDI)* – allows Java components to discover and look up data and objects by their names. It is included in the Java SE platform but has additional requirements specified by the Java EE platform.

- *Java API for XML Processing (JAXP)* – provides support for SAX and DOM APIs for parsing XML documents, as well as for XSLT transformations. It is included in the Java SE platform.

- *Java API for XML Web Services (JAX-WS)* – provides support for both, Web Service clients and endpoints following the WS-I Basic Profile specification.

- *Java Connector Architecture (JCA)* – allows resource adapters to heterogeneous sources to be plugged into a Java EE product. The connector architecture defines a set of system-level contracts between the Java EE server and the adapter. These contracts cover security as well as connection, transaction, and thread management.

- *Java Authentication and Authorization Service (JAAS)* – enables services to authenticate users and enforce access controls by implementing the Pluggable Authentication Module framework.

- *Java Management Extensions (JMX)* – enables management of Java EE servers using Java objects.

The certification exam demands sufficient understanding of the above services and APIs. These are all relevant in the day-to-day WebLogic Server administration, operations, and troubleshooting tasks. These services will be analyzed in greater depth in subsequent chapters.

Oracle Fusion Middleware

Oracle Fusion Middleware is a collection of enterprise software products from which Oracle WebLogic Server is a part. Oracle Fusion Middleware includes products and tools for many solutions including the following:

- Service Oriented Architecture

- Business Process Management

- Business Intelligence

- Content Management

- Identity Management

SOA and BPM products implement standards-based infrastructure to connect applications and systems with each other, and to orchestrate business activities in a workflow. BI tools allow for integrating data and support decision making based on business performance against key indicators. Content solutions are central repositories from which documents and business media can be managed. Identity solutions allow for centralized management of users, identities, and roles, and enable federated access and authentication.

Products in the Fusion Middleware family are Java components, implemented as Java enterprise applications that run on a Java container. Oracle WebLogic Server provides the foundation on which these products will run. Once installed, several of these products can be configured to run interdependent and integrated among each other as well as with other products such as Oracle Database.

Some of the Java components of Oracle Fusion Middleware include Oracle WebLogic Server, Oracle Service Bus, Oracle SOA Suite, and Oracle BPM Suite.

Oracle WebLogic Server

Oracle WebLogic Server 12c is a Java EE 6 specification compliant Java application server. There are three WebLogic Server licensing offerings:

- Oracle WebLogic Server Standard Edition – Includes the Core Oracle WebLogic Server plus Oracle TopLink, which is Oracle's ORM framework; Oracle Application Development Framework and Oracle WebTier, which includes Oracle HTTP Server.

- Oracle WebLogic Server Enterprise Edition – Includes all Oracle WebLogic Standard Edition features plus WebLogic Server clustering and Java SE advanced platform, which includes the Java Mission Control and Java Flight Recorder tools for profiling and diagnosing a JVM instance.

- Oracle WebLogic Server Suite – Includes all Oracle Enterprise Edition features plus Oracle Coherence Enterprise and Active GridLink for RAC to optimize connectivity with Oracle RAC Databases.

Oracle WebLogic Server is certified to run on Windows, Linux, Solaris, and other UNIX operating systems on top of Java SE platform version 7[2].

---

[2]The full details of certification and interoperability for WebLogic Server 12c can be found in the Oracle Fusion Middleware Supported System Configurations page at URL: http://www.oracle.com/technetwork/middleware/ias/downloads/fusion-certification-100350.html.

New Features in WebLogic Server 12c

The improvements in Oracle WebLogic Server 12c version 12.1.2 are significant and very exciting for experienced WebLogic Server administrators. As explained before, these improvements come either as a result of the implementation of the Java EE 6 specification, or as added value to WebLogic Server as a Java EE product.

The changes listed and described in this section are not comprehensive. The ones introduced here will also be analyzed in greater depth in subsequent chapters.

Updates Required by Java EE 6

The following are the salient changes in features and technologies that were added to WebLogic Server as part of its implementation of the Java EE 6 specification:

- *Profiles* – A profile in Java EE is a configuration of the platform for a specific class of applications. All profiles share a set of common features and add the required functionality according to the types of applications that the profile supports. WebLogic Server has compatible implementations with the Java EE 6 Web profile and with the Java EE 6 Full Platform.

- *Java API for Restful Web Services (JAX-RS)* – defines an API for the development of Web Services applications based on the REST architectural style. Services are deployed as Servlets in web containers. JAX-RS version 1.1 is defined in JSR 311.

- *Managed Beans* – are lightweight Plain Old Java Objects that support resource injection, life cycle callbacks, and interceptors. Managed beans can now be used anywhere in a Java EE application, not just in web modules using JavaServer Faces. Managed Beans version 1.0 are defined in JSR 316.

- *Contexts and Dependency Injection (CDI)* – provides a way for developers to use enterprise beans and JavaServer Faces together. CDI version 1.0 is defined in JSR 299.

- *Bean Validation* – defines an API for validating data in JavaBeans components. With this, validation constraints can be defined in a single place, mainly through annotations, and then shared across multiple layers. Bean Validation version 1.0 is defined in JSR 303.

- *Updates to EJB specification* – session bean interfaces have now been made optional, just like other enterprise beans were. Singleton beans have been introduced, as well as support for running EJBs directly on a Servlet container. These updates have been introduced with EJB 3.1, which is defined in JSR 318.

- *Updates to Servlet specification* – web containers must now support that certain types of objects, such as serializable and EJB, may be stored in HTTPSession objects, and also that when a session is moved from one JVM to another, all objects of supported types must be accurately recreated on the target JVM. Among other changes, these updates have been introduced with Servlet 3.0, which is defined in JSR 315.

- *Updates to JavaServer Faces specification* – annotations can be used instead of a configuration file to specify managed beans. JSP has been replaced by Facelets as standard display technology. Implicit navigation and Ajax support has been included. These updates have been introduced with JavaServer Faces 2.0, which is defined in JSR 314.

Other Functionality Changes and Additions

WebLogic Server 12c version 12.1.2 also includes changes and additions to its functionality as a Java EE product. The following is a partial list of the new features:

- *Installation features* – a JDK is no longer included with any product installers. Also, only generic installers are available, which can be used on any supported production platform. The ZIP installer is still available from Oracle OTN and is still intended for development use only.

- *Configuration features* – OHS and ODI system components of Oracle Fusion Middleware can now be configured in a WebLogic Server domain. Managed servers can now be added to an expandable server group.

- *WebSockets* – support for IETF RFC 6455 has been added. This provides two-way, full-duplex communication over a single TCP connection.

- *TopLink* – now supports JSON bindings and RESTful persistence for JPA entities as well as NoSQL database support.

- *Server Templates* – eases administration by allowing for the definition of certain attributes in a template. Such attributes can be changed in a single place, and take effect on all server instances that use the template.

- *Dynamic Clusters* – are based on server templates and enable easy expansion of a cluster. The number of server instances required at peak load is specified when configuring the cluster. WebLogic Server will at runtime create the required number of server instances and configure them accordingly.

- *Simplified JMS configuration* – JMS servers and persistent stores can now directly target a cluster. This is further enhanced by dynamically scaling JMS resources in a dynamic cluster.

Conclusion

Oracle WebLogic Server is the premier Java application server product from Oracle, and the foundation of the Fusion Middleware and Fusion Applications range of products. Experienced WebLogic Server administrators and their employers had anticipated some of the new features and functionality upgrades available in the 12c release series for some time. It is an exciting time to become a WebLogic Server 12c certified administrator.

Recommended Exercises

1. Review the full certification requirements and interoperability matrix for Oracle WebLogic Server 12c version 12.1.2.

2. Download the Oracle WebLogic Server 12c binary installers for Linux.

3. Install a Linux server virtual machine and modify its networking configuration to make it accessible from your workstation.

Certification Questions

1. Enterprise applications may run directly on top of the Java SE platform.

   a. True

   b. False

2. What are the certified Java SE versions to run Oracle WebLogic Server instances?

   a. All the latest

   b. Java SE 7 only

   c. Java SE 6 only

   d. Java SE 6 and 7

   e. Any

3. What fundamental component of the Java EE architecture is provided by an application server?

   a. The virtual machine

   b. The runtime environment

   c. The database drivers

   d. The management console

   e. None of the above

4. Provides support for creating Web Service clients and endpoints using a REST architectural style:

   a. JAXP

   b. JAX-WS

   c. JMX

   d. All of the above

   e. None of the above

5. What edition of WebLogic Server should I license if I intend to use
    the Oracle JVM profiling tools?

    a. WebLogic Server Standard Edition

    b. WebLogic Server Enterprise Edition

    c. WebLogic Server Suite

    d. All of the above

    e. None of the above

Coming Up

This high-level overview of the technologies that represent the foundation of the
Oracle Fusion Middleware family of products is useful to remember the critical role
that WebLogic Server plays. The next chapter will introduce the first set of tasks that an
administrator performs in everyday work.

CHAPTER 2

Installation and Updates

In this chapter we deal with installing and updating Oracle WebLogic Server. As a matter of sheer preference, this book employs Linux as the operating system of choice to describe the product installation, configuration, and other administration procedures. This will not be a concern for administrators who prefer other operating systems since Oracle has made a pretty good effort to provide a consistent administration experience across all supported platforms.

For instance, as indicated in the previous chapter, product installers that are currently provided to be used in production environments are generic installers, as opposed to previous versions in which they were operating system dependent installers.

Note Installer help messages still have references to other types of installers even though Oracle has discontinued their general availability.

These generic installers are provided in the form of executable Java archives and their use is consistent across all supported operating systems. This is true also with most, if not all, of the WebLogic Server administration tools and procedures. Administrators will simply have to apply the notions and concepts presented to the file formats, locations, scripting environments, and other details of other supported operating systems.

In order to install a WebLogic Server environment that can be used to run production applications, an administrator needs to cover much more than just running the product installer. The process involves understanding what constitutes a certified configuration, choosing the right distribution according to the intended use of the product, making sure that all requirements are met, defining the installation details, selecting an installation method, and running the product installer. Figure 2-1 depicts the complete effort.

© Gustavo Garnica 2018
G. Garnica, *Oracle WebLogic Server 12c Administration I Exam 1Z0-133*,
https://doi.org/10.1007/978-1-4842-2562-2_2

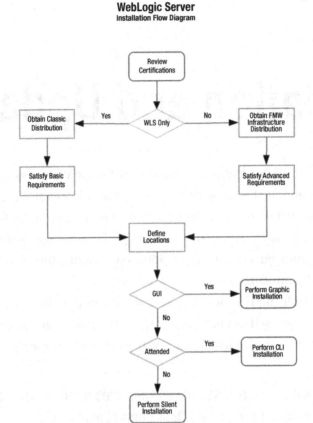

Figure 2-1. *Flow chart of the recommended process to install WebLogic Server environments*

Supported Configurations

Oracle Fusion Middleware end users sometimes engage in rational conversations regarding how they may or may not use WebLogic Server. The part of that conversation that refers to what can legally be done with the licensed product is beyond the contents of this book. However, from the technological perspective, there is a clear line that differentiates the scenarios in which the use of WebLogic Server is supported by Oracle and those in which it is not. Supported scenarios are defined by the possible configurations listed in the Oracle Fusion Middleware certification matrix.

The matrix is available in the form of a Microsoft Excel file, composed of multiple spreadsheets that contain information regarding several Oracle Fusion Middleware products. The spreadsheet named System contains information relevant to understand

WebLogic Server configurations that are certified and therefore supported by Oracle. The information is organized in columns as follows:

- Product

- Release

- Processor

- Operating system version

- Operating system update type

- Operating system update level

- Operating system type (32-bit or 64-bit)

- JDK vendor

- JDK version

- JDK type (32-bit or 64-bit)

- Exceptions and additional information

Each column header permits sorting the information to display a quick view of whether or not a given combination of technologies has been certified by Oracle. For example, an administrator might want to find out what WebLogic Server configurations are supported by Oracle on SPARC. Unselecting all but the SPARC option in the Processor column header will result in a list of rows indicating that it is possible to run WebLogic Server on SPARC, on Oracle Solaris 10 or 11 only, and that in both cases Oracle JDK is the only certified JDK. Figure 2-2 shows this view in the certification matrix.

Product Offering	Release	Processor	OS Version	OS Update Type	OS Update Level	OS 32/64	Oracle App 32/64 Bit	JDK Vendor	JDK Version	JDK 32/64 Bit
ALL	FMW 12.1.2.0.0	Oracle Solaris on SPARC (64-bit)	10	Update	9+	64	64	Oracle JDK	1.7.0_15+	64
ALL	FMW 12.1.2.0.0	Oracle Solaris on SPARC (64-bit)	11	Update	0+	64	64	Oracle JDK	1.7.0_15+	64
*JDKVERSION	. A plus sign (+) after the fourth digit in the version number indicates that this and all higher versions of the JRE/JINIT/JDK extensions are certified. For example, 1.7.0_15 certified.									

Figure 2-2. *Extract of the Oracle Fusion Middleware Certification Matrix sorted to display support for WebLogic Server on Solaris SPARC*

It is not uncommon to learn that an administrator decided to try, and actually managed, to install and run a variant of a certified configuration, for example, by using an unsupported JDK. The Oracle certification matrix does not imply that such a configuration is not technically feasible, but only that Oracle will not support it. Running unsupported configurations is usually a risk that corporations will refuse to take in their production systems. Even so, this is not an absolute conclusion because the prospect of running an unsupported configuration might arise and be fully justified in certain technological scenarios. For instance, a very large corporation had set a deadline to discontinue using IPv4 in their infrastructure at a time when Oracle had not yet certified some of their middleware products to communicate using IPv6 only. They assessed that the gains outweighed the risks and decided to move forward and run their Oracle Fusion Middleware environments outside of the certified configurations, and succeeded in doing so. A bold move like this is clearly not for every organization; it should only be made after having carefully planned how to work around or mitigate any resulting issues.

Fusion Middleware Infrastructure

WebLogic Server administrators are often tasked with installing and configuring environments that support Oracle Application Development Framework. In a nutshell, Oracle ADF is a framework that is built on Java EE standards and open source technologies to deliver infrastructure services that facilitate development of enterprise applications. Before the 12c release, administrators had to install, on top of WebLogic Server, a product called Oracle Application Developer, which included the Oracle ADF runtime and Oracle Enterprise Manager. Since the 12c release, Oracle offers a new distribution package named Fusion Middleware Infrastructure. This new distribution bundles together WebLogic Server with ADF, Enterprise Manager, and a few additional components. When using the Fusion Middleware Infrastructure distribution installer, these components are installed together in a common location. This new distribution is an ideal foundation for administrators who will be supporting ADF and/or other Oracle Fusion Middleware products in their environments.

The base topology that can be created from the Fusion Middleware Infrastructure installer includes a DB host, requires an Oracle database, and is a very good starting point to configure an environment for high availability. The traditional WebLogic Server installer available in releases 11g and prior is still available in 12c.

Product Requirements

Once a certified configuration has been selected, but before the Oracle WebLogic Server installer is run, several product requirements must be satisfied. These include CPU and memory, disk space, networking, and a Java SE platform. All of these are described in the following sections.

Administrators who support environments in which the Middleware Infrastructure distribution is used to install WebLogic Server, or in which additional Fusion Middleware products are used, will need to satisfy some advanced requirements such as installing a database management system and using it to create the corresponding Fusion Middleware product schemas. Such details are not covered by the 1Z0-133 certification exam and are therefore outside the scope of this book.

CPU and Memory Requirements

The Oracle Fusion Middleware System Requirements and Specifications page [1] defines the set of minimum requirements for systems on which WebLogic Server will be installed. WebLogic Server requires at least one 1 GHz CPU and 4 GB of physical RAM, plus at least 4 GB of swap space. This requirement is the same across all supported operating systems [2].

For a development environment where all components reside on a single JVM, these minimum settings should be enough. Production environments require more than one JVM to be configured to run as a cluster. As a general rule for environments running more than one JVM in the same system, Oracle recommends considering a minimum of 3 GB of available memory for the operating system itself and any other processes, and 3 GB more of available memory for each JVM. Again, this is just a statement of the minimum requirements for a multi-JVM system. The optimal configuration of a production environment should be defined by performing a formal capacity planning exercise, which should account for this as well as for other derived settings such as the number of file descriptors per process and the number of processes required [3].

---

[1]The Oracle Fusion Middleware System Requirements and Specifications document is available at http://docs.oracle.com/cd/E23104_01/sysreqs1213/sysrs.htm.

[2]The Oracle Fusion Middleware System Requirements and Specifications document is available at http://docs.oracle.com/cd/E23104_01/sysreqs1213/sysrs.htm.

[3]On Linux operating systems, the following limits should be increased in the /etc/security/limits. conf file: soft – nofile – 4096, hard – nofile – 65536, soft – noproc – 2047, hard – noproc – 16384.

Disk Space

An installation of WebLogic Server with default settings will take close to 900 MB of disk space. Oracle states that at least 2.5 times this space is also required in temporary space during the installation process.

Networking

WebLogic Server 12c supports IPv4, IPv6, or dual-stack networking configurations. The topology in which WebLogic Server runs determines the applicable configuration mode. In the product documentation, Oracle defines five supported topologies and lists the IP versions for WebLogic Server in each one of them. In short, when WebLogic Server runs on an IPv6 only system, the rest of the topology, such as front-end proxies and back-end database management systems, should also run on hosts configured with IPv6 only. The rest of the topologies mandate either an IPv4-only or a dual-stack configuration, the definition of which depends on what products are in use in a given topology, and on what IP configurations the underlying hosts have.

Java SE

Often, organizations already have other systems in place when they decide to introduce Oracle middleware to their existing shops. It is likely that they will already have defined their choice of processor type, and they will probably also have narrowed down their operating system options to a couple of types or versions.

Regardless of the processor, operating system type and version, all certified configurations of WebLogic Server version 12.1.2 require Java SE 7, update 15, or later [4]. The recommended general practice is to always use the latest update of the supported Java SE platform version unless there are valid reasons for using a specific update version.

Java SE 7 reached the end of free and public updates on April 2015, and the latest available update is number 80 [5]. Subsequent Java SE 7 updates are published by Oracle in its support website for customers with a support license. Java SE releases 8 or 9 are not certified for Oracle WebLogic Server version 12.1.2.

---

[4]Elsewhere in the documentation library, the required Java SE 7 update for WebLogic Server version 12.1.2.0.0 is 55 or later.

[5]The last public update of Java SE 7 is available from the Java Archive Downloads page at http://www.oracle.com/technetwork/java/archive-139210.html.

Installation Overview

The process of running the WebLogic Server installer is quite straightforward. The actual installation will mostly just unpack the files onto the target file system. Performing the installation locally on a fairly modern system takes just a couple of minutes [6].

Assuming that the Java SE platform binaries have been included in the system path, the installer can be run by the following command:

```
java -jar fmw_12.1.3.0.0_wls.jar
```

As expected, the installer provides information regarding options using the help (-help) argument. One useful option is to have the installer ignore the results of the system requirements check (-ignoreSysPrereqs), useful for example when installing the product on an unsupported operating system. Conversely, an administrator may just want to have the installer check if her system is supported but not install the product just yet (-executeSysPrereqs). The installer supports additional arguments that will be reviewed in the next section.

The installation process is comprised of a few steps where configuration information is passed to the installer, and a few other steps in which confirming information is presented to the user.

Oracle keeps track of product installations in a UNIX or Linux system by creating a product inventory. The first step in the installation process is to define a location for the product inventory and specifying an operating system group that will have write permissions to the inventory directory. The installer will also create a script named createCentralInventory.sh in the inventory directory, which if run by root, will create an inventory pointer file named oraInst.loc in a standard system-wide location. Subsequent product installations or upgrades will recognize the presence of a central inventory and will not prompt an administrator to create one.

The second step is defining the WebLogic Server installation directory, which is referred to as the Oracle home [7] and its location is referred to as the value of the ORACLE_HOME environment variable in the product documentation. This directory

---

[6]The actual time the installation will take will be longer if installing on a remote machine by forwarding the display.

[7]Administrators of Fusion Middleware 11g referred to this location and variable as the middleware home and MW_HOME respectively, but this has been dropped by Oracle starting with the 12c release series.

is a read-only location that will contain product binaries and library files. It is a recommended practice to keep this location separate from the location where the runtime product configuration information is located.

The third step is choosing an installation type. The WebLogic Server installer offers three choices: WebLogic Server, Coherence, and Complete with Examples. Each type comprises several feature sets. Feature sets of several Fusion Middleware products may coexist on the same Oracle home.

The following is a list of all feature sets available in the WebLogic Server distribution, grouped by product, with a small description of their purpose or function:

- *Core server*

  - Core application server (WebLogic Server runtime with full support for Java EE 6)

  - Coherence product files (distributed data management and caching services)

  - Web 2 HTTP Pub-Sub server (a publish-subscribe server based on the Bayeux protocol)

  - WebLogic SCA (container for applications that use the SCA set of standards)

  - WebLogic client jars (to be used with RMI clients that use the T3 proprietary protocol)

- *Administrative tools*

  - Administration console language help files (additional languages of the online help)

  - CIE WLS config (required by the configuration tools)

- *Database support*

  - Third-party JDBC drivers (drivers for systems such as Microsoft SQL Server) [8]

  - WebLogic evaluation database (Apache Derby)

---

[8]My Oracle Support document ID 1969871.1 includes SQL Server, DB2, Sybase, and Derby in the list of installable third-party drivers.

- *Open source components*

  - Jackson (JSON processor)

  - Jersey (JAX-RS official implementation)

  - Apache Maven (build management tool)

- *Examples*

  - Server examples (sample applications to demonstrate key WebLogic features)

  - Coherence examples (sample applications to demonstrate key Coherence features)

- *Oracle installation infrastructure*

  - OPatch (tool for updating and patching WebLogic Server)

Selecting the option "Complete with Examples" will include all feature sets available. The difference between Complete and the WebLogic installation option is that the latter does not include sample applications nor the evaluation database. Likewise, the WebLogic installation option includes database support and WebLogic client JARs that the Coherence installation type does not.

Once an installation type is selected, the installer will verify the system requirements, including if the operating system and the Java SE platform used are supported. If the results of the check are positive, the installer continues by requesting an email address and the password of a My Oracle Support account to subsequently inform the administrator of any security updates. This is an important but optional request. When declined, an administrator must ensure to stay on top of the latest security information released by Oracle to update the WebLogic Server environment.

In the next step, the installation tool will present a summary of the choices made and allow saving the installation configuration to a file. If confirmed that everything is as desired, the product files will be extracted and installed. The final step will again present a summary that will include the Oracle home location, the location of the log file written by the installer, and the list of feature sets installed.

Installation Methods

The WebLogic Server 12c release series has two installation methods available: graphic and silent. The previous section described the installation process from the perspective of a graphic installation. The console method that was available in previous versions is not available in 12c.

The silent installation method is a convenient method to perform an installation on a remote system in which X11 forwarding is not enabled or when manually running the installer is not an option. The silent installation method is best for automating the installation process when managing a large number of systems.

As reviewed in the previous section, the installer requires some information to configure the installation. Running the installer tool in silent method requires a response file from which this information will be read. The summary screen of the installer running in graphical mode allows saving such a response file that will contain the selections made in previous screens. This can then be used as a template for creating response files for other systems.

In addition to the response file, running the installer in silent mode requires a file that by convention is named oraInst.loc that, as the name implies, is a pointer to the inventory location. This file must contain the same two pieces of information that the first step of the graphic installer requires in the following format:

```
inventory_loc=/path/to/inventory/location
inst_group=group_name
```

The absolute path to this file must be passed to the installer as a command-line argument. The installer will also require an indication that it must run on silent mode, as well as the absolute path to the response file.

The response file must contain all other pieces of information gathered by the installer tool in graphic mode. The most important of these are the location of the Oracle home and the install type. The rest of the lines require information regarding declining or accepting notification of security updates. For the sake of brevity, the contents of the response file are not shown. The following is the complete command to run the installer tool in silent mode:

```
$JAVA_HOME/bin/java -jar fmw_12.1.3.0.0_wls.jar -silent -invPtrLoc /path/
to/oraInst.loc -responseFile /path/to/env.rsp
```

The text output of a silent installation displays the results of the tool executing the various system requirements checks, reading the response file, and a progress bar of the installation, followed by a message stating if the installation completed successfully.

Installation Structure

Either installation method results in the exact same installed structure in the target file system. The following directories and files will be created by the installer after a successful run:

- *coherence* (core Coherence product files)

- *install* (files related to installation run)

- *inventory* (product inventory that is local to this Oracle home)

- *OPatch* (patch and update tool)

- *oracle_common* (libraries required by WebLogic Server)

- *oraInst.loc* (pointer to local inventory)

- *oui* (installer tool product files)

- *wlserver* (core WebLogic Server product files)

At this point, the WebLogic Server installation has been successful and the system is ready for product configuration.

Updating and Patching

Experienced administrators in releases previous to 12c had to use one tool to update and patch WebLogic Server and another tool to update and patch other Oracle Fusion Middleware products. OPatch has been consolidated as the only tool available to perform patching and updating. The OPatch version included is 13.1.0.0. OPatch requires Oracle Universal Installer, which gets installed in any WebLogic Server installation type. Eventually both tools, OPatch and OUI, may require being updated or patched. In order to maintain proper functionality, both tools must be maintained in the same version. The OUI version can be verified in the ORACLE_HOME/oui/oraparam.ini file, and the OPatch version can be checked by running ORACLE_HOME/OPatch/opatch with the version command.

The following types of product updates are released by Oracle, are downloadable from the My Oracle Support site, and must be processed by OPatch:

- *Interim* (contains fixes available between product releases)

- *Bundle* (contains fixes available between patch sets)

- *Security Patch Update* (security fixes, released quarterly)

- *Patch Set Update* (fixes that address the top 50 WLS critical bugs, released quarterly)

The general process for using OPatch is as follows:

1. Identify, download, and extract patch.

2. Review specific patch or update instructions in the README.txt file included.

3. Set ORACLE_HOME and OPatch locations in PATH.

4. Verify that the OPatch inventory is sane (opatch lsinventory).

5. Apply update (opatch apply PATCHDIR).

6. Verify that issues addressed have been resolved.

It is possible to verify that all prerequisites for a patch or update are present in the Oracle home by running the **apply** command passing the -report argument. Patches may also be rolled back by using the rollback command of opatch. Applying or rolling back multiple patches is possible by using the **apply** and **rollback** commands of opatch. This requires passing the -id argument followed by a list of patch identifiers. Log files of either apply or rollback operations are created after each operation.

It is a recommended practice to create a specific directory to extract all patches and updates applied to an Oracle home directly under the OPatch directory.

De-installation

The product removal tool is available at ORACLE_HOME/oui/bin/deinstall.sh. If a WebLogic Server environment has already been configured and has JVMs running, these must be stopped before attempting to run the product removal tool. Once the de-install tool has been run, the Oracle home directory may be manually removed.

Recommended Exercises

1. Perform an installation of WebLogic Server 12c version 12.1.2 using the Complete with Examples installation type and save the corresponding response file.

2. Edit the response file to define a different Oracle home and a different installation type.

3. Perform a silent installation of WebLogic Server 12c version 12.1.2 using a response file.

4. Review the two Oracle homes just installed by contrasting the resulting file system structures.

Certification Questions

1. Select the operating systems certified to run WebLogic Server 12c in production environments:

   a. Red Hat Linux 7

   b. Ubuntu Linux 14.04

   c. Microsoft Windows 7

   d. Mac OS 10.5

   e. Oracle Solaris 11

2. Select the product distribution types supported to run WebLogic Server in production environments:

   a. Physical media

   b. WebLogic Server JAR file

   c. Middleware Infrastructure JAR file

   d. ZIP distributions

   e. All of the above

3. Select the option that lists the correct components of the standard installation topology:

    a. One administration server, one managed server, one machine, one domain

    b. Two administration servers, two managed servers, two machines, one domain

    c. One administration server, one cluster, two managed servers, one machine, one domain

    d. None of the above

    e. All of the above

4. Select all of the supported installation methods:

    a. Graphic

    b. Console

    c. Silent

    d. Remote

    e. Local

5. Select the required command to apply a security patch.:

    a. bsu -install

    b. bsu -apply

    c. opatch install

    d. opatch apply

    e. opatch secure

Coming Up

For most WebLogic Server users, installing WebLogic Server is a relatively standard procedure; however, the configuration effort is a road with many slopes. In the next chapter we cover the main configuration concept: domains.

CHAPTER 3

Domains

In this chapter we discuss Oracle WebLogic Server domains and its components: the domain structure in file system and the methods available to create and configure a domain. We also walk through the domain configuration flow and discuss the steps required to configure a domain spanning multiple hosts, one of several required actions to configure WebLogic server in high availability.

We also touch on WebLogic Scripting Tool or WLST, which is an administration tool highly useful in automating WebLogic Server administrative tasks. A brief mention is made of how WLST works, such as connectivity and run modes, enough to understand how to use WLST to accomplish the task of configuring a domain.

Definition

A domain is the logical unit that comprises all components and services that make up a WebLogic environment. A domain always includes one and only one administration server that acts as a centralized domain configuration controller and is commonly named AdminServer. A typical WebLogic domain also contains one or more managed servers. Business applications are deployed and run on managed servers. Managed servers can be organized into clusters. A single domain may contain one or more clusters.

Domains that run one or more managed servers are commonly configured with a component named node manager whose purpose is to perform administrative actions on managed servers on behalf of the administration server, such as controlling server life cycle. All of these domain components are JVM processes.

© Gustavo Garnica 2018
G. Garnica, *Oracle WebLogic Server 12c Administration I Exam 1Z0-133*,
https://doi.org/10.1007/978-1-4842-2562-2_3

A domain includes also other types of components such as domain services and application resources; these include data sources, messaging destinations, security providers, etc. These types of components are deployed and configured on top of the domain JVMs. Configuration management in a WebLogic Server domain is commonly done through the administration console that is deployed on the administration server, as well as through custom JMX clients talking with the administration server [1]. Communication between cluster members is achieved using T3 [2] over RMI.

Domain Components

The logical major components of an Oracle WebLogic Server domain are servers. These may play different roles, and may have logical associations within a domain. The following is a simple classification of the domain components.

- Administration server – Single point of control and distribution of configuration in the domain. It also monitors the health and performance of managed servers, including the domain services and applications deployed on them.

- Managed servers – Upon starting, each managed server contacts the administration server to get a read-only copy of the domain configuration. Managed servers are used to run business applications and other domain services. Failure of the administration server does not negatively impact the operation of managed servers.

- Clusters – Comprised of one or more managed servers. Clusters facilitate scalability, fail-over, and load balancing, which are typically required in environments where increased performance, throughput, and availability are mandatory.

---

[1]JMX is a technology included in Java SE platform, useful to build managing and monitoring solutions, and is the underlying standard used in WebLogic Server administration.

[2]JVMs in a WebLogic domain open T3 channels to communicate with other JVMs. T3 includes multiplexing and point-to-point heartbeats to determine connection availability. It is also possible to use T3 over SSL if the required certificates configuration has been completed.

- Coherence Clusters – Support in-memory, distributed caching for applications [3].

Product Installation and Domains

A domain may run from a single product installation on a single host. In fact, multiple domains may run from a single product installation, either in a single host, or running from an installation on shared storage accessible to each participating host.

The determination to how many product installations will be required to run a particular WebLogic Server environment is a question of scope and business purpose. For example, an administrator may need to run multiple domains for multiple business units, and he may decide to run a single product installation for each domain. He may then be able to maintain different patch set levels on each WebLogic Server installation, according to the requirements of the applications of each business unit. From the technological perspective, the factors that come into play are manageability and independence.

Domain Topology

For the purposes of our analysis, Figure 3-1 depicts a basic domain topology comprised of a single host configured with one machine, one cluster made up of two managed servers, the administration server, and a node manager.

---

[3]Coherence Clusters are different from WebLogic Server clusters. When as part of the domain configuration a cluster is configured, it is a WebLogic Server cluster, not a Coherence cluster.

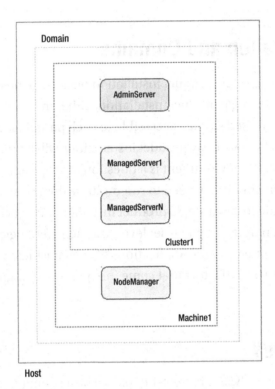

Figure 3-1. *Basic Domain Topology*

In this diagram, the boxes represent JVM processes and the dotted lines represent logical boundaries of the WebLogic Server domain, machine, and cluster definitions. In environments where a domain spans multiple hosts, the cluster can also cover up to as many hosts as the domain does. Unlike this, the machine definition and the node manager are designed to remain on an individual host in a single domain. This is so, precisely to enable a single administration server to manage and control any number of clusters and managed servers in disparate hosts. However, if desired, multiple machine definitions can exist in a single host, as long as they all belong in different domains.

Domain Structure

As mentioned before, it is an Oracle recommended practice to maintain the directory where the product installation is stored, separate from the product configuration. Despite this recommendation, the configuration wizard will by default suggest to create the domain in a path such as *ORACLE_HOME/user_projects/domains/domain_name*.

Most WebLogic Server administrators will instead define a directory that contains separate directories for product installation and product configuration. In this latter directory the *domains/domain_name* directory can be created. It is a convention also to suffix the name of the domain directory with the string: *_domain*. Unless there is a need to use a different name for the domain directory, it is not a bad idea to stick to this convention but it is by no means a requirement.

Whatever the location and names defined, the following directories will be created in the target directory:

- **autodeploy** – Depending on the domain configuration, at regular intervals WebLogic can scan this directory for files of type EAR, WAR, or JAR and automatically deploy them.

- **bin** – Contains server life-cycle control scripts. Other scripts may be added to this directory, for example, as hooks to modify the behavior of the JVM using command-line arguments.

- **config** - Main domain configuration directory, includes information about the deployment state of all servers in the domain.

- **config/jdbc** – Contains system modules configuration for JDBC.

- **config/jms** – Contains system modules configuration for JMS.

- **console-ext** – Contains files that represent customization of the administration console.

- **init-info** – Contains files used when creating the domain.

- **lib** – JAR files found by WebLogic in this directory are added to the CLASSPATH of each server instance.

- **pending** – Contains files representing domain configuration changes requested but not yet activated.

- **security** – Contains critical files of the security configuration of the domain, including those used in processes such as file encryption and decryption.

- **servers** – Contains a directory for each server instance that has been started in the host.

- **servers/server-name/data** – Contains files representing the persistent state of this particular server instance.

- **servers/server-name/security** – Contains security files required to run this particular server instance, such as the one containing the credentials to query the administration server for configuration information.

- **servers/server-name/logs** – Contains log files of this particular server instance.

- **servers/server-name/tmp** – Contains temporary data of this particular server instance.

- **servers/server-name/cache** – Contains processed data used in this particular server instance.

The content of the logs, tmp, and cache directories of each managed server should be left alone at runtime. However, it is possible to discard their contents once the corresponding server instances have been shut down.

Configuration Repository

The *config.xml* file located in the config directory conforms to an XSD schema and represents the main configuration repository for the domain. Even though with sufficient XML/XSD knowledge it is possible to edit the file directly, it is recommended to do so only through the administration console, deployed on the AdminServer and accessible through the /console context, or through a JMX client that will interact with the in-memory representation of the configuration that is kept by the administration server.

At runtime, the config.xml should never be manually updated. Given that the administration server manages changes to the config.xml file through a specific process, manually editing the file may interfere with such process and could result in domain corruption. Also, since the configuration is contained in the config.xml file, it is by nature not distributed; therefore any updates done to config.xml files in the file system structures of managed servers will be overwritten by the administration server upon restart.

Security credentials maintained in configuration files are in encrypted form only.

Configuration Methods

Creating and configuring a domain can be performed using one of several methods: the configuration wizard, WLST, or the pack and unpack commands. The scripts to execute all of these methods can be found in the *ORACLE_HOME/wlserver/common/bin* directory.

- **Configuration Wizard** – Learning about the general options available to configure a domain is best achieved by using the configuration wizard. It supports a GUI that guides an administrator through a series of screens that require entering the necessary information to define and configure domain components. The configuration wizard can be run by executing the config.sh file ([4]). The configuration wizard may also be run from remote systems that have been configured with display forwarding.

- **Pack and Unpack commands** – For administrators whose task is to replicate or distribute existing domains, the pack.sh and unpack.sh commands offer a simple, one-step invocation that will get the job done efficiently.

---

[4]To prevent slowness when creating domains on Linux systems, the installation wizard JVM should be configured to use the non-blocking system entropy device by specifying -Djava. security.egd=/dev/./urandom as value of the environment variable CONFIG_JVM_ARGS.

- **WLST** – Seasoned professionals working to automate domain creation, update, and extension can benefit from using WLST, which is a CLI scripting environment based on Jython. It offers a large set of scripting functions implemented specifically to perform WebLogic Server administrative actions. WLST can be run either online or offline. Running it online means operating as a JMX client, connecting to an administration server, and is analogous to operating on the administration console. Running it offline is analogous to running the configuration wizard. Running WLST offline is the right approach to create domain templates, create domains, or modify existing domains. WLST offers functions such as *readDomain(path)* or *readTemplate(file)* to build in-memory representations of domains that can be customized, and *createDomain(path)* or *writeTemplate(file)* to persist the configured in-memory representation of a domain to file system. WLST also has three operation modes, interactive, script, or batch mode and embedded (in Java programs). WLST can be run by executing the wlst.sh script to enter interactive mode, or by passing a .py script containing the desired code to execute, including WebLogic Server function invocations.

Domain Templates

Regardless of the method involved, domain management always involves domain templates. A domain template defines the full set of resources that a domain is comprised of. When WebLogic Server is installed, it comes with a set of predefined templates, which can be found in the *wlserver/common/templates/wls* directory.

The basic WebLogic Server domain template is wls.jar. It defines the necessary security configuration and the administration server. Because it has no dependencies, it can be used as the basis to create more complex domain configurations.

Other types of domain templates include extension templates and reconfiguration templates. The former can only be used to add functionality to an existing domain, as opposed to creating domains from scratch; the latter are provided by Oracle to facilitate certain domain updates.

Planning Domain Configuration

Creating a domain is the process of defining and configuring all WebLogic Server components and services required by the business purpose the domain will serve, using a tool to deploy the corresponding configuration to file system. Therefore, preparing to create and configure a domain requires an administrator to define the number of servers, the IP address or DNS names and port numbers they will use; the number of hosts that will participate in the domain and whether or not the managed servers will be members of a cluster, as well as the number of clusters the domain will support. All of these components will require an identification that must be unique in the domain. Also, the combination of IP addresses or DNS names and port numbers must be available in their corresponding network [5].

A domain has two server startup modes: development and production. Either one of them must be selected, depending on the purpose of the domain. The choice of server startup mode has an impact on security. Development mode will allow starting servers without entering administration credentials and has a different number of threads in their execution pool, logs a different amount of information by default, and has different operation timeouts.

Servers in a domain that will be supported by multiple product installations must all run the same product and patch level version.

Configuration Flow

Figure 3-2 shows the full process of creating and configuring the basic domain topology described in this chapter, from the perspective of an administrator using the configuration wizard.

---

[5]Even though it is not explicitly required by the domain configuration, the corresponding firewall rules must be in place to allow inbound network communications as well as communications between the servers in the domain.

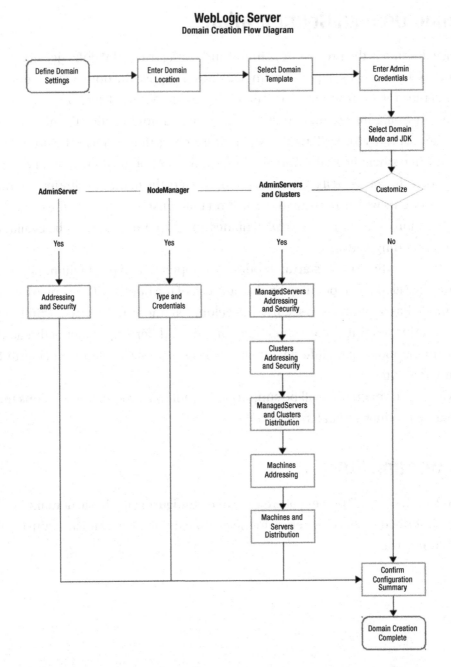

Figure 3-2. *Domain creation flow diagram*

This flow diagram shows that the first group of screens gather general information about the domain including the template that will be used as domain source, the name and location of the domain, the administration credentials, the domain mode, and the JDK that all JVMs will use.

The next screen allows choosing which subsequent portions to customize, the choices are administration server, node manager, managed servers, and clusters. If no further customization is made, the domain creation can proceed and will result in a domain that only has the minimal components to be functional, meaning the administration server with default configuration values.

If an administrator chooses to select any of the customization options, additional steps will be dynamically added to the wizard. In these additional screens the customization information is provided. The flow diagram displays the type of information required when customizing each item.

The last screen displays the configuration summary. The summary has different views that allow an administrator to verify the different perspectives in which domain components will be distributed, such as clusters and machines. Once this information has been reviewed, the actual domain creation and configuration can be started. As expected, the wizard will display a progress bar, indicating the actions in progress until complete.

Domain Propagation

The base topology depicted in the diagram at the beginning of this chapter included only one host. Production environments will typically start with two hosts, sometimes spanning dozens of hosts working together under a single domain configuration.

As mentioned before, the size of a domain is not determined solely considering technological factors, but is also a matter of scope and business purpose of the applications that will be deployed on this infrastructure.

From the technological perspective, WebLogic Server can support domains with several clusters, each with dozens of managed servers running on a similarly large number of hosts.

However many hosts comprise a WebLogic Server environment, a domain is created and configured first in one host, and is then propagated to the rest of the hosts. This process is performed by using two configuration tools mentioned in the previous section: the pack and unpack commands. Scripts to run these commands are located in the *ORACLE_HOME/wlserver/common/bin* directory.

Pack Command

The pack.sh script is used as an efficient, one-step command to create domain templates from existing domains. This tool cannot be used to customize domains. The pack.sh command creates a template by taking a snapshot of a fully functional domain. The pack command can produce either domain templates or managed server templates.

Domain templates can be used to create full copies of the source domain, or can be used as a starting point for further customization using other tools, such as the configuration wizard or WLST.

Managed server templates include only a subset of the domain resources, just enough to create the managed server structure on the file system of a host participating in a domain. This is precisely the type of template required to propagate the configuration of a domain to other hosts whose responsibility as domain members will only be to run managed servers. The pack command can be used to create a domain template as follows:

```
./pack.sh -domain=/path/to/source_domain -template=/path/to/domain_
template.jar -template_name=MyDomain -log=/path/to/pack.log
```

The pack command receives as arguments the path to the domain that will be packed, the path to the domain template that will be created, name inclusive, a template name, and optionally a log file.

Creating a managed server template requires adding the argument: -managed=true to the command above.

Unpack Command

The unpack.sh script is the counter part of the pack.sh script. It is also executed as an efficient, one-step command but it is used to create domains from existing templates. The unpack command used with a domain template can create a domain and optionally customize the administration username and/or password, the JDK path, the domain mode, the node manager configuration, as well as specifying an applications directory when needed.

If used with a managed server template, no customization is available because the template will use the configuration settings specified by the administration server in the source domain. The unpack command can be used to create a domain from a template as follows:

```
./unpack.sh -template=/path/to/domain_template.jar -domain=/path/to/target_
domain -log=/path/to/unpack.log
```

The unpack command takes as arguments the path to the domain template and the path to the location where the domain will be created by expanding the contents of the domain template. Customization when using a domain template is optional. It is available through the following arguments:

```
-user_name=USER -password=PASS -app_dir=/path/to/apps -nodemanager_
type=TYPE⁶ -nodemanager_home=/path/to/nodemanager -java_home=/path/to/jdk
-server_start_mode=MODE
```

The available customization options with the unpack command include setting the Node Manager type, either plan or SSL; the path to the Node Manager home location; and a server start mode, either development or production.

Propagation Process

Assuming that WebLogic Server has already been installed and updated in each of the hosts that will run the managed servers in a domain, propagating the domain configuration will simply involve running the pack command to create a managed server template, transferring the template to each of the hosts that will run the managed servers, running the unpack command on each of them and start the servers.

Upon startup, the managed servers will connect with the administration server to obtain a fresh copy of the configuration and will be ready to process requests for any deployed applications.

---

⁶Configuring node manager is the topic of the next chapter.

Recommended Exercises

1. Using the configuration wizard, create a domain that defines a cluster with two managed servers and a machine definition for the host.

2. Review the structure and contents of the main configuration file config.xml.

3. Using the pack command create a domain template and a managed server template from the created domain.

4. Using the configuration wizard, use the domain template just created with the pack command to create a new domain, adding the definition of a second cluster comprised of two additional managed servers.

5. Use the readTemplate() function and explore the representation of the domain template in WLST.

Certification Questions

1. How many servers can be designated as administration servers in a domain?

    a. One and only one

    b. More than one

    c. Two

    d. Any

2. Each managed server in a domain requires its own product installation to run.

    a. True

    b. False

3. Is it possible to run more than one domain in a single host?

    a. True

    b. False

4. What format is used to persist the domain configuration?

    a. A database schema

    b. A set of XML files

    c. In-memory

5. Select the tools that enable domain configuration and customization:

    a. The configuration wizard

    b. The administration console

    c. WLST

    d. The pack and unpack commands

    e. All of the above

Coming Up

Once a domain has been created, its servers are ready to be started and used. Before this, it is important to review the purpose and configuration of the node manager component as it is required to enable communication between the administration server and the managed servers. Node manager is the subject of the next chapter.

CHAPTER 4

Node Manager

Oracle WebLogic Server Node Manager is an optional but recommended WebLogic Server utility. Any domain configuration that defines at least one managed server will benefit from configuring and using Node Manager to control server start and shutdown, including automatic restart.

In this chapter we first look briefly at the components that interact with Node Manager at the domain level and thoroughly discuss its configuration options. We end this chapter by reviewing the most common operations performed by Node Manager.

Overview

Oracle WebLogic Server Node Manager comes in two versions, one Java-based and one script-based. Both serve the same purposes but the Java-based version is, by far, the one used most commonly. It is actually the default version in WebLogic Server 12c and has had its configuration significantly simplified. Some of the recommended practices to managing Node Manager in previous WebLogic Server versions have now become the default practices, including the scope in which Node Manager is used.

A new screen is part of the WebLogic Server 12c configuration wizard that requires selecting the node manager type and credentials[1]. If administrators select per-domain Node Manager, as opposed to choosing manual setup, the wizard will create a default configuration that is ready for immediate use. This configuration is complete with security credentials, configuration properties, domain association and control scripts already in the right place, all of which and more was commonly manually performed by administrators of previous product versions. Figure 4-1 displays the Node Manager screen from the WebLogic Server Configuration Wizard.

---

[1]The semantics for type in the said screen is that of the WebLogic Server managed beans and defines whether the domain is configured per-domain or per-host, rather than reference its implementation.

© Gustavo Garnica 2018
G. Garnica, *Oracle WebLogic Server 12c Administration I Exam 1Z0-133*,
https://doi.org/10.1007/978-1-4842-2562-2_4

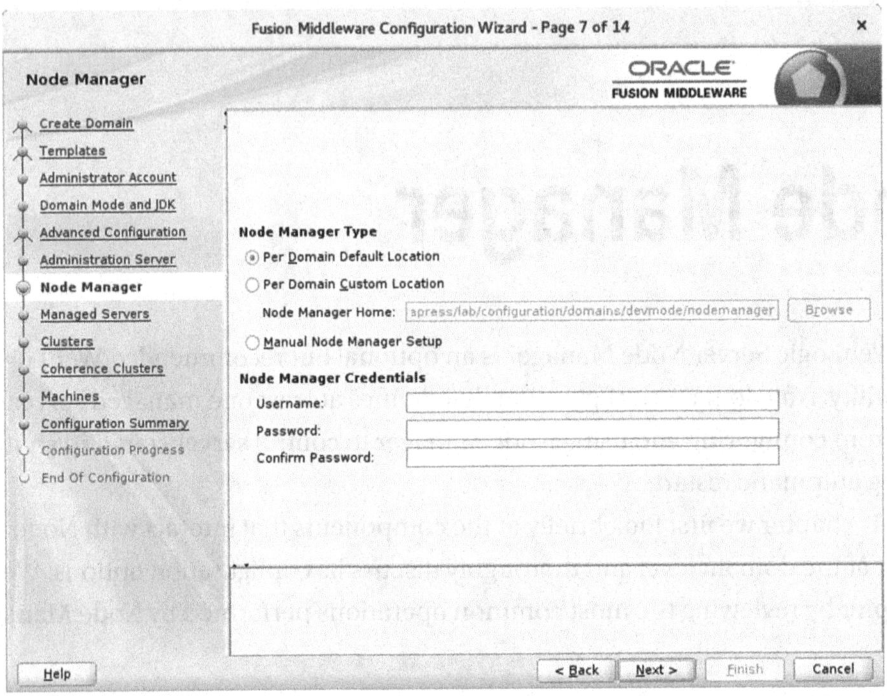

Figure 4-1. *Configuration Wizard Node Manager screen*

As indicated previously, the default Node Manager version is implemented in Java and runs as a JVM process just like servers do, although it is by default configured to have a much smaller foot print on the system. The main configuration of the Java Node Manager is kept in a properties file. It supports one-way SSL to secure its communications with other domain components.

The script-based Node Manager is implemented in UNIX/Linux shell scripts and depends on SSH for security and communications. This makes the Java-based Node Manager the only alternative in Windows environments.

Node Manager Interactions

Once configured, Node Manager can be used to start and control any of the servers in the same WebLogic machine in which it resides, including the Administration Server. Node Manager will then also be able to receive requests from the Administration Server to perform control commands on the managed servers. These requests may have originated in the Administration Console or come from other JMX clients. Figure 4-2 shows a diagram of the components with which Node Manager interacts, and the flow of communication.

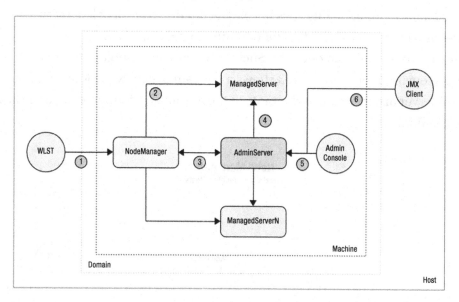

Node Manager
Logical View - Single Host

Figure 4-2. *Node Manager logical view in a single-host domain configuration*

The following interactions are displayed in the diagram:

1. An administrator connects to Node Manager using WebLogic Scripting Tool.

2. Node Manager may directly start, stop, and restart any WebLogic server instances in the same machine.

3. The Administration Server will contact Node Manager with control requests to be performed on managed servers.

4. The Administration Server will contact managed server instances directly, in order to perform graceful shutdown operations[2].

---

[2]Graceful shutdown procedures transition a server instance through a series of states, from running to shutdown, by allowing existing HTTP sessions to be terminated gracefully over a configurable length of time.

5. The Administration Console can be used to request control operations on managed servers.

6. Custom JMX clients can connect to the Administration Server in order to request control operations on managed servers.

Node Manager functionality goes beyond facilitating control of local server instances; it is even more important for domains containing clusters that are distributed across more than one host. Such is the common topology used in production environments. Figure 4-3 shows a diagram of how Node Manager is used to control server instances that are remote to the Administration server, and the flow of communication.

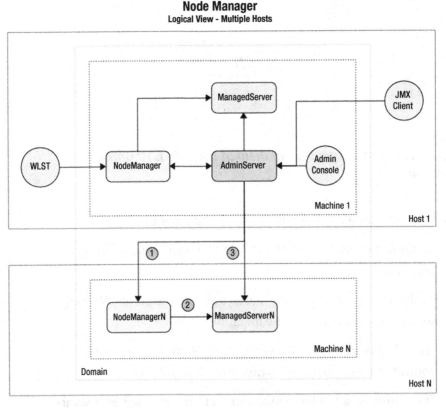

Figure 4-3. *Node Manager logical view in a multiple-host domain configuration*

Besides the interactions shown in the previous diagram, the following interactions are depicted:

1. An Administration Server will contact a remote Node Manager process over a network channel, with control requests to be performed on remote managed server instances.

2. The remote Node Manager process may directly start, stop, and restart any WebLogic server instances local to the same machine in which it resides.

3. The Administration Server will also attempt to contact managed server instances directly, in order to perform graceful shutdown operations[3].

Configuration

There are two configuration modes available for Node Manager: per-domain and per-host. The default configuration mode is per-domain. Even though the per-host mode is still available, even in previous versions, Node Manager was commonly configured on a per-domain basis. The per-host configuration enables using a single Node Manager process to manage server instances and machines that belong in different domains. It appears that the per-domain configuration trend was known to Oracle as it streamlined its configuration and made it the automatic and default choice.

Since the per-domain configuration of the Java-based Node Manager is the default choice, and in practice it is commonly used, this chapter will devote most of the remaining content describing this approach.

The configuration process prepares the files that contain the information that will be used at runtime to determine how to bootstrap the Node Manager JVM itself, how to initialize server instances, and how to connect to them, as well as how to authenticate users who request to perform control operations.

As explained before, Node Manager is automatically configured and is readily available by simply opting for per-domain configuration, providing credentials and

---

[3]If an Administration Server does not succeed in contacting a managed server directly, it will fall back to request Node Manager to perform a non-graceful shutdown operation instead.

defining a WebLogic machine. The settings created by this automated configuration
may also be manually overridden by running a few commands in a WLST session, or by
modifying the corresponding screens using the Administration Console.

Automatic Configuration

The automatic Oracle WebLogic Server Node Manager configuration performed by the
domain configuration wizard defines that the JVM process will listen for requests on
localhost, port 5556. While defining the machine in the same configuration wizard, it
is possible to change this to a DNS name or IP address and port number combination.
This piece of configuration information must match exactly the CN field of the SSL/TLS
certificate used by Node Manager.

The default configuration automatically associates Node Manager to the domain in
question, meaning that Node Manager will be authorized to perform control operations
on all server instances that belong to it. This is done by creating a file that maps the
domain names to their root directories.

The credentials entered will be encrypted and saved to file system. Remote Node
Manager processes are only authorized to perform operations on server instances on
behalf of the Administration Server after propagating these credentials to them. This is
done by running the *nmEnroll* command in WLST.

Thus, a Node Manager client will only be authorized to perform control operations if
the user is successfully authenticated and if the server instance in question belongs to a
domain registered in the Node Manager configuration.

By default, Node Manager is configured to use SSL with demonstration certificates
which must be replaced with custom certificates [4]. The demonstration certificates must
never be used in production environments. Even though it is highly insecure and not
advisable even for non-production environments, it is possible to disable using SSL in
Node Manager communication channels altogether.

There are several additional pieces of configuration automatically created by
the configuration wizard. These include other default settings such as the properties
required to start a server for the first time. A full description of the configuration files
appears in this chapter in subsequent sections.

---

[4]In corporate environments, there is usually a group or individual in charge of issuing SSL
certificates. This entity is commonly an intermediate CA of a trusted CA. If this is not available
for your environment, and for training or other non-production purposes, the alternative is to
use self-signed certificates.

Manual Configuration

An administrator may use Oracle WebLogic Server Scripting Tool to configure or reconfigure Node Manager settings that were automatically created by the configuration wizard. This is one alternative to perform the configuration if manual node manager was selected in the configuration wizard.

As indicated before, WLST allows navigating the managed beans structure that represents a domain configuration[5]. The following example, Listing 4-1, will set or modify Node Manager listen address and port, type, and credentials of a domain named "sample," created at the following location: "/opt/oracle/domains/sample". Other Node Manager properties are available readable and writable at the same managed beans location.

Listing 4-1. Manual Node Manager configuration

```
cd ORACLE_HOME/oracle_common/common/bin
./wlst.sh

readDomain("/opt/oracle/domains/sample")⁶
cd("/")
cd("NMProperties")
set("ListenAddress", "127.0.0.1")⁷
set("ListenPort", 7001)
cd("/")
cd("SecurityConfiguration/sample")
set("NodeManagerUsername", "nodemanager")
set("NodeManagerPasswordEncrypted", "newPassw0rd")⁸
setOption("NodeManagerType", "PerDomainNodeManager")
updateDomain()
```

---

[5]The WebLogic Server managed beans structure can be navigated using commands such as *cd*, *ls*, and *pwd*, much like those found in file systems in a UNIX command shell.

[6]The absolute path to the domain home was selected at the time the domain was created using the Configuration Wizard. If no custom path for the DOMAIN_HOME was specified, the location will be ORACLE_HOME/user_projects/domains/DOMAIN_NAME.

[7]The listen address for a server can be either the DNS name, the hostname, or the IP address of the machine where the server will run.

[8]Despite the name of the property, the password here can be entered in plain text, and WebLogic Server will take care of storing it encrypted.

Structure and Properties

Oracle WebLogic Server Node Manager maintains its configuration in several files. It will also depend on several files created for each server instance it will control. Similarly, the Node Manager process will write in a dedicated log file and will also keep a log file for each server instance.

Configuration Files

Node Manager maintains the following configuration files:

- nodemanager.properties – This is the main Node Manager configuration file

- nm_password.properties – This file contains the encrypted node manager credentials

- nodemanager.domains – This file contains the names and locations of the associated domains

- nodemanager.process.id – This file contains Node Manager OS process ID

- nodemanager.process.lck – This file represents an internal Node Manager lock

Node Manager will create or otherwise use the following files for each server instance:

- boot.properties – This file contains user credentials used by Node Manager to start this server

- startup.properties – This file maintains the server startup properties last passed to Node Manager by the Administration Server[9]

- SERVER_NAME.lck – This file contains an internal Node Manager lock ID

---

[9]These properties correspond to the server startup attributes found in the ServerStartMBean managed bean.

- SERVER_NAME.pid – This file contains the corresponding server instance OS process ID

- SERVER_NAME.state – This file contains a string describing the internal server state

Log Files

Node Manager maintains the following log files:

- nodemanager.log – This file contains entries for events and operations made on server instances of the associated domains, such as when a server is started, stopped, or shut down. It also includes entries for other node manager events, such as when Node Manager detects that a server has failed.

- SERVER_NAME.out – This file is created by Node Manager when it starts a server instance. It contains entries for both standard out and standard error messages.

The contents of these files are also accessible using the Administration Console or the WLST *nmLog* and *nmServerLog* commands. The default operation is for Node Manager to append to these files although configuring rotation is possible. Server instances create and maintain their own log files, in addition to those created by Node Manager.

File Locations

The location of the Oracle WebLogic Server Node Manager configuration files depends on the type of node manager selected in the domain configuration wizard. As expected, when working with a domain that has a default, per-domain node manager configuration, the configuration files can be found under the domain root directory, whereas with a per-host node manager configuration, the corresponding files are located under the product home root directories.

The exact location of the configuration files for a per-domain Node Manager configuration is:

- nm_password.properties – DOMAIN_HOME/config/nodemanager

- nodemanager.properties & nodemanager.domains – DOMAIN_HOME/nodemanager

- startNodeManager.sh & stopNodeManager.sh – DOMAIN_HOME/bin

The exact location of the configuration files for a per-host Node Manager configuration is:

- nodemanager.properties & nodemanager.domains – ORACLE_HOME/oracle_common/common/nodemanager

- startNodeManager.sh & stopNodeManager.sh – ORACLE_HOME/wlserver/server/bin

Properties

As indicated before, the properties that control how Node Manager performs its work are found in the nodemanager.properties file. These properties may also be overridden at the command line when creating the Node Manager process. A listing of the core properties and an explanation of their purpose follow:

- ListenAddress – DNS name or IP address on which the Node Manager process will listen for requests, default value: localhost

- ListenPort – Port number on which the Node Manager process will listen for requests, default value: 5556

- LogFile – Location and name of the file where the Node Manager process will write its messages, default value: DOMAIN_HOME/nodemanager/nodemanager.log

- LogLimit – Maximum size of the log file when using log rotation, default value: 0

- LogCount – Maximum number of log files to keep when using log rotation, default value: 1

- LogAppend – Whether to append to an existing log file when the Node Manager process starts, default value: true

- LogLevel – Verbosity of the messages written by log manager, default value: INFO

- CrashRecoveryEnabled – Whether or not attempt to restart a failed server instance, default value: false

- StartScriptEnabled – Whether to use a specific script to start server instances, default value: true

- StartScriptName – Name of the script that will be used to start server instances, default value: startWebLogic.sh

- StopScriptEnabled – Whether to use a specific script to stop server instances, default value: false

- DomainsFile – Location and name of the file that contains the associated domain names and locations

- DomainRegistrationEnabled – Whether to accept dynamic domain associations from node manager clients, default value: false

- AuthenticationEnabled – Whether to authenticate clients against the domain, default value: true

- NativeVersionEnabled – Whether to use native libraries in the Node Manager process, default value: true[10]

- StateCheckInterval – The length of time that Node Manager will wait to check the state of server instances it started, default value: 500 (milliseconds)

- NodeManagerHome – Location and name of the directory where the configuration and log files are stored

- JavaHome – Location and name of the directory where the JDK is installed

---

[10]It is strongly advisable to maintain the value of NativeVersionEnabled set to true as changing it will limit the ability of Node Manager to recognize the status of a server instance process and to recover crashed instances.

- SecureListener – Whether to use SSL/TLS on the network channel, default value: true

- Keystores – Indicates the type of keystore configuration that Node Manager will use, available values are the same of a server instance: DemoIdentityAndDemoTrust, CustomIdentityAndJavaStandardTrust, CustomIdentityAndCustomTrust

- JavaStandardTrustKeyStorePassPhrase – The password required, if any, by the underlying Java trust keystore. Required when the SSL keystores configuration is set to CustomIdentityAndJavaStandardTrust

- CustomIdentityKeyStoreFileName – Location and file name of the Node Manager identity certificate that contains its private key. Required when the SSL keystores configuration is set to CustomIdentityAndJavaStandardTrust or CustomIdentityAndCustomTrust

- CustomIdentityKeyStorePassPhrase – Password to the keystore that contains the identity certificate private key. Required when the SSL keystores configuration is set to CustomIdentityAndJavaStandardTrust or CustomIdentityAndCustomTrust

- CustomIdentityPrivateKeyPassPhrase – Password to access the private key from the identity certificate. Required when the SSL keystores configuration is set to CustomIdentityAndJavaStandardTrust or CustomIdentityAndCustomTrust

- CustomIdentityAlias – String used to refer to the private key in the identity keystore, defined when the private key was first loaded into the keystore

SSL Configuration

As stated in the beginning of this chapter, the automatic configuration installs and configures SSL demo certificates to encrypt Node Manager traffic. In general terms, SSL uses public key encryption, which requires a key pair, a private key, and a public key. Data encrypted using the public key can only be decrypted using the private key. In this scenario, a key pair must be generated and configured for Node Manager. The public key contains information about the owner, such as its DNS name or IP address in the CN field. The public key is embedded in a digital certificate, and the private key along with the digital certificate comprise the server identity. The data embedded in the digital certificate is verified and signed by a certification authority that is commonly well known and trusted. Anyone who trusts the certificate authority will also trust the digital identity of Node Manager.

As indicated before, Node Manager is configured with one-way SSL, meaning that Node Manager will present its digital certificate to clients, but clients will not be required to present their digital identity in a certificate. The Node Manager digital identity will be used to encrypt Node Manager traffic. At this point, it should be fairly obvious that maintaining the demonstration SSL certificates configured by default should be replaced with a custom digital identity for Node Manager.

Obtaining digital certificates in established corporations is usually as simple as requesting them from the group that is in charge of generating them. When this is not available, it is also possible to generate the digital identity certificates and also sign them. In terms of the technologies involved, this can be just as secure as having a well-known and trusted certificate authority sign them, but the certificates thus signed will not be trusted by anyone. For training purposes, this should be enough. In this book we will not go into the details of creating a CA, generating the digital identity, and signing it, but we will assume that the digital certificate is already available. In order to replace the demonstration certificate with a custom identity certificate, the following steps should be followed:

1. Set the Keystores property to one of the custom options: CustomIdentityAndJavaStandardTrust or CustomIdentityAndCustomTrust.

2. Set the values of the CustomIdentityKeyStoreFileName and CustomIdentityKeyStorePassPhrase properties to the name and location of the keystore that contains the private key as well as its corresponding password.

3. Set the value of the CustomIdentityPrivateKeyPassPhrase and CustomIdentityAlias properties to the password to the private key and the alias name which was used when populating the keystore with the private key.

Choosing Java standard trust over custom trust essentially means that we will use the trust keystore that was provided as part of the Java SDK that we are using[11]. This keystore has been populated with the identity certificates of many well-known certificate authorities. It is however not very relevant to the Node Manager SSL configuration as we do not need to use these certificates to authenticate and trust client certificates.

If we choose to customize trust as well, we will need to provide a keystore location and file name that must be populated with the identity certificates of the certificate authorities whose signed certificates we choose to trust.

If we choose to use the Java standard trust, we must set the corresponding password in the JavaStandardTrustKeystorePassPhrase property. The well-known password of the *cacerts* keystore is, not surprisingly: *changeit.*

Operation

As explained throughout the chapter, Node Manager enables an administrator to start server instances both locally and remotely, to constantly monitor their state, and to automatically restart them when they crash. This is a very important feature for Oracle WebLogic Server production environments that are commonly required to stay up and running at all times. Node Manager also plays a role in more advanced WebLogic Server functionality such as what is termed Whole Server Migration, which further enhances the availability of a domain by migrating server instances from a failed host to a healthy one. It is also a recommended practice to leverage Node Manager for regular operations on server instances.

Each host participating in a domain should be configured to run Node Manager as an operating system service. For hosts running Microsoft Windows, this can be performed by simply running the installNodeMgrSvc.cmd script[12]. There is also a corresponding uninstallNodeMgrSvc.cmd script.

---

[11]The Java standard trust keystore of the Oracle JDK 1.7.0+ is located at JAVA_HOME/jre/lib/security/cacerts.

[12]The StartScriptEnabled and NativeVersionEnabled properties of the Java-based Node Manager are not supported on Microsoft Windows.

For UNIX/Linux hosts, the startNodeManager.sh and stopNodeManager.sh scripts are suitable to be invoked from *init* scripts, which enables Node Manager to be effectively run as a UNIX/Linux operating system service.

The StartScriptEnabled and StopScriptEnabled properties in the configuration allow customizing the events surrounding startup and shutdown of the Node Manager process. This is useful in cases where, for example, a shared volume should be mounted before the process is created, and unmounted after the process has exited.

In general terms, the custom start script would run the preparation tasks before invoking the startNodeManager.sh script. Conversely, the custom stop scripts would first invoke the stopNodeManager.sh script and then run the clean-up tasks.

Start the Administration Server

The first step after a domain has been created and Node Manager has been configured and started is to start the Administration Server. This is achieved by connecting to Node Manager using WLST, and then having Node Manager start the Administration Server instance.

Before actually creating corresponding JVM process, Node Manager will first use its registered domains file (nodemanager.domains) to determine the domain root location; it will then authenticate the administrator using the credentials provided against those available in the domain in encrypted format, and it will determine the initial startup properties. The following WLST example, Listing 4-2, commands perform this process on a sample domain that has Node Manager configured to listen on the default port:

Listing 4-2. Start the Administration Server

```
cd DOMAIN_HOME/bin
./startNodeManager.sh &

cd ORACLE_HOME/oracle_common/common/bin
./wlst.sh

nmConnect("nodemanager", "newPassw0rd", "127.0.0.1", "5556", "sample", "/
opt/oracle/domains/sample", "ssl")
nmStart("AdminServer")
```

Start Managed Servers

Once the Administration Server has started, it is a trivial step to start the managed servers configured to run on the same WebLogic Server machine as the command is the same that was used to start the Administration Server, just passing the name of a managed server instead. Before creating a managed server instance, Node Manager will obtain the corresponding startup properties from the Administration server.

Managed servers will be started using the same root directory as Node Manager. When no root directory is explicitly specified, the domain root directory is used by default in a path such as: DOMAIN_HOME/servers/SERVER_NAME.

Automatic JVM Restart

Node Manager is able to restart crashed server instances as long as both of the following conditions are met:

1. They must have been started using Node Manager

2. The CrashRecoveryEnabled property in Node Manager or the AutoRestart attribute in the server instance are enabled

The need to restart a server instance is determined by checking the JVM process exit code or its last known state, both of which are tracked by Node Manager. Managed server instances contact the Administration server to obtain a copy of the latest domain configuration. If the managed server is unable to contact the Administration server for this purpose, it will start in Managed Server Independence mode if enabled in the domain, which as the name suggests, will cause the server to continue operating independently of the Administration server, using the last copy it received of the domain configuration.

Crash Recovery

Crash recovery is different from automatic JVM restart in that the Node Manager process will attempt certain recovery actions immediately upon starting, including:

1. Check for any lock files created

2. If lock files exist but a process with the corresponding ID does not, Node Manager will attempt to restart the required server instances

3. If the process ID exists, Node Manager will attempt to verify if it belongs to a WebLogic Server JVM by attempting to access an internal management servlet that is available in each server instance; if it is not able to, Node Manager will attempt to restart the required server instance

Recommended Exercises

1. Run the Domain Configuration Wizard and select the manual node manager setup option, then configure Node Manager manually using WLST.

2. Configure Node Manager timed log rotation with a short duration and verify that new log files are created.

3. Configure Node Manager on a non-default listen address and port.

4. Enable server restart in the Node Manager configuration and kill a managed server instance to force Node Manager to restart the JVM.

5. Customize the Node Manager SSL configuration using custom identity certificates.

6. Create init scripts to configure Node Manager to run as a service on UNIX/Linux.

Certification Questions

1. What are the two Node Manager implementations available on WebLogic Server 12c?

   a. Java-based and script-based

   b. Java-based and Windows-based

   c. Windows-based and UNIX/Linux-based

   d. Java-based and Bash-based

2. WebLogic Server Node Manager can control server instances in more than one domain.

   a. True

   b. False

3. Select the supported options to secure Node Manager traffic:

   a. One-way SSL

   b. Two-way SSL

   c. Passphrase

   d. SSH

   e. All of the above

4. Node Manager is capable of automatically restarting any WebLogic Server instance.

   a. True

   b. False

5. What is the WLST command to configure Node Manager on multiple WebLogic Server machines?

   a. configure()

   b. createConfig()

   c. nmAuthorize()

   d. nmEnroll()

Coming Up

After learning how to configure Node Manager and how to use it to start and automatically restart server instances, it is now time to review the details of how a server instance JVM is configured. Servers are the subject of the next chapter.

CHAPTER 5

Servers

The central component of a WebLogic Server domain is a server instance, or more specifically, a JVM that is running the WebLogic Server main class. In this chapter we discuss in detail what options are available for an administrator to configure and run such a server instance, both the default options, and how to customize the setup process for cases when the standard procedure may not suit the needs of a particular environment.

Standard Startup

Notwithstanding the process that is followed to configure the environment to run an Oracle WebLogic Server instance, either administration servers or managed servers, the command that is issued to create the JVM is always the following:

```
java weblogic.Server
```

Programmers and system administrators that support the Java platform will quickly recognize that this runs the Java program, which is part of the Java JDK that was installed ahead of WebLogic Server. This command creates a Java virtual machine as an operating system process and, by passing weblogic.Server as an argument, it runs the WebLogic Server main class. The JVM requires additional information to determine where to find the weblogic.Server class, its dependencies, and it also requires additional configuration to work as expected by the designers of the weblogic.Server program. This information, along with additional configuration details, is also supplied as part of the command in the form of several system properties.

© Gustavo Garnica 2018
G. Garnica, *Oracle WebLogic Server 12c Administration I Exam 1Z0-133*,
https://doi.org/10.1007/978-1-4842-2562-2_5

Available Methods

A server instance is provided the essential information to run, including essential configuration for any WebLogic Server JVM, as well as certain customizations to make it run in the environment where it is created, through one of the following methods:

1. Using startup scripts

2. Using WLST and Node Manager

3. Using the Administration Console and Node Manager

All methods will come down to the same command invocation we just mentioned. However, there are slight differences in the setup process, in other words, in the way the command invocation is built.

The next few sections explore how the standard startup scripts provide the required configuration information to create and run the JVM[1]. Understanding how the command is built gives an administrator the ability to run server instances manually[2]. This requires an administrator to also manually set all of the startup configuration options, including both environment variables and system properties. Understanding how to do this enables an administrator to also put these options together in a custom script, which could then be used to also perform other preparatory tasks before the actual command invocation. Even though this approach may be useful in certain situations, Oracle reserves the right to make changes to the requirements of the weblogic.Server class, for example, by removing or adding libraries to the classpath as part of a product update, which would obviously break custom startup scripts. Therefore, this information is intended to give administrators a better understanding of the requirements to run a WebLogic Server instance, rather than substituting the standard startup methods.

---

[1]At runtime, a WebLogic Server instance accepts other configuration options than just those provided at startup. These are additional options in general complement, rather than override, the configuration options provided at startup.

[2]Oracle recommends not to manually invoke java weblogic.Server to start server instances in production environments.

Standard Scripts

When a WebLogic Server domain is created, it includes the following scripts[3], which are used in the standard process of starting and shutting down server instances:

- startWebLogic

- startManagedWebLogic

- setDomainEnv

- setStartupEnv

- setWLSEnv

- commEnv

The first four scripts are part of the domain configuration and are found in the DOMAIN_HOME/bin directory, and the last two are located in the ORACLE_HOME/wlserver/bin and ORACLE_HOME/wlserver/common/bin directories, respectively. Figure 5-1 shows the order in which the standard scripts are invoked to build the command to start a server instance.

---

[3]Oracle provides scripts for both UNIX/Linux (*.sh) and Microsoft Windows (*.cmd) environments.

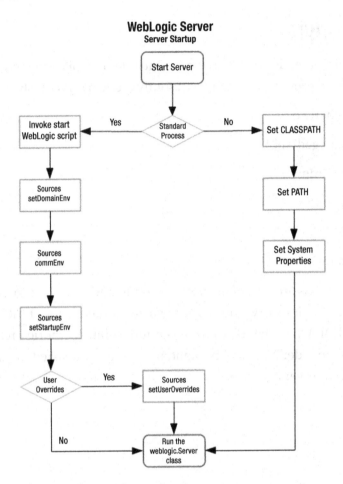

Figure 5-1. *Flow of invocation of standard server startup scripts*

As shown on the left in the flow diagram, the standard server instance startup process begins by invoking the startWebLogic script[4]. This script will in turn invoke the rest of the scripts[5] in a specific order to properly build the complete command and set the required environment variables. On the right, the generic steps to successfully configure and start a server instance are also listed. In other words, the steps on the right roughly describe what those on the left perform.

---

[4]The startWebLogic and startManagedWebLogic scripts do not require Node Manager to be running in order to start server instances. The same is true of the WLST startServer command, which can be used to start both administration and managed server instances. The startManagedWebLogic scripts, however, require an administration server to be up and running before use.

[5]Oracle advises against calling the setDomainEnv script directly.

The descriptions that follow do not list the actions performed in each line of each of the standard scripts, but will rather just describe the actions that are considered fundamental in building the configuration that will be used to start up server instances.

The startWebLogic Script

There are actually two scripts named startWebLogic: one is located in the DOMAIN_HOME directory and the other in the DOMAIN_HOME/bin directory. The first script will simply set the DOMAIN_HOME variable and then invoke the second script.

The script starts by setting a user mask of 027, which means that all files created by the JVM process will be fully accessible to the process owner, readable by the main group to which the process owner belongs, and inaccessible to the rest of the world. Kudos to Oracle for setting by default yet another best practice.

The script sets the DOMAIN_HOME, ensuring that is set for when the script in the bin directory is called directly and then it sources the setDomainEnv script.

The setDomainEnv Script

It starts by setting the WL_HOME variable to the absolute path of the ORACLE_HOME/wlserver directory. It then sets the JAVA_HOME variable to the absolute path to the JDK that was used to install WebLogic Server. It does this after evaluating several other variables including those containing the JDK vendor name and the JVM type.

If the SERVER_NAME variable is not set, it will set it to the value of AdminServer. This has the effect of WebLogic Server by default attempting to start an Administration server unless explicitly told to start a managed server. The script will next process any arguments passed to the script. If production is passed, the variable DOMAIN_PRODUCTION_MODE is set to true. At this point, the script sources the commEnv script.

The commEnv Script

The script checks whether both the WL_HOME and MW_HOME variables are set. If they are not, it will display an error message and exit with a status code of 1. Then, if only the MW_HOME has not been set, it will define it with a value of one directory above of that which the MW_HOME directory points to and source itself again to ensure these variables are set.

Resuming Execution of setDomainEnv

The script then sets the WLS_HOME variable to the value of the server directory under the WL_HOME directory. After this, it evaluates several variables and at the end, if it is a HotSpot JVM it sets the heap size to 256 megabytes minimum and 512 megabytes maximum, as well as a permanent generation size of 128 megabytes minimum and 256 megabytes maximum. At this point the script sources the setStartupEnv and setUserOverrides scripts if they exist.

The setStartupEnv Script

The script sets the STARTUP_GROUP variable to AdminServerStartupGroup if the value of the SERVER_NAME variable is AdminServer. Then, it will ensure that the POST_CLASSPATH variable includes the following library:

```
WL_HOME/oracle_common/modules/com.oracle.cie.config-wls-online_8.1.0.0.jar
```

The setUserOverrides Script

Near the end of the standard process shown in the flow diagram, an optional script named setUserOverrides script may be invoked. The provision to have a WebLogic Server instance automatically source this script when present is a very much appreciated improvement in Oracle WebLogic Server 12c.

Creating a script with this name is actually the Oracle supported method to customize the configuration and startup process of a WebLogic Server instance, as opposed to modifying or substituting the standard startup scripts, for the reasons explained before. A setUserOverrides can be used, for example, to include additional libraries in the server classpath or to define the heap size of the JVM.

WebLogic Server administrators working with product versions prior to 12c resorted to a similar approach to apply customizations, that is, creating a script that was simply invoked from the right place in one of the standard startup scripts.

Since the invocation to source the setUserOverrides script has been made part of setDomainEnv script logic, it will not be lost when the setDomainEnv script is replaced by product updates, etc. Furthermore, the setUserOverrides script will be picked up by the pack tool that is used to propagate domain configuration to other servers.

A setUserOverrides script on Linux is implemented using shell scripting. The following sample setUserOverrides.sh script can be used to set the heap size of the JVM. The script simply appends our required options to the existing options defined in the JAVA_OPTIONS variable:

Listing 5-1.   Sample setUserOverrides.sh script

```
#!/usr/bin/env bash

JAVA_OPTIONS="${JAVA_OPTIONS} -Xms4096m -Xmx4096m"
```

The sample code above will set the minimum and maximum heap size of all server instances to 4 gigabytes.

Completing Execution of setDomainEnv

The setDomainEnv script again resumes execution by setting the value of the MEM_ARGS variable to the value of the USER_MEM_ARGS if it carries a value. It then adds the system properties weblogic.home and wls.home to the JAVA_PROPERTIES variable. It also sets the system property weblogic.management.server to the value of the ADMIN_URL variable. After this, it will ensure that the POST_CLASSPATH variable includes the following library:

```
WL_HOME/server/lib/xqrl.jar
```

The script will then set the SERVER_CLASS variable to the value of weblogic.Server and appends the value of JAVA_PROPERTIES to the JAVA_OPTIONS variable, and also appends the system property weblogic.ProductionModeEnabled with a value of true when the PRODUCTION_MODE variable also has a value of true.

If the variable WEBLOGIC_EXTENSION_DIRS is defined, its value will be added to JAVA_OPTIONS using the system property weblogic.ext.dirs. The script will finally ensure that the value of the CLASSPATH variable is set to the values of the PRE_CLASSPATH, WEBLOGIC_CLASSPATH, and POST_CLASSPATH variables.

Completing Execution of startWebLogic

At this point, the script sets the weblogic.management.username and weblogic.management.password system properties to the values of WLS_USER and WLS_PW respectively. At this point, the script will echo messages to display the values of MEM_ARGS, CLASSPATH, and PATH.

To conclude the server startup configuration, the script adds to JAVA_OPTIONS the system properties launch.main.class to the value of SERVER_CLASS, launch.class.path to the value of CLASSPATH, and launch.complete to the value of weblogic.store.internal. LockManagerImpl.

The script will then echo messages to display the values of JAVA_HOME, JAVA_VM, and java -version and the WebLogic Server invocation line, followed by the actual command execution. Once the JVM has been created, the following message is shown in the corresponding server log file:

```
<TIMESTAMP> <Notice> <WebLogicServer> <BEA-000360> <The server started in
RUNNING mode.>
```

Verifying that this message appears in the log file is one of several actions that an administrator should perform to confirm that a server instance started correctly.

Path, Classpath, and System Properties

As shown in previous sections, the standard configuration settings of a WebLogic Server instance are defined in both, environment variables and system properties. In a WebLogic Server instance, several system properties are defined that are product specific. Other system properties and some environment variables are commonly defined for any Java program. These include the PATH and CLASSPATH variables.

The PATH variable in WebLogic Server has the same purpose as it does in any non-Java environment. It is defined to include a series of directories that contain binaries. After setting this variable, such binaries will be conveniently available to be run without having to type the full path to their location.

The CLASSPATH variable is defined specifically for every Java program. It is meant to tell the JVM where to find the classes required to run an application of a certain type, such as a WebLogic Server instance. CLASSPATH entries can include specific JAR files or directories with wildcards to include files without stating their individual names. The order in which CLASSPATH entries are included does matter in case of duplicate JAR files. The first one that is found will be used and the rest will be ignored.

There are two simple ways to inspect the startup configuration of a server instance, either looking at the corresponding server log file or by using a tool to interrogate the JVM for these settings.

As explained before, there will be messages that output the content of the PATH, CLASSPATH, and JAVA_OPTIONS variable. This latter variable will include the system properties and values that have been set.

There are several tools that can be used to interrogate the JVM such as jcmd and jstat, both of which are included in the Oracle JDK. The jcmd tool is a pretty simple but powerful tool[6] for inspecting the JVM configuration and can also perform other important tasks on the server process.

Sample Configuration Values

The following are default PATH, CLASSPATH, and system properties as defined for an administration server instance. These settings are essentially the same that an administrator will find in a WebLogic Server environment whose configuration has not been customized beyond the basic options available during domain creation.

The sample environment that produced these settings runs on Fedora Linux with Oracle JDK 7 installed using the RPM package. Oracle WebLogic Server 12c is installed at /home/gustavo/Mine/apress/lab/product, and the sample domain configuration is located at: /home/gustavo/Mine/apress/lab/configuration/domains.

Sample PATH Value

Listing 5-2. Default value of the PATH variable from the log file of an administration server

```
PATH=/home/gustavo/Mine/apress/lab/product/wlserver/server/bin:/home/
gustavo/Mine/apress/lab/product/wlserver/../oracle_common/modules/org.
apache.ant_1.9.2/bin:/usr/java/jdk1.7.0_80/jre/bin:/usr/java/jdk1.7.0_80/
bin:/usr/local/bin:/usr/local/sbin:/usr/bin:/usr/sbin:/home/gustavo/.local/
bin:/home/gustavo/bin
```

The output above shows that among other entries, the location of the JDK binaries, as well as the WebLogic Server binaries, are included in the value of the PATH variable. These two are always required to run and manage server instances.

---

[6]The jcmd tool is part of the Oracle JDK set of tools. Help is available by running: jcmd PID help where PID is the number of a JVM process.

Sample CLASSPATH Value

Listing 5-3. Default value of the CLASSPATH variable from the log file of an administration server

```
CLASSPATH=/usr/java/jdk1.7.0_80/lib/tools.jar:/home/gustavo/Mine/apress/
lab/product/wlserver/server/lib/weblogic_sp.jar:/home/gustavo/Mine/apress/
lab/product/wlserver/server/lib/weblogic.jar:/home/gustavo/Mine/apress/lab/
product/wlserver/../oracle_common/modules/net.sf.antcontrib_1.1.0.0_1-0b3/
lib/ant-contrib.jar:/home/gustavo/Mine/apress/lab/product/wlserver/modules/
features/oracle.wls.common.nodemanager_2.0.0.0.jar:/home/gustavo/Mine/
apress/lab/product/wlserver/../oracle_common/modules/com.oracle.cie.config-
wls-online_8.1.0.0.jar:/home/gustavo/Mine/apress/lab/product/wlserver/
common/derby/lib/derbyclient.jar:/home/gustavo/Mine/apress/lab/product/
wlserver/common/derby/lib/derby.jar:/home/gustavo/Mine/apress/lab/product/
wlserver/server/lib/xqrl.jar
```

The code above shows that the CLASSPATH variable includes the following JAR files by name:

- tools.jar

- weblogic.jar

- weblogic_sp.jar

- ant-contrib.jar

- com.oracle.cie.config-wls-online_8.1.0.0.jar

- oracle.wls.common.nodemanager_2.0.0.0.jar

- derbyclient.jar

- derby.jar

- xqrl.jar

The tools.jar file includes JDK tools and utilities. The weblogic.jar file contains some of the core WebLogic Server classes. The weblogic_sp.jar file is automatically included in the CLASSPATH by the commEnv script although it may not be present in a WebLogic Server installation. Its purpose is to enable administrators to apply a product patch without having to update the domain CLASSPATH by renaming the patch JAR file to weblogic_sp.jar and copying it to the WL_HOME/server/lib directory.

The ant-contrib.jar file includes classes supporting Ant tasks that are used by WebLogic Server. The com.oracle.cie.config-wls-online_8.1.0.0.jar includes classes that are used by the configuration wizard. The oracle.wls.common.nodemanager_2.0.0.0.jar obviously includes files that are used to support the Node Manager features. The derbyclient.jar and derby.jar include the Apache Derby client. The xqrl.jar implements XQuery support for WebLogic Server.

How the CLASSPATH Is Built

In the sample system, the WebLogic Server classpath was built in the following specific sequence:

1. The com.oracle.cie.config-wls-online JAR is added to the POST_CLASSPATH variable in the setStartupEnv script

2. The derbyclient and derby JARs are added to the DATABASE_CLASSPATH variable in the setDomainEnv script

3. The POST_CLASSPATH is appended values from the DATABASE_CLASSPATH in the setDomainEnv script

4. The xqrl JAR is added to the POST_CLASSPATH in the setDomainEnv script

5. The CLASSPATH variable is set to the value of the POST_CLASSPATH variable in the setDomainEnv script

6. The WEBLOGIC_CLASSPATH variable is set to include the following JARs: tools, weblogic, weblogic_sp, ant-contrib and oracle.wls.common.nodemanager in the setDomainEnv script

7. The CLASSPATH variable is prepended the value of the WEBLOGIC_CLASSPATH in the setDomainEnv script

8. The CLASSPATH variable is defined to the same value in the startWebLogic script

Sample System Properties

Listing 5-4. Default JVM flags and system properties from the log file of an administration server

```
Starting WLS with line:
/usr/java/jdk1.7.0_80/bin/java -server   -Xms256m -Xmx512m
-XX:CompileThreshold=8000 -XX:PermSize=128m  -XX:MaxPermSize=256m
-Dweblogic.Name=AdminServer -Djava.security.policy=/home/gustavo/Mine/
apress/lab/product/wlserver/server/lib/weblogic.policy  -Xverify:none
-Djava.endorsed.dirs=/usr/java/jdk1.7.0_80/jre/lib/endorsed:/home/
gustavo/Mine/apress/lab/product/wlserver/../oracle_common/modules/
endorsed -Xms4096m -Xmx4096m  -da -Dwls.home=/home/gustavo/Mine/
apress/lab/product/wlserver/server -Dweblogic.home=/home/gustavo/Mine/
apress/lab/product/wlserver/server -Dweblogic.utils.cmm.lowertier.
ServiceDisabled=true  weblogic.Server
```

The code above shows the following JVM flags:

- Xms and Xmx

- XX:CompileThreshold

- PermSize and MaxPermSize

- weblogic.Name

- java.security.policy

- Xverify

- java.endorsed.dirs

- wls.home

- weblogic.home

- weblogic.utils.cmm.lowertier.ServiceDisabled

The memory values shown in the previous listing are the standard values for an Oracle HotSpot JVM running on a 64-bit Linux OS and represent the contents of the MEM_ARGS variable in the standard scripts.

The heap size is set to range from 256 megabytes up to 512 megabytes, with a permanent generation size set to range from 128 megabytes to 256 megabytes. The CompileThreshold option is a performance flag to indicate that there should be 8000 method invocations or code iterations before code compilation. These values can be overridden in a setUserOverrides script. The actual heap size can be identified in the subsequent Xms and Xmx definition, which takes precedence over the first. It can also be reviewed by querying the JVM flags using the jcmd tool. The value of none in the Xverify flag disables bytecode verification. The java.security.policy specifies the location of the Java Security Manager policy file for WebLogic, which is the weblogic.policy file located in the server/lib directory of the product installation. The java.endorsed.dirs sets the location of the directory where libraries may be placed to override packages in the JDK. The weblogic.Name system property is set to the server name, in this case AdminServer. The wls.home and weblogic.home are both references to the WL_HOME directory.

The complete list of system properties defined in a running server instance the JVM may be obtained using a variety of methods, for instance, by using the VM.system_properties option of jcmd.

Additional System Properties

WebLogic Server defines a large set of additional system properties that can optionally be used to configure a server instance at startup. These properties can actually be used to override the server configuration that is kept in the domain repository. Unless persisted in the config.xml file, these settings would only last until the server instance is restarted.

As shown in Listing 5-4, these system properties are specified in the command line using a capital D, followed by the property name and its intended value, such as:

```
-Dweblogic.Name=AdminServer
```

The following list of properties is a small subset of the full range of options available. The purpose of each can be derived from their names:

- weblogic.Domain

- weblogic.ProductionModeEnabled

- weblogic.management.server

- weblogic.Name

- weblogic.ListenAddress

- weblogic.ListenPort

- weblogic.ssl.ListenPort

- weblogic.security.SSL.minimumProtocolVersion

- weblogic.system.BootIdentityFile

- weblogic.log.FileName

- serverType

The weblogic.management.server specifies the URL that must be used to contact the administration server in a given domain. The serverType property can take a value of wlx in which case, the server instance will be a lightweight instance that will not load the EJB, JMX, and JCA subsystems.

Manual Startup

As indicated in the beginning of this chapter, starting an Oracle WebLogic Server always invokes the Java command passing the weblogic.Server class. Doing so without the proper startup configuration as discussed will result in a JVM process created but that will not be able to properly function as a WebLogic Server instance of any kind.

As shown, the classpath is comprised of the JAR files that are required by the weblogic.Server class to perform its work. This set of JARs is subject to change, potentially frequent change indeed – either by system administrators who include additional JAR files to complement server functionality, connectivity, etc., or by Oracle, in the form of product updates.

Product patches may add, substitute, or remove from this set of JARs at any time, which appears to be the main reason for recommending administrators not to create their own startup process for server instances, but rather work with the standard process, customizing at the standard points, such as adding JAR files to one of the several directories defined for this purpose, according to the required visibility scope, or by implementing the changes in a setUserOverrides script.

Server Instance Selection

When the weblogic.Server command is run, it will always look for a domain configuration in the standard location, meaning a directory named config that includes a config.xml file. It will inspect this file and will run an administration server named AdminServer if it is defined; otherwise it will run a server named myserver if it is defined.

If no config.xml file can be found at the expected location, the command will prompt to create one. This configuration file will contain the definition of a single server instance named myserver. The command will also prompt for basic configuration information to customize this server instance, such as the required security credentials. The command would then start this server as an administration server.

From this we can see that the weblogic.Server command will by default attempt to start an administration server in an existing domain. If the environment where the command is run does not point to an existing domain with an administration server defined, then it will create one.

Running the Command

In the context of all the information discussed in this chapter, a viable process to start a server instance from the command line would be as follows:

1. Source the setWLSEnv script from the WL_HOME/server/bin directory[7].

2. Append additional entries to the CLASSPATH environment variable to be at least what was described before[8].

3. Identify the required system properties and values, according to the function of the server instance that will be started.

4. Change to the DOMAIN_HOME directory and run the java weblogic.Server command. The system properties defined must be specified in the command line between the java and the weblogic.Server words.

---

[7]Just running the setWLSEnv script will not be enough, it must be sourced to the current environment so that the environment variables defined will remain after the script has completed. In Linux systems this can be accomplished in several ways, the simplest is perhaps running: . ./setWLSEnv.sh, using a dot and a space before the script name.

[8]This will require the values described in steps 1 through 5 of the "How the Classpath Is Built" section in this chapter.

As discussed before, depending on the values passed to the Java command, the weblogic.Server program could actually be used to create a domain, since the program will actually prompt to create a domain configuration when it is unable to find one in the directory from where the command is run. This approach can only be used to create domains with a single instance, and cannot modify existing domains.

In general, one should include properties to define the heap size at least as big as the sample values shown above. If those settings are omitted, the JVM will very quickly run into memory issues. If starting an administration server is planned, one should at least include the weblogic.Name property as well. In addition, to start managed servers, the administration server should already have been started, and the weblogic.management. server property must also be included.

Credentials

When a new domain is created, the administration credentials are provided, encrypted, and saved. Each server instance will have a separate file whose contents are encrypted and which cannot be reused across server instances. Each time a server instance is started, the right credentials must be used. Depending on the domain start mode, either development or production, these credentials must be provided by pointing to the boot.properties file where they reside, or they must be typed in the command line.

In Oracle WebLogic version 12.1.2 both username and password may be specified using a pair of system properties. However, these properties have been deprecated and they should not be used as they remain visible on the command-line invocation throughout the life of the JVM process.

Recommended Exercises

1. Using the standard process start both an administration server and a managed server and review the contents of the CLASSPATH, PATH, MEM_ARGS, and command line used.

2. Manually set the CLASSPATH and start both an administration server and managed server passing the minimum necessary system properties for a WebLogic Server instance.

3. Implement a setUserOverrides script to customize the server configuration.

4. Manually start a server instance and verify if it applies the customizations from the setUserOverrides script.

Certification Questions

1. A server instance may be started using several commands.

   a. True

   b. False

2. What is the name of the standard script to start a managed server instance?

   a. startServer

   b. startWebLogic

   c. startManagedServer

   d. startManagedWebLogic

3. Which script sources the setUserOverrides script to apply configuration customizations?

   a. setDomainEnv

   b. startWebLogic

   c. startServer

   d. None of the above

4. Oracle WebLogic Server provides standard server start scripts for each supported platform.

   a. True

   b. False

5. What is the correct method to add a library to a server instance configuration?

   a. The PATH

   b. The CLASSPATH

   c. A system property

   d. All of the above

Coming Up

In our next chapter, we will talk about the details of the configuration management process in WebLogic Server, including how the underlying Java technology solves the challenge of a file-based configuration repository, as well as what tools are available to perform changes to the domain configuration.

CHAPTER 6

Configuration Management

All WebLogic Server domains drift from the original settings of its node manager and server instances at one point or another. This obviously happens more frequently with domains that are used for development and pre-production purposes, but the fact that it also happens on production environments as well makes it critical to gain the necessary understanding of the configuration management process.

In this chapter, we review the architecture of the components that represent the configuration of a WebLogic Server domain at runtime, how changes to these are made, persisted and distributed, as well as the tools available to perform configuration changes.

As explained in a previous chapter, the main domain configuration values are maintained in the config.xml file located in the DOMAIN_HOME/config directory. This config.xml file contains references to other XML files that describe the settings of several WebLogic subsystems[1]. Together they comprise the domain configuration repository.

If we think about the distributed architecture of Java EE middleware systems, such as WebLogic Server, where server instances are spread across multiple hosts, and then we consider that the domain configuration repository is file-based, we will quickly recognize that maintaining such configuration system presents an important synchronization challenge. The solution to this lies in WebLogic Server implementation and use of Java Management Extensions or JMX technology, to manage the entire domain configuration.

---

[1]Not every single configurable option can be found in the XML configuration files. WebLogic Server will not explicitly state in these files its default configuration values.

© Gustavo Garnica 2018
G. Garnica, *Oracle WebLogic Server 12c Administration I Exam 1Z0-133*,
https://doi.org/10.1007/978-1-4842-2562-2_6

Java Management Extensions

Java Management Extensions is a management and monitoring technology. Oracle WebLogic Server uses JMX for both purposes. Administrators use this technology all the time while interacting with server instances.

JMX technology is a natural way to instrument manageability to Java applications. Its architecture defines three tiers. The first tier contains the components, named managed beans or MBeans, instrumenting the resources subject to monitoring and management. The second tier is the MBean server or agent, which controls access to the MBeans. The third tier enables remote client access to the MBeanServer through connectors or adaptors, depending on the type of client.

JMX clients can be generic applications such as JConsole or Java Mission Control, which come bundled with the Oracle JDK and can be used to manage JMX instrumented applications, WebLogic Server included; or they can be custom built, such as a client with an adaptor that enables access to the API to consume monitoring data in an SNMP console.

Oracle WebLogic Server implements all three tiers. This implementation comprises the tools and utilities through which a domain configuration is managed.

There are two main JMX clients included in all WebLogic Server installations: WebLogic Scripting Tool or WLST, and the Administration Console. Although we have briefly mentioned WLST in previous chapters, we will now describe in detail its operation and scope. We will also review the main aspects and operation of the Administration Console. Besides these two tools, WebLogic Server MBeanServer and its collection of MBeans can interoperate with custom-built JMX clients.

Architecture

An Administration Server in a WebLogic Server domain has two hierarchies of configuration MBeans. Both of these sets resemble the domain configuration as defined in the config.xml file structure. One of these hierarchies is used as a read-only set of MBeans and contains the current configuration state of the domain. The second hierarchy is editable, and is used as a staging area to perform configuration changes. Likewise, Administration Servers will also maintain a second set of temporary configuration files to keep track of the pending configuration changes as they occur.

Managed servers in a domain do not have an editable configuration MBean hierarchy. Both administration and managed server instances also maintain a set of runtime MBeans that contain information about their runtime state.

During startup, Administration Servers will instantiate its configuration MBean hierarchies from the values kept in its file-based configuration repository. Managed Servers will contact the Administration Server to receive a copy of the latest domain configuration files before instantiating its read-only hierarchy of configuration MBeans. Once this process is complete, each server instance in a domain will have identical information in-memory of the domain configuration.

Figure 6-1 illustrates the architecture of the JMX components and their relationship to the configuration repositories in a WebLogic Server domain.

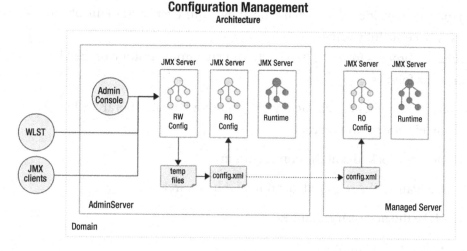

Figure 6-1. *JMX Architecture in a WebLogic Server domain*

Configuration Management

At runtime, JMX clients can modify the configuration MBeans maintained by the Administration Server. As expected, a transactional process is in place to manage the changes. This process involves a lock that clients must acquire to work on the editable configuration and release once they are done.

The modifications performed will be saved to the Administration Server's editable hierarchy of configuration MBeans as well as to a set of temporary configuration files that maintain the pending changes. Up to this point, a client may still roll back his changes, which will simply remove them from both the editable MBean hierarchy and temporary files, without affecting the runtime behavior of any of the server instances in the domain.

When clients request changes to be made permanent on the domain, a distribution process named activation is triggered, during which an attempt will be made to propagate the changes to all server instances across the domain. This involves sending the updated configuration files to all managed servers and having them update their configuration MBean hierarchies accordingly.

During the activation phase, a managed server receiving the updated configuration may reject the changes because of perceived inconsistencies or other circumstances. In these cases, changes will not be activated and the client that requested activation will receive a notification of the activation error. Additional work might be required to understand and resolve the inconsistency before attempting activation again.

Depending on the type of configuration data that is being modified, deleted, or added, changes may be applied dynamically, immediately upon successful activation, or when they are considered non-dynamic, they require a restart of the affected server instances to become fully active.

The change process from the perspective of an administrator can then be summarized as follows:

1. Use a JMX client to connect to the editable MBeans hierarchy in an administration server.

2. Obtain a lock to edit the configuration.

3. Navigate to the required location in the hierarchy.

4. Make the necessary changes.

5. Save the changes made.

6. Verify that the changes made are correct.

7. Request activation of the changes made.

8. Release the edit lock.

At any time in steps 4 to 6, an administrator may undo the changes made in an edit session. The edit lock acquired in step 2 will be retained by an administrator, even after server restarts, if not explicitly released; therefore, common sense and good system administration practices are in order around its use[2].

---

[2]The edit lock acquired by an administrator may be forcefully released by another administrator if required.

The configuration management pattern discussed up to this point covers pretty much any changes an administrator will perform on domain and server instance configuration data. This means pretty much every topic we have discussed about WebLogic Server administration in the preceding chapters.

Administration Console

The Administration Console is a web application. It is a front end to a JMX capable back end. As every WebLogic Server domain has an Administration Server, so every Administration Server has an Administration Console.

It is perhaps the tool most widely used by administrators of WebLogic Server domains. It has pretty good cross-browser support and has a pretty solid design, making it easy for new administrators to get used to it. Despite its ease of use, it is pretty broad in scope, covering many functions to manage domain configurations and to monitor server instances.

The Administration Console is started by default and accessible via the host address and port number configured when the domain was created. Its application context is /console.

When running a domain in production mode, the Administration Console is immediately accessible upon Administration Server start. When the domain is configured to run in development mode, the Administration Console is deployed when the server first detects that its context is requested.

If the administration server was configured with SSL, the corresponding port must be used to access the Administration Console. If the SSL configuration is running with the default values, which is with the SSL demo certificates, the browser will refuse access with a warning stating that the certificates were issued by an unknown authority. As mentioned in a previous chapter, this must be corrected by updating the configuration with custom certificates that are issued by a well-known certificate authority[3]. Figure 6-2 shows the login page of the Administration Console.

---

[3]Most organizations configure domains that reside in internal networks with self-signed certificates, which are every bit as secure in terms of the encryption process.

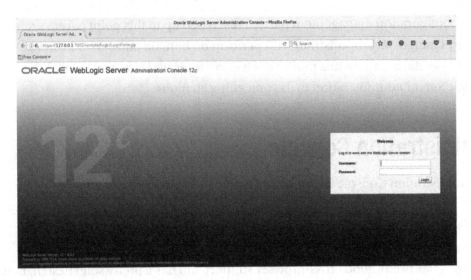

Figure 6-2. *Login page of the WebLogic Server Administration Console*

The Administration Console may be used to configure and work with domain components such as node manager; the administration and managed server instances; and to create, modify, and delete individual components and the properties of these components. It can also be used to access and view diagnostic information of the running server instances.

Security

The Administration Console in production systems is commonly protected by creating the Administration Server in a host without direct access to the Internet, then allowing access to it through a protected network only. It is not that uncommon to see environments in which administrators have decided to create the administration server in a DMZ. In environments like this, the Administration Console may be disabled when not in use.

At the application level, the console leverages the domain security system[4]. The domain security system architecture supports the definition of roles, groups, and users. Authorization levels are defined at the role level, which are granted to groups. Users are then added to a group whereby they inherit the corresponding authorization level.

---

[4]The domain security system details will be reviewed in a subsequent chapter.

When creating the domain, the credentials of a user are defined. A user is created with those credentials in the Administrators group, which has the administration role.

Out of the box, the domain security realm includes four roles: Administrators, Operators, Deployers, and Monitors, with matching groups. The monitor role is commonly of special interest in production environments as it effectively allows read-only access to the Administration Console.

GUI Layout

The Administration Console GUI has three sections that are most frequently used when working with the domain configuration: the Change Center, the Domain Structure, and the Main Panel where the properties of the selected domain component are displayed. Figure 6-3 shows the landing page of the Administration Console.

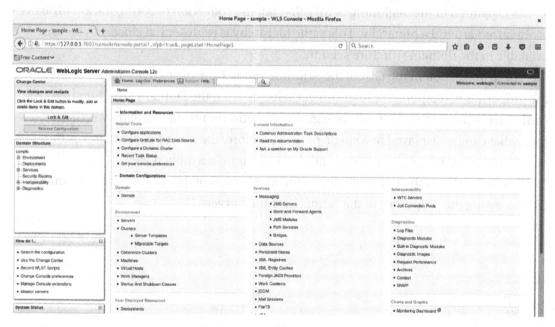

Figure 6-3. *Landing page of the WebLogic Server Administration Console*

The Change Center is displayed on the upper-left corner of the GUI. It is used to acquire or release the lock on the underlying editable MBeans hierarchy. From here, it is possible to access a table that lists all changes made to the domain configuration. From this table, it is also possible to either activate or undo all changes that have been made but not yet activated, and to see which of those are non-dynamic and require a server restart.

The Domain Structure is displayed below the Change Center. It is implemented as a tree structure that has the following main branches:

- Environment

- Deployments

- Services

- Security Realms

- Interoperability

- Diagnostics

The Environment branch enables access to the main domain components, such as servers, clusters, and machines. The Security Realms branch contains by default a single entry named *myrealm*, which provides access to the configuration of the security system.

As explained in the beginning of this chapter, the collection of configuration MBeans is organized around a hierarchy. This same hierarchy is represented closely in the tree available in the domain structure section.

The third section in the GUI of the Administration Console or Main Panel displays the properties corresponding to the object selected from the Domain Structure tree. The configurable properties available for a given configuration component may be larger than what can be displayed in a single page. Therefore, the main panel organizes the configuration properties in sections and displays them in a tabbed view.

Figure 6-4 shows the tabs available in the main panel of the Administration Console when viewing the properties of the Administration Server.

Figure 6-4. *Tabbed access to groups of properties of the AdminServer in the Administration Console*

The information in the main panel appears by default in form fields that are grayed out and not editable, unless an edit lock is acquired.

Again, depending on the domain component selected, the information available may also appear split in two sections in the main panel, where the most common values are readily shown in the upper part of the panel, with a secondary or advanced section initially hidden from view, but accessible at the bottom of the page.

Figure 6-5 shows the link to display the advanced section available in the main panel of the Administration Console when viewing the properties of the Administration Server.

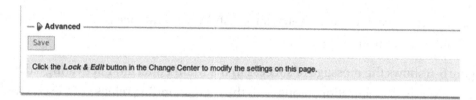

Figure 6-5. *Advanced Properties section of the AdminServer in the Administration Console*

Configuration Management Using the Administration Console

The Administration Console may be used to perform all types of changes to the domain configuration from the simplest, involving just a dynamic property change, to the most complex, including those that require the creation of multiple interdependent components, such as creating a cluster made up of several new managed servers. However complex the change at hand, the fundamental process to edit the configuration remains the same.

The following is the list of actions that the configuration management process involves when using the Administration Console, regardless of what change to the domain configuration is involved:

1. Log in to the Administration Console using the credentials of a user in the Administrators group.

2. Click on the Lock and Edit button in the Change Center.

3. Select the required domain component, etc., in the Domain Structure tree.

4. Make the necessary changes to the properties displayed in the Main Panel.

5. Save the changes made by clicking on the Save button at the top or bottom of the Main Panel.

6. Verify that the changes made are correct by reviewing the messages displayed in the Main Panel.

7. Request activation of the changes made by clicking on Activate Changes on the Main Panel.

8. For changes that are activated successfully, the edit lock is released automatically.

Figure 6-6 shows the message of success in the Main Panel after activating a dynamic change in a server configuration, along with the corresponding release of the edit lock in the Change Center.

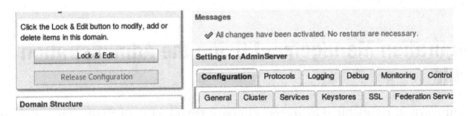

Figure 6-6. *Message of successful activation of dynamic changes using the Administration Console*

WebLogic Scripting Tool

In previous chapters, brief mentions were made about the WebLogic Scripting Tool. It was presented as an auxiliary tool to create and update domains when working in offline mode, and as a JMX client when working in online or connected mode. It was introduced as a tool capable of interpreting commands in Jython language as well as of executing WebLogic Server specific methods, either interactively or from a script.

WLST supports Jython version 2.2 implementation of the Python language and runs on the JVM. Even though it has more limited features than a full-fledged Python interpreter, it covers pretty much all programming needs of WebLogic Server system administrators.

Whereas the Administration Console provides a nice graphical user interface, is easy to learn and comfortable for non-repetitive tasks, WLST is geared for automation.

WLST can obviously be used in one-time tasks, but when used to automate work its real value becomes apparent. It is common to see experienced WebLogic Server administrators performing most repetitive actions through a set of scripts they wrote from scratch. Therefore, it is a good idea to spend time becoming familiar with Jython, the WebLogic Server MBean hierarchies, and the WLST environment.

WLST is not part of a WebLogic Server domain. It is available in both UNIX/Linux and Windows versions at the *wlserver/common/bin* path in every WebLogic Server product installation directory. The following code shows how to run WLST, and it shows its command prompt. The code below requires setting the ORACLE_HOME environment variable first.

Listing 6-1. Running WLST and its command prompt

```
cd $ORACLE_HOME/wlserver/common/bin
./wlst.sh

Initializing WebLogic Scripting Tool (WLST) ...

Welcome to WebLogic Server Administration Scripting Shell
Type help() for help on available commands

wls:/offline>
```

Security

As indicated before, in order to work with WLST online, a connection to the Administration Server must be established. The first action to secure the WLST environment is to always use a network channel that is TLS protected for this communication.

By default, when the administration server is configured to use SSL/TLS, it will encrypt communications using the demonstration certificates issued by Oracle. These certificates should be substituted. Failing to do so makes a WebLogic Server domain prone to DOS or MIM attacks[5]. It is strongly recommended to replace these demonstration certificates.

---

[5]Two types of attacks that WebLogic Server may be subject to are DOS and MIM. The following are two good introductory articles on them: https://www.arbornetworks.com/blog/asert/ddos-attacks-on-ssl-something-old-something-new/ and https://en.wikipedia.org/wiki/Man-in-the-middle_attack.

As explained before, this involves determining whether or not a CA is in place at your organization. If there is one, an administrator will simply have to request custom certificates for each of the hosts participating in the domain. If there is no internal CA, the alternative is either setting up a CA, or acquiring certificates from a well-known CA.

Once the certificates have been acquired, the information regarding the demonstration certificates in the domain configuration is simply replaced with the information of the new certificates. This process can be performed using either the Administration Console or WLST[6].

Once the communication has been established securely with the Administration Server, proper credentials must be provided to access the in-memory representation of the domain configuration, for both reading and writing.

These credentials are exactly those used to log in to the Administration Console. They reside in a realm in the WebLogic Server security subsystem. By default, these credentials are defined when the domain is created. Additional users and credentials may be created, as discussed in the beginning of this chapter.

After WLST validates the credentials provided, the required access level will be granted, which means granting access to either the read-only or read-write MBean hierarchies.

The following code shows a WLST session in which a connection to the Administration Server is made using the *connect()* command.

Listing 6-2. Connecting to an Administration Server

```
wls:/offline>connect("weblogic", "aPassw0rd", "127.0.0.1:7001")
Connecting to t3://127.0.0.1:7001 with userid weblogic ...
Successfully connected to Admin Server "AdminServer" that belongs to domain
"sample".

Warning: An insecure protocol was used to connect to the
server. To ensure on-the-wire security, the SSL port or
Admin port should be used instead.

wls:/sample/serverConfig>
```

---

[6]The procedure to replace the demonstration certificates provided by Oracle will be reviewed in detail in a subsequent chapter dedicated to review WebLogic Server security.

The WLST code prompt changes from `wls:/offline>` to `wls:/sample/serverConfig>`, reflecting that the server is now connected to the server configuration MBean hierarchy in our domain named *sample*.

In this example, a connection was established using an unprotected network channel, and because of this we are shown a warning. When connecting using a TLS protected channel, the warning is not displayed.

In order to successfully establish a secure connection between WLST and the administration server using demonstration certificates, one must ensure that the system property weblogic.security.SSL.ignoreHostnameVerification=true is set.

Executing Commands

Once in the WLST prompt, either online or offline, we are able to execute commands interactively; both Jython language commands and WebLogic Server specific functions are available, and the output of such commands or functions is immediately displayed on screen.

The quintessential *Hello World!* program in WLST is familiar to Python and Jython programmers as it only involves calling the `print()` method and passing our message to have it displayed to standard output. The following code (Listing 6-3) shows the output of this example.

Listing 6-3. WLST interactive Hello World! program

```
wls:/sample/serverConfig> print('Hello World!')
Hello World!
wls:/sample/serverConfig>
```

As we can see, WLST interprets the sentence, displays the result, and returns to the command prompt, ready to receive additional commands.

WLST supports executing commands in a file, and there are two ways of doing this, either by invoking the WLST script and passing the file name that contains the commands as the first argument, or by entering interactive mode and executing the Jython function `execfile()` and passing the same file name. In both cases, the file is parsed and evaluated as a series of statements and are then interpreted.

When working with WLST online, choosing either scenario implies that an administrator will connect to an administration server interactively and then execute a batch of commands in a file, or that the connect statements will be included in the file to be passed to WLST. This has obvious security implications. As usual, the recommendation is that credentials should never be stored in plain text anywhere, ever.

The following code shows the same program as in Listing 6-3 but in batch mode. The first line simply creates the batch Jython file with our Hello World program, and the second passes our file to WLST to be run in offline mode.

Listing 6-4. WLST batch Hello World! program

```
echo "print('Hello World! - batch')" > hello.py
./wlst.sh hello.py

Initializing WebLogic Scripting Tool (WLST) ...

Welcome to WebLogic Server Administration Scripting Shell
Type help() for help on available commands

Hello World! - batch
```

A third method to run commands in WLST, which is perhaps less practiced than batch or interactive mode. This involves embedding the WLST interpreter using the WebLogic Server class `weblogic.management.scripting.utils.WLSTInterpreter` in a Java program. This scenario may be required when administrative actions must be carried out as part of other Java applications. Additionally, WLST can also be invoked from Ant tasks and as a Jython module, although these are simply variations of the methods described.

WLST Commands

The most common WebLogic Server specific commands in WLST can be grouped in the following categories:

- Control – Connect and disconnect from administration servers and edit domains in offline mode

- Tree – Used to switch between available MBean hierarchies

- Browsing – Used to navigate the MBean hierarchies

- Editing – Used to perform changes to the writable MBean hierarchy

- Life Cycle – manage the state of server instances

- Node Manager – Similar to life cycle commands, executed through a running Node Manager instance

There are other types of commands such as those used for application deployment and those used to obtain runtime information from a specialized WebLogic Server monitoring subsystem called WLDF[7].

In a somewhat logical order, an administrator will typically first choose the WLST mode, depending on the task at hand, then select the right MBean hierarchy and will start browsing and viewing or editing the MBean attributes available.

The domainConfig() and serverConfig(), as well as domainRuntime() and serverRuntime() commands, will change the location to the read-only MBean hierarchies representing the current domain and server configuration and runtime information, respectively.

The edit() command will change the location to the read-write MBean hierarchy where changes to the domain configuration may be performed. The startEdit() command acquires the lock on the writable MBean hierarchy. All of these commands are available only in WLST online mode.

Browsing the MBean hierarchies was designed to resemble navigating a UNIX/Linux file system hierarchy where commands such as cd(), pwd(), and ls() offer the expected behavior of changing to a specific path, displaying the current position, and listing the objects available at the current position.

WLST also includes the special variable **cmo**, which stands for current management object and which represents the current MBean instance. This variable is commonly used, in connection with the most common editing commands such as set() and get() to invoke the corresponding methods in the current MBean instance. The following example from a WLST session that is already connected to an administration server can be used to change the listen port of the administration server from default 7001 to 9999. The example (Listing 6-5) includes changing to the editable MBean hierarchy, navigating to the administration server MBean, and modifying the corresponding property.

---

[7]Monitoring is the subject of the next chapter where the functionality offered by WLDF will be reviewed.

Listing 6-5. Changing the Listen Port of an Administration Server

```
wls:/sample/serverConfig> edit()
Location changed to edit tree. This is a writable tree with
DomainMBean as the root. To make changes you will need to start
an edit session via startEdit().

For more help, use help('edit')

wls:/sample/edit> startEdit()
Starting an edit session ...
Started edit session, please be sure to save and activate your
changes once you are done.

wls:/sample/edit !> cd('/Servers/AdminServer')
wls:/sample/edit/Servers/AdminServer !> print(cmo)
[MBeanServerInvocationHandler]com.bea:Name=AdminServer,Type=Server

wls:/sample/edit/Servers/AdminServer !> cmo.getListenPort()
7001
wls:/sample/edit/Servers/AdminServer !> cmo.setListenPort(9999)
wls:/sample/edit/Servers/AdminServer !> cmo.getListenPort()
9999
```

When working in batch mode, it is often useful to save the output of the commands executed to a file for verification and analysis. This can be accomplished by calling the commands `redirect()` and `stopRedirect()`. The `redirect()` command takes a file name as an argument, and optionally an indication of whether to still display the output of the commands.

In the example above, an administrator would still have to validate, save, and activate the changes, using the corresponding `validate()`, `save()` and `activate()` commands, in order for the change management process to be completed.

One final consideration regarding the WebLogic Server commands in WLST has to do with reading and writing encrypted values, such as passwords stored in MBeans[8]. The representation of an encrypted value in an MBean hierarchy is stored as an encrypted byte array.

---

[8]Encrypted MBean properties end with the suffix Encrypted, for example: SystemPassword Encrypted of the AdminServer MBean of type Server.

In a previous chapter, it was stated that in WLST offline, encrypted values can be edited by simply passing the new, un-encrypted string to the set method.

In WLST online, the special method encrypt() may be used to create an encrypted byte array that can be set to an encrypted property of an MBean. The encrypt() method requires the string to be encrypted, and the absolute path to the DOMAIN_HOME directory. The following example shows how to encrypt the SystemPassword property in the administration server MBean.

Listing 6-6. Changing the encrypted SystemPassword of an Administration Server

```
wls:/sample/edit/Servers/AdminServer !> set('SystemPasswordEncrypted',
encrypt('aNewPwOrd', '/home/gustavo/apress/lab/configuration/domains/
sample'))
```

Configuration Management Using WLST

Regardless of whether WLST is being used interactively or in batch mode, the configuration management process remains the same. The following is the list of actions involved when using WLST online:

1. Connect to the administration server using the credentials of a user in the Administrators group by calling the connect() method.

2. Change to the writable MBean hierarchy by calling the edit() method.

3. Acquire the lock on the MBean hierarchy by calling the startEdit() method.

4. Select the required domain MBean, etc., by browsing to the correct location using any of the browse commands available.

5. Make the necessary changes to the properties available by calling the set() method or the exposed methods of the CMO.

6. Validate that the changes made are correct by calling the validate() and/or showChanges() methods.

7. If necessary, revert the changes made by calling the undo() and/or cancelEdit() methods.

8. Save the changes made by calling the save() method.

9. Request activation of the changes made by calling the activate() method.

10. Release the lock on the editable MBean hierarchy by calling the stopEdit() method.

The following is a complete change management example using WLST in which the dynamic SSL listen port of a managed server is disabled.

Listing 6-7. Disabling the SSL Listen Port of a managed server

```
./wlst.sh

Initializing WebLogic Scripting Tool (WLST) ...


Welcome to WebLogic Server Administration Scripting Shell
Type help() for help on available commands

wls:/offline> connect('weblogic','welcome1','127.0.0.1:7001')
Connecting to t3://127.0.0.1:7001 with userid weblogic ...
Successfully connected to Admin Server "AdminServer" that belongs to domain
"sample".

Warning: An insecure protocol was used to connect to the
server. To ensure on-the-wire security, the SSL port or
Admin port should be used instead.

wls:/sample/serverConfig> edit()
Location changed to edit tree. This is a writable tree with
DomainMBean as the root. To make changes you will need to start
an edit session via startEdit().

For more help, use help('edit')
You already have an edit session in progress and hence WLST will
continue with your edit session.
```

```
wls:/sample/edit !> startEdit()
Starting an edit session ...
Started edit session, please be sure to save and activate your
changes once you are done.

wls:/sample/edit !> cd('/Servers/mserver1/SSL/mserver1')
wls:/sample/edit/Servers/mserver1/SSL/mserver1 !> print(cmo)
[MBeanServerInvocationHandler]com.bea:Name=mserver1,Type=SSL,Server=mserv
er1
wls:/sample/edit/Servers/mserver1/SSL/mserver1 !> set('Enabled',False)

wls:/sample/edit/Servers/mserver1/SSL/mserver1 !> showChanges()

All changes that are made but not yet activated are:

MBean Changed : com.bea:Name=mserver1,Type=SSL,Server=mserver1
Operation Invoked : modify
Attribute Modified : Enabled
Attributes Old Value : true
Attributes New Value : false
Server Restart Required : false

wls:/sample/edit/Servers/mserver1/SSL/mserver1 !> validate()
Validating changes ...
Validated the changes successfully

wls:/sample/edit/Servers/mserver1/SSL/mserver1 !> save()
Saving all your changes ...
Saved all your changes successfully.

wls:/sample/edit/Servers/mserver1/SSL/mserver1 !> activate()
Activating all your changes, this may take a while ...
The edit lock associated with this edit session is released
once the activation is completed.
Activation completed
```

Recommended Exercises

1. Using WLST online, change the non-dynamic property listen address of the administration server.

2. Using WLST offline, change any encrypted property, verify that it is stored encrypted.

3. Using WLST online, create a new managed server.

4. Using WLST offline, delete an existing managed server.

5. Verify in the Administration Console the effect of calling the `startEdit()` method.

Certification Questions

1. The edit lock on acquired on a WLST session is released automatically when closing the session.

   a. True

   b. False

2. What is the group in the WebLogic Server security realm that effectively has read-only access to the Administration Console?

   a. Readers

   b. Monitors

   c. Watchers

   d. All of the above

3. What types of configuration changes may be reverted in a WebLogic Server domain?

   a. Saved

   b. Activated

   c. None

   d. All

4. What are the arguments to the `encrypt()` method to create
    encrypted byte arrays in WLST?

    a. String to encrypt

    b. String to encrypt, encryption algorithm

    c. String to encrypt, property to update

    d. String to encrypt, domain path

    e. None of the above

5. It is possible to automate all types of domain configuration
    changes using WLST.

    a. True

    b. False

Coming Up

In our next chapter, we will review the logging subsystem and WLDF, two excellent
alternatives to monitor and troubleshoot runtime behavior of domain components.

CHAPTER 7

Logging and Monitoring

All middleware environments eventually face circumstances that affect the availability of their subsystems and of the applications running on them. Oracle WebLogic Server administrators must anticipate these events by closely monitoring the behavior of the JVM and reviewing the information available in log files, which can be useful before and after these events occur.

In this chapter, we discuss monitoring and logging services, how server subsystems use them, how to configure them, and how to access and interpret their messages.

Logging

The fundamental purpose of logging is to provide a mechanism whereby which information about certain events in a system can be broadcast and persisted for interested parties to access and use.

Logging in Oracle WebLogic Server originates in various locations, including server subsystems and deployed applications. The content in this section deals with logging from the perspective of the server and its subsystems rather than from an application. However, most of the information is applicable to application logging as well.

© Gustavo Garnica 2018
G. Garnica, *Oracle WebLogic Server 12c Administration I Exam 1Z0-133*,
https://doi.org/10.1007/978-1-4842-2562-2_7

In short, Oracle WebLogic Server subsystems produce log messages using an internal framework[1] and distribute them using Java APIs, either *java.util.logging*[2] or Apache Log4J[3].

System administrators do not work directly with the logging APIs used by WebLogic Server to produce and distribute messages, unless, for example, when they require a custom output channel. However, gaining a good understanding of the role of these components in the logging process provides a better comprehension of how logging works in WebLogic Server, and how to properly configure them to suit the needs of a particular environment.

Figure 7-1 shows that logging is a two-phase process. In the first phase log messages are produced, and in the second phase log messages are distributed to the configured output channels.

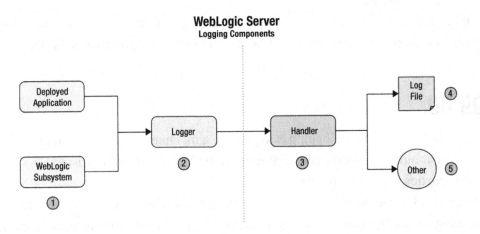

Figure 7-1. *WebLogic Server logging components*

As shown above, WebLogic Server subsystems send log messages to *Logger* objects that use *Handler* objects to distribute these messages to certain configured destinations, such as log files.

---

[1]WebLogic Server provides support for applications to produce messages and send them to the server log without using its standard catalog.

[2]The Java logging API URL is `https://docs.oracle.com/javase/7/docs/api/java/util/logging/package-summary.html`.

[3]The Apache Log4J open source project URL is `http://logging.apache.org/log4j/`.

The points in Figure 7-1 highlight key logging components. First, the source (1) of interesting events, and second, what logger (2) and handler objects (3) are available to enable direct access to the messages produced through the required output channels (4 and 5).

As indicated before, our analysis focuses on WebLogic Server subsystems logging. Depending on the WebLogic Server features used in a particular environment, the server log file will include logging messages from different subsystems such as, for example, the core server subsystem, HTTP, EJB, JDBC, JTA, and JMS.

By default, a server instance is able to distribute messages to standard out, server log files, the domain log file, memory buffer, and JMX. A server log file always contains messages from all subsystems and deployed applications.

Rather than just opening a log file and start searching for relevant strings in the log file, in order to understand the causes for a specific event, an experienced administrator will have a certain expectation of what the system should do, how it should behave, and will configure logging to contain precise and sufficient information about events where the system deviates from the anticipated behavior. It will also forward relevant messages through interesting channels.

Loggers and Handlers

A quick look at the server log file of a WebLogic Server instance that has just started up shows several different types of messages. For those particular messages to have reached the log file, they must have first been handed to a pair of Loggers: Message Catalog Logger and Server Logger, and must have been distributed by the File Handler to the actual log file. All of this occurs as per the default server logging configuration.

The association between loggers and handlers is made by subscription. Several handlers may be interested in messages published by a particular logger and subscribe to it. In fact, that is the default configuration for certain server messages that, in addition to appear in the server log file, are also broadcasted to the domain log file.

Thus, a certain log message will reach a particular output channel if there is a handler subscribed to the particular logger that will process it.

Both loggers and handlers use severity levels and filters to select the log messages they are interested in processing. Handlers may also use additional objects such as formatters and localizers to further process the log message.

Message Severity

The severity assigned to a message is an expression of the impact of the event on the subsystem reporting it, going from the lowest level assigned to events occurring in normal conditions; to the most critical, which often indicates service interruption or meaningful failure.

The severity levels in WebLogic Server log messages are, from the highest impact to the lowest are the following:

- Emergency
- Alert
- Critical
- Error
- Warning
- Notice
- Info
- Debug
- Trace

Note   Messages in severities notice and higher will, by default, always appear in standard out.

When a subsystem is configured to output messages of severity trace, it will often mean to produce very verbose output[4]. Most of the regular messages produced by a subsystem occur in info and notice severity levels.

Messages in warning and error levels should always be of concern to administrators. Messages of critical, alert, and emergency levels should never be disregarded as most of the time they will mean that subsystem functionality has been impaired and that QoS has been severely degraded.

---

[4]In production systems, use the Debug and Trace logging levels with caution, keeping in mind that the server will need to use much more resources than usual to process such levels of verbosity.

It is not uncommon that when users report service degradation or outright disruption to a WebLogic Server administrator, messages of the three highest severity levels will most certainly be found in the corresponding WebLogic Server log files.

An experienced administrator will therefore have special interest in any messages in notice and warning levels as they could be used to prevent situations from escalating and becoming critical issues.

Message Attributes

The log messages produced by WebLogic Server subsystems contain several attributes. An administrator will use the values of these attributes to select and filter out interesting log messages. The following log message attributes are consistently available, regardless of what subsystem produces the message:

- Timestamp

- Severity

- Subsystem

- Origin

- User ID

- Transaction ID

- Context ID

- Milliseconds

- Message ID

- Message text

The timestamp attribute contains the locale-formatted[5] date and time when the message was created.

The origin of the message includes the DNS name of the host, the server instance name, and an ID of the thread where the message originated.

---

[5]The JVM will resort to the OS configuration to determine the locale and format to use to display the log message timestamp.

Inclusion of transactional and contextual identifiers in the message is optional, depending on whether the log message was created as part of a transaction and whether or not correlation information is associated with the message.

The message ID is a six-digit identifier with a BEA- prefix. This ID is associated with the WebLogic Server internal message catalog.

All of the previous message attributes may be considered metadata of the actual event. Information is used to classify and persist the situation that occurred within a server subsystem. The core event information an administrator is interested in is likely contained within the last attribute, the message text.

Listing 7-1 is an example of a log message obtained from a domain log file that shows in detail the message attributes discussed above. The four pound signs at the beginning of the log message indicate that it originated in a server log file.

Listing 7-1. Log message from a domain log file

```
####<Jan 14, 2017 3:34:04 AM CST> <Notice> <WebLogicServer> <redhat.
garnica.mx> <AdminServer> <[STANDBY] ExecuteThread: '2' for queue:
'weblogic.kernel.Default (self-tuning)'> <<WLS Kernel>> <> <>
<1484386444248> <BEA-000365> <Server state changed to STARTING.>
```

Available Log Files

A WebLogic Server instance is configured to always work with at least one log file; this is referred to as the server log file and can be considered the main log file for that particular instance. Depending on the features in use in the server, there may be other log files available.

In this file, an administrator can find information about the startup and shutdown processes of the server instance, as well as an aggregation of messages from several subsystems.

The server log file has the same name as the server instance by default. Both, the server log file name and its location are configurable. The default location is the *logs* directory in the server root, which is located in the *servers* directory in the domain root.

For example, in my local Linux environment, I have a domain named *sample* that has a managed server named *mserver1*. Starting from the domain root, the path to the server log file is:

```
sample/servers/mserver1/logs/mserver1.log
```

By default, each server instance will also print a subset of its log messages with severity NOTICE and higher to standard out. However, for instances started using Node Manager, both standard out and standard error are redirected to a log file that is also named as the server instance, but has an *.out* extension. Thus, if *mserver1* server is started using Node Manager, both log files, mserver1.log and mserver1.out, will be found in the same *logs* directory[6].

In addition to the server log file, some subsystems also maintain logs of their own activity. The default location of these log files is also the *logs* directory specified above.

The logs of two subsystems are of interest to most WebLogic Server system administrators: the HTTP and JTA subsystems.

The HTTP subsystem writes its messages by default to a log file named *access.log*. This log file is useful to audit HTTP access to applications deployed on the server instance, including internal applications such as the Administration Console. Its messages are formatted differently from the server log file. Since the HTTP subsystem works as an embedded HTTP server, its log file format resembles the log files of other HTTP Servers such as Apache httpd or Nginx.

The following is an example message found in the *access.log* file in the administration server of my local environment.

Listing 7-2. Log message from the HTTP subsystem

```
127.0.0.1 - - [03/Dec/2016:00:50:39 -0600] "GET /favicon.ico HTTP/1.1" 404
1164
```

In this message, we see the IP address of the requestor, a timestamp, a string containing the method used to perform the request, the resource requested, as well as the HTTP version used. We also see the status code used in the HTTP response.

The JTA subsystem keeps a log of all transactions committed. This means distributed transactions in which the server has taken part, and for which it has a confirmed responsibility. Therefore, this is a critical log for the server to be able to recover from catastrophic system failure.

---

[6]Node Manager also keeps its own log file named nodemanager.log, located in the nodemanager directory in the domain root. This file contains its own server startup and status messages

Unlike other log files, JTA keeps this file in binary format. The location of the transaction logs is specified as the *default persistent store*[7], which takes a directory location.

Other subsystems such as JDBC and JMS, when they are in use by the server, will also maintain separate log files. Both of these subsystems will create directories in the *logs* directory and will keep their log files in them.

Finally, one other log file every WebLogic Server administrator must be aware of is the domain log file. This log file has the same name as the domain and is located in the *logs* directory of the administration server. For example, in my local Linux environment, starting from the domain root, the path to the domain log file is:

```
sample/servers/AdminServer/logs/sample.log
```

Each server instance in the domain has a subset of its messages broadcasted to the domain log file. This makes the domain log file a convenient place from which to monitor the general status of the domain.

Note   Messages in debug and lower severities will not be forwarded from server log files to the domain log file.

When using the domain log file, administrators must be aware that messages in the domain log file are not updated in any way and that they will appear in the order in which they are aggregated, meaning that timestamps of the messages reflect the time when they were produced, in their original server instance.

Viewing Log Files

Oracle WebLogic Server includes enough functionality for basic log analysis right from within the Administration Console. This is available from the *Domain Structure* panel, under *Diagnostics*, then *Log Files* in the navigation tree. From here, administrators select a log file, apply a time filter to its messages, and search through the resulting messages.

---

[7]It is also possible to also store transaction logs in a database instead of in the file system. Either option is configurable using the Administration Console, in the Default Store section of the Services page under the General tab of the corresponding server.

The first page lists all log files available in the domain. This includes the domain log file as well as several log files per server instance, such as the server log file and the HTTP subsystem log file. Figure 7-2 shows a listing of the log files available in a sample domain.

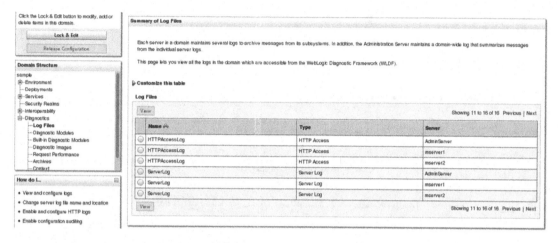

Figure 7-2. *Summary of Log Files page*

The desired log file will be displayed after selecting it and clicking the *View* button. Log file contents are displayed in a table whose columns correspond to log message properties according to the type of log file selected.

The option *Customize This Table* allows changing the default message filter. It is possible to filter messages from a specific time range, such as several minutes, hours, or days, as well as from an arbitrary time span. The filter customization also allows selecting which message attributes are displayed and to customize message pagination, going from 10 messages per page up to 5 thousand.

Note   If the log page selected does not show any messages, it is usually due to the log filter time frame applied being too narrow.

The actual log file content is displayed in a new page that contains a table whose caption changes to reflect the type of log file that is being displayed. Messages are listed as rows in this table. Figure 7-3 shows how filtered log messages appear after having selected the server log of an administration server.

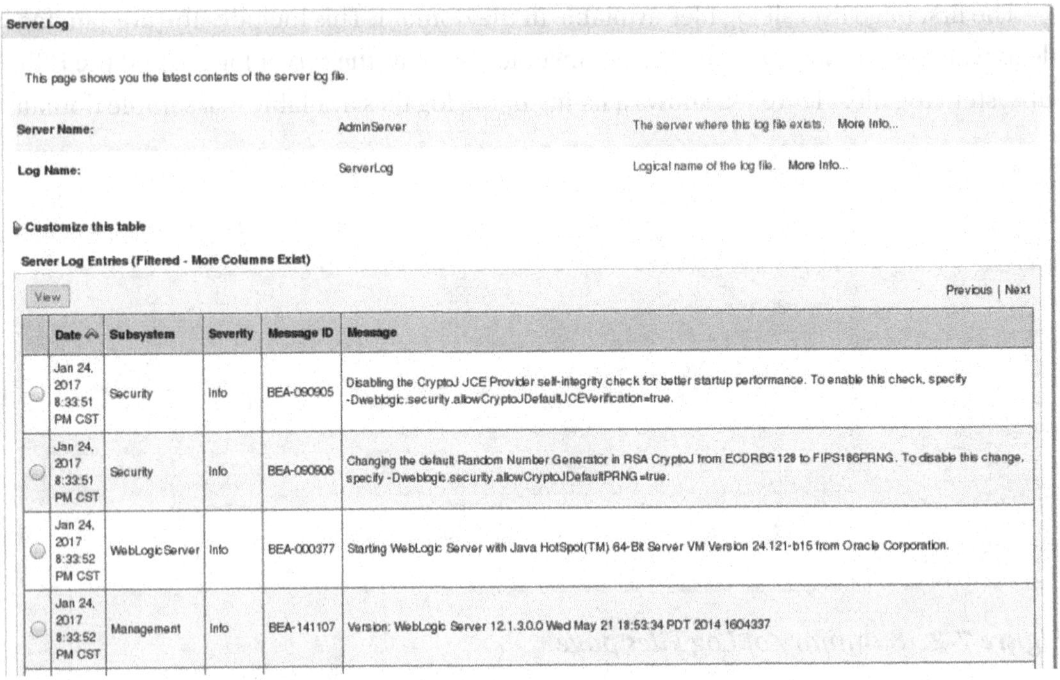

Figure 7-3. *Log File page*

Once an interesting log message appears, selecting it and clicking the *View* button will open yet another page containing all of its attributes and values.

Troubleshooting a WebLogic Server domain by reviewing log files using these pages is not practical in most scenarios.

Administrators will commonly analyze log files using other tools such as those that enable them to read their messages in near-real time, for instance, the Linux *tail* command, or to search for specific phrases across many log files such as the *grep* command. Also, when administrators are tasked with monitoring a large number of servers, log aggregation services such as Splunk or SumoLogic are better suited for the job.

The functionality described above is useful for quick glances at log files without having to log in to different hosts where server instances reside.

Configure Logging

There are many scenarios in which a WebLogic Server administrator should modify the logging configuration. As indicated before, the log file name and location are customizable, along with log file rotation and other details concerning the actual files containing the log messages[8].

However, administrators may be more interested in changing the configuration to filter out certain messages, or to increase the logging volume to view messages in a non-default severity, such as when enabling DEBUG messages in a particular subsystem. This is all done at the server level.

The main settings page of each server instance contains a *Logging* tab that provides access to configure its logging services. The following are the most common options an administrator will want to customize:

- Log file name and location – absolute or relative path plus file name

- Log file rotation[9]

    - Rotation type – either by size or by time

    - Rotation size – expressed in KB

    - Rotation time – either an hour of the day or an interval in hours

    - Whether to limit the number of log files

    - Number of log files to keep

    - Rotation target directory

    - Whether the log file should rotate at server start

---

[8]Changing log file name and location, log rotation type, and directory, and whether or not to rotate the log file at startup will require a server restart to become active.

[9]In production mode, WebLogic Server will by default rotate the file when it reaches 5MB in size and will not rotate the log file upon server start.

- Logging volume

  - General minimum severity – sent to all logging destinations

  - Selective minimum severity – for server log, domain log, and standard out

  - General standard out and error redirection – sent to all logging destinations

  - Domain log buffer size – batch of messages to buffer before forwarding to the domain log

Logging Filters

Custom log filters control what messages are published based on their attributes. Once a filter has been created, it is available for use by default in the server log, standard out, and the domain log.

Filters can be created from the Administration Console, navigating to the domain *Configuration* and *Log Filters* tab. Since log filters are created at the domain level, they are available for use in any server instance in a domain.

A filter is created by giving it a name and attaching expressions to it. The expressions are formed by putting together a message attribute with an operator and a value. Multiple expressions can be added to a single filter, and the expressions can be further combined to describe the right condition that will filter the messages as desired.

The message properties available for use in filters are the following: Date, Severity, Subsystem, Machine, Server, Thread, UserID, TXID, ContextID, Timestamp, MsgID, and Message.

The operators available are equals, less than, greater than, less than or equal, greater than or equal, not equal, like, matches, in, and, or, and not.

The like operator accepts two wildcards: the percent sign to match any string of zero or more characters, and a period to match any single character.

The matches operator compares against a regular expression, and the in operator matches against a predefined set of values.

Figure 7-4 shows two expressions in a sample filter.

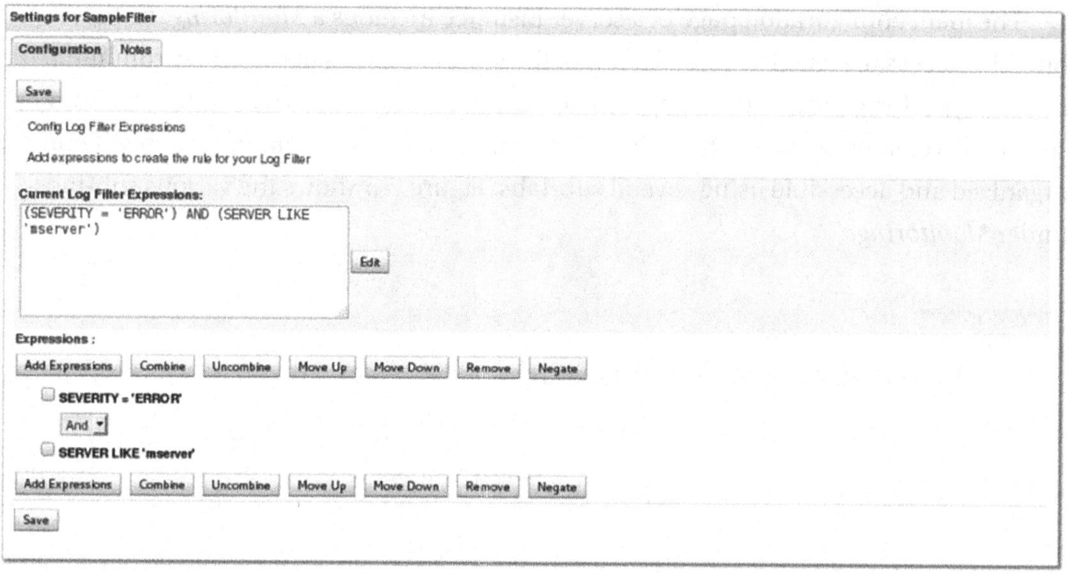

Figure 7-4. *Two sample expressions in a log filter*

The example expressions above would cause that only messages of severity error, in servers whose name includes the *mserver* string, are published to the log destination on which the filter is applied.

Log filters are an excellent feature available to WebLogic Server administrators to facilitate server and subsystem troubleshooting.

Monitoring

Just like with analyzing log files, WebLogic Server administrators monitor their environments using a variety of tools, several of which are beyond the scope of Oracle middleware.

Unlike logging services, WebLogic Server includes a robust framework for server diagnostics, the WebLogic Diagnostic Framework, or WLDF. In fact, the logging filters reviewed in the previous section used a query language that is part of WLDF.

WebLogic also includes basic tools to monitor server instance health. The certification exam objectives cover only basic monitoring from the Administration Console and the *Monitoring Dashboard*.

Monitoring is available for server instances and their subsystems. This section focuses on monitoring server instances.

The main configuration page of a server instance includes a *Monitoring* tab that provides access to statistical information of the several aspects of the server runtime, including performance, networking, threads, timers, workload, as well as to data from several server subsystems such as JDBC, JMS, and JTA. The information is conveniently organized and accessible using several sub-tabs. Figure 7-5 shows the various sub-tabs under *Monitoring*.

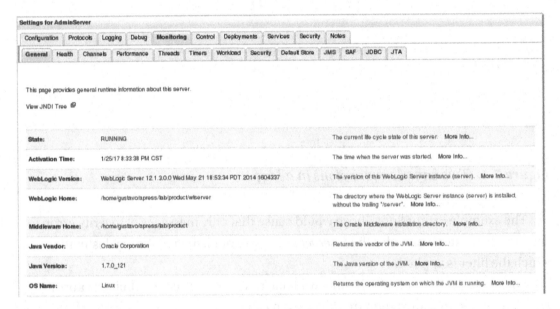

Figure 7-5. *Monitoring a server instance in the Administration Console*

The General tab is selected by default. It displays general information about a server instance, including the current state of the JVM, the date and time when it was started, the WebLogic Server installation directory, what Java version is powering the JVM, and the OS name and version.

The *View JNDI Tree* link in this page opens a new window from which an administrator can determine whether a particular Java object is available for use in the JVM[10].

---

[10]Java Directory Naming Interface or JNDI is an API that maintains a type of directory service for software components and allows Java software clients to discover objects by name.

At the bottom of this page a second table is displayed, which contains a list of what services and API versions are supported by this particular server instance; this includes, for example, the versions of core Java EE services such as EJB, JDBC, Servlet, and so forth.

Server Health

Core server health status[11] is available in the *Health* tab. It is reported by WebLogic Server in one of several states including:

- OK – Server is healthy.

- Warning – Services could have problems in the future.

- Critical – Something must be done to prevent service failure.

- Failed – Service has failed and must be restarted.

- Overloaded – Service is functioning normally but with too much work.

WebLogic Server takes into account the health of several components and subsystems to determine the overall server health, and reevaluates its assessment continuously at regular intervals. Server health is determined by the less healthy component or subsystem evaluated.

Whereas the *General* and *Health* tabs report general statistics, the *Channels, Performance, Threads,* and *Workload* tabs display distinct core server runtime data as follows:

- Channels – Network statistics including the number of connections as well as incoming and outgoing bytes and messages.

- Performance – JVM memory and heap utilization, as well as process and system CPU load[12].

- Threads – Statistics about the server thread pool and the behavior of individual threads.

- Workload – Statistics of the pending and completed requests of each of the work managers in the server instance.

---

[11]These states are defined in the weblogic.health.HealthState class from the WebLogic API.
[12]From this page JVM garbage collection can be forced and thread stacks can be dumped.

The statistics found in these four sections influence and are influenced by the work done in other subsystems such as JDBC, JMS, and JTA.

The subject of memory allocation in the Java Virtual Machine, including garbage collection algorithms and their intricacies, are well outside the scope of the first WebLogic Server certification exam for administrators, though in practice it is very desirable knowledge to have when working with production environments, where performance and capacity are two core requirements. Understanding the information contained in the Threads and Workload tabs is just as critical.

In very broad terms, WebLogic Server automatically manages thread allocation, concurrency, and synchronization and does so using a single thread pool and execute queue. The number of threads in the thread pool is automatically increased or decreased.

The execute queue considers priorities to determine order of execution. The basic mechanism available for administrators to influence when requests are assigned to threads, thus altering the priority of execution, is a work manager. WebLogic Server comes configured out of the box with several work managers assigned to certain internal components. Additional work managers may be created and assigned to applications.

Monitoring Dashboard

The *Monitoring Dashboard* presents diagnostic data of servers and applications in charts or graphs. It is accessible in the home page of the Administration Console, at the lower-right corner under *Charts and Graphs*. Figure 7-6 shows a dashboard displaying a line point chart of the thread pool of two server instances.

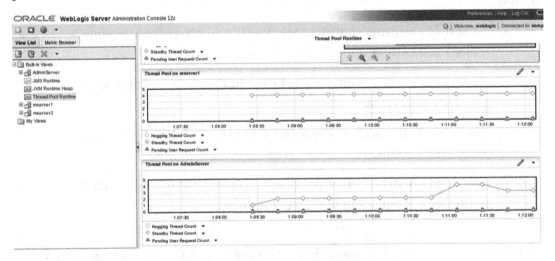

Figure 7-6. *Monitoring Dashboard displaying a chart*

The diagnostics information available in the *Monitoring Dashboard* proceeds from the same sources as the monitoring pages, which is from runtime MBean attributes. However, in addition to presenting live runtime data, it is integrated with WLDF and can present information from archived diagnostic data.

Working with WLDF deserves a dedicated chapter, as it offers important functionality to create watches, alerts, and also integrates with monitoring tools using standards such as SNMP. For these reasons however, WLDF is outside the scope of this chapter.

The Monitoring Dashboard includes several metrics and views that receive input from live runtime data. Configuring a dashboard is just a matter of selecting the view or metric from the left panel, selecting the type of chart of graph on the right panel, and clicking on the start button on the top-left corner of the screen to start seeing live data displayed.

This brief introduction should be enough to highlight the value of the logging and monitoring information available. If coupled with educated intuition and common sense, it can be used to find root causes and define corrective actions for misbehaving environments. Experienced administrators are likely to use additional tools to support their research.

Recommended Exercises

1. Enable debug mode in the server log file of a managed server.

2. Identify the message IDs of the startup and shutdown messages in any server instance.

3. Customize the rotation configuration of a server log file in order to have it rotate upon server restart and every 5 minutes.

4. Create a log message filter to display only messages of severity CRITICAL and apply it to the server log file of an administration server.

Certification Questions

1. It is possible to define a custom log message severity.

    a. True

    b. False

2. What type of Java object distributes log messages to a destination?

    a. Logger

    b. Log4J

    c. Handler

    d. All of the above

3. It is possible for applications to send custom log messages to the server log file.

    a. True

    b. False

4. WebLogic Server can report information about operating system users logged in the system.

    a. True

    b. False

5. Which contains statistical information about the number of threads allocated?

    a. Channels

    b. Performance

    c. Workload

    d. None of the above

Coming Up

In our next chapter, we will review the concepts of network channels and virtual hosts in WebLogic Server.

CHAPTER 8

Networking

The Oracle WebLogic Server configuration wizard permits configuring a listening address as well as SSL and non-SSL port numbers for each server instance in a domain. Even when administrators do not specify listen addresses, WebLogic Server instances will, by default, accept incoming requests through all configured network interfaces in the host where they reside, including the loopback interface and using the *localhost* string.

This represents the minimal network configuration required to have functional server instances that will listen to and accept requests over the network[1].

Since it is unlikely that these simple settings satisfy the requirements for network traffic in most production environments, WebLogic Server supports much more granular networking configurations to enable more precise control over the traffic associated with server instances.

Network Channels

Network channel is the name given by Oracle to the piece of WebLogic Server configuration that defines a network connection to a server instance. The basic and default network configuration editable using the domain configuration wizard is also defined in terms of network channels, and it is stored in the *ServerMBean* and *SSLMBean* objects.

---

[1]Reaching a WebLogic Server instance from outside the host where it is running also depends on whether or not traffic destined to the network address specified in the configuration is permitted.

© Gustavo Garnica 2018
G. Garnica, *Oracle WebLogic Server 12c Administration I Exam 1Z0-133*,
https://doi.org/10.1007/978-1-4842-2562-2_8

Custom network channels created by administrators are stored in instances of the *NetworkAccessPointMBean* object[2].

For obvious reasons, server instances complete network channel setup nearly at the end of their initialization, when all other subsystems are ready to process requests received over the network. Listing 8-1, which shows example log messages from an administration server, shows the default network channels ready to begin accepting connection requests.

Listing 8-1. Log messages indicating the status of the default network channels

```
<Jan 31, 2017 1:52:21 AM CST> <Notice> <Server> <BEA-002613> <Channel
"DefaultSecure" is now listening on 127.0.0.1:7002 for protocols iiops,
t3s, ldaps, https.>
<Jan 31, 2017 1:52:21 AM CST> <Notice> <Server> <BEA-002613> <Channel
"Default" is now listening on 127.0.0.1:7001 for protocols iiop, t3, ldap,
snmp, http.>
```

A network channel was set up to support secure protocols and a separate channel is set up to support their counterpart but insecure protocols. Again, this is the default and most basic use of network channels in a server configuration.

Purpose

Network channels are used by administrators to address or comply with complex network requirements, such as the following:

- Security

- Quality of service

- Traffic segmentation

- Observability

- Performance

By creating and activating separate network channels, an administrator indeed segments the network traffic associated with the corresponding WebLogic Server instances.

---

[2]Custom network channels inherit values from the default network channel for properties that are left undefined.

Administrators may choose to utilize these channels in their WebLogic Server domains according to several criteria, such as performance and/or quality of service of the underlying network, application protocols used, traffic encryption, and so forth.

By doing this, administrators will also be implicitly facilitating network monitoring by making it easier to differentiate traffic, etc.

Configuration

Network channels are server-instance specific, and a single instance may have a number of network channels[3].

Network channels are uniquely identified by a combination of listen address, port number, and protocol(s) supported.

Network channels can be configured using both the Administration Console and WLST. When using the console, additional network channels can be created in the Channels page under the Protocols page of the server configuration.

Figure 8-1 shows the location in the Administration Console of the page where custom network channels are created and configured.

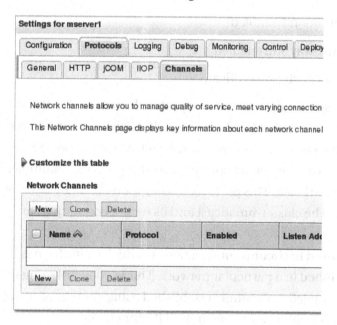

Figure 8-1. *Network Channels configuration page*

---

[3]Be aware that when multiple network channels are created on a single network interface, there will be some overhead due to context switching.

When a network channel is created, it is given a name, after which its properties may be customized.

The name of a network channel is relevant for certain types of channels as we shall see later. The following properties of a network channel can be customized:

- Name

- Protocol

- Listen address

- Port number

- External listen address

- External port number[4]

- Whether the channel:

  - Is enabled or disabled

  - Supports tunneling

  - Supports HTTP

  - Is outbound enabled

  - Is two-way SSL enabled

  - Enforces client-certificate

A network channel supports standard protocols such as HTTP and HTTPS, LDAP and LDAPS, IIOP and IIOPS, SNMP, as well as the WebLogic Server proprietary protocols T3 and T3S, admin, cluster-broadcast, and cluster-broadcast-secure.

The T3 protocol and its secure counterpart support packet multiplexing and are used to transport RMI data. This protocol also supports WebLogic server to server communications. The cluster-broadcast and its secure counterpart are used for unicast broadcasting.

Tunneling is used to circumvent situations in which traffic from certain ports and protocols is prohibited in a particular network. This is done by letting the restricted traffic go over a connection or tunnel established using another protocol, for example, when configuring T3 traffic to go over an HTTP connection.

---

[4]The external listen address and port number must be specified for scenarios such as when running asynchronous web services that expect a callback.

Outbound enabled specifies that a network channel may be used to initiate WebLogic server-to-server communications.

Channel Types

Network channels can be classified by their function in two groups, internal and external. As their names imply, internal channels are used for internal, WebLogic Server-only traffic, as opposed to external or client traffic. Internal traffic can be further subclassified in three types: cluster communication, session replication, and administrative traffic.

When creating a network channel that will be used for either cluster broadcast or replication, the name of the channels must be the same across all cluster members[5], and in the case of replication, the selected protocol should be t3.

A custom network channel may be created and activated dynamically on a server instance; however, be aware that when a channel is made inactive, or altogether deleted, it will not end traffic gracefully.

Note   Clustering is the subject of the next three chapters.

Administration Port

It is a recommended practice for production environments to enable a channel specifically for the purpose of separating client or application traffic from administrative traffic.

It is not uncommon for servers that are behaving badly to become completely irresponsive, including to intervention by an administrator. By enabling the administrative port, access to all server instances will be guaranteed, as administrative traffic will not compete with application traffic at any time.

---

[5]Replication channels for clusters are not configured with SSL protection by default.

The administration port is enabled at the domain level, and when it is, it activates another default network channel[6], the default administration channel.

Once activated, all managed servers will start using exclusively this new channel to communicate with the administration server.

The following example log message (Listing 8-2) shows the administrative network channel activated.

Listing 8-2. An Administration Channel has been activated.

```
<Jan 28, 2017 1:31:30 PM CST> <Notice> <Server> <BEA-002613> <Channel
"DefaultAdministration" is now listening on 127.0.0.1:9002 for protocols
admin, ldaps, https.>
```

Attempting to enable the administration port and channel on a host with more than a single JVM but with a single NIC, and therefore a single IP address, which is typically the configuration of a development environment, will fail because each server instance will attempt to bind to the same listen address and port number. The process will only succeed for the first JVM. The following example log message (Listing 8-3) shows this error.

Listing 8-3. Error activating the administration channel

```
<Jan 28, 2017 2:31:30 PM CST> <Critical> <WebLogicServer> <BEA-000362>
<Server failed. Reason: [Server:002653]The servers administration channel
conflicts with the Administration Servers channel.>
```

The solution to this is to either assign multiple NICs and IP addresses so that each JVM has a different listen address. The alternative is changing the administration port in each server instance from its default number 9002. Figure 8-2 shows the location in the Administration Console where the administration port can be overridden for each server instance.

---

[6]Enabling the administration port requires a full domain restart to become active.

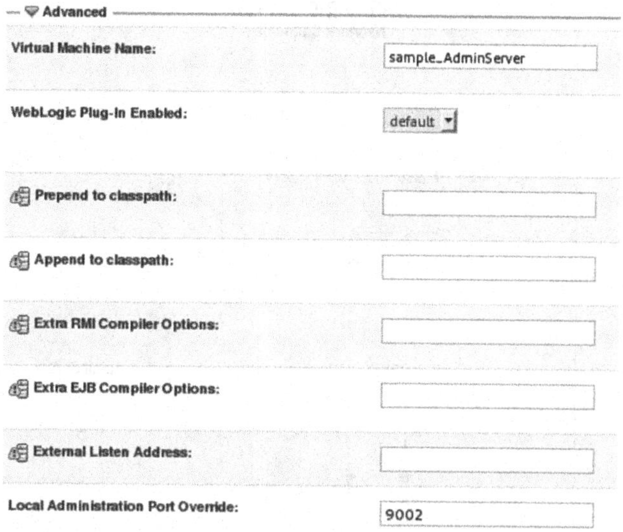

Figure 8-2. *Administration Port override page*

In production environments, this situation is not expected because production hosts are often multi-homed systems that have an adequate number of IP addresses configured.

Sample Use

The following example illustrates how network channels could be used to configure a production environment. The following network requirements are assumed:

1. Only HTTPS client traffic is allowed through the firewall.

2. All administrative traffic should be SSL protected and accessible only from a secured network.

3. Cluster and replication traffic should be on a high-speed fabric network such as InfiniBand.

4. Transactional traffic from EJBs should be logged and monitored.

Figure 8-3 shows how such an environment could be configured. The domain includes three hosts with a cluster of two managed servers.

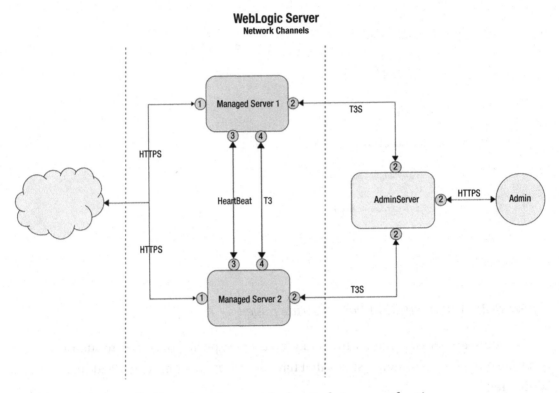

Figure 8-3. *Sample diagram of network channels in a production environment*

The diagram on the previous page could be realized by having three NICs configured in the servers that host the managed servers, assuming that link for channels 3 and 4 is high speed.

Virtual Hosts

One additional feature that WebLogic Server has beyond its functionality as a Java EE application server is that it can also serve static content as a web server that is HTTP 1.1 compliant.

When considering a virtual host configuration in WebLogic Server, a recommended step is to ensure that managed servers listen for requests on privileged ports 80 and 443, in order to avoid having to specify a port number in destination URLs.

However, in order to avoid having to run JVM processes with elevated privileges, WebLogic Server has the ability to employ Unix *setuid* and *setgid* commands to delegate ownership of the JVM process to a non-privileged OS user, right after binding to privileged ports.

This can be configured either while running a domain configuration wizard, as part of the WebLogic Server machine definition, or at any time in the Administration Console, under *Machines* in the main navigation tree[7].

A virtual host in WebLogic Server works the same way as a virtual host configuration in web servers such as *Nginx* or *Apache httpd*.

In essence, when WebLogic Server receives a request for a DNS name that has been configured as a virtual host, it determines what server or cluster has been configured to process such request, and sends the request to that particular server or cluster, which in turns determines what application will handle the request.

Virtual hosts can be defined using the Administration Console, also using the corresponding option in the main navigation panel.

For each virtual host defined, WebLogic Server can take a specific configuration comprised of individual HTTP parameters and access logs.

A virtual host may also have assigned a network channel as a source from which to process incoming requests.

In development environments where DNS names are not an option, the */etc/hosts* file in Unix/Linux systems can be edited to add the desired names, along the localhost string or loopback address.

Once the desired DNS names are resolvable, the embedded HTTP server in WebLogic Server will start routing requests to server instances configured as targets of virtual hosts.

Recommended Exercises

1. Create and activate a custom replication channel for a cluster.

2. Identify the changes to a JVM process, at the OS level, when a new network channel is configured and activated.

---

[7]This may also be configured using WLST by editing the properties of the UnixMachineMBean, using methods setPostBindUIDEnabled and setPostBindGIDEnabled.

3. Completely disable access to non-secure protocols by creating and configuring custom network channels.

4. Start a server instance listening on privileged ports 80 and 443, and configure the corresponding machine to delegate ownership to the *nobody* user.

Certification Questions

1. Select all protocols supported by the default secure channel:

    a. HTTPS

    b. T3S

    c. SNMP

    d. Cluster-broadcast-secure

    e. All of the above

2. What objects store the default network channels configuration?

    a. NetworkAccessPointMBean

    b. ServerMBean

    c. ConfigurationMBean

    d. SocketMBean

    e. None of the above

3. Select all required properties to configure a cluster replication channel:

    a. Tunneling

    b. HTTP Enabled

    c. Outbound

    d. External listen address

    e. External port

4. It is possible to configure two network channels using the same listen address and port number as long as:

   a. They both support secure protocols

   b. They both support different protocols

   c. They both support the same protocols

   d. It is not possible

   e. All of the above

5. When no listen address has been specified in any network channel, the following occurs:

   a. Server instances fail to start

   b. Server instances bind to localhost and loopback

   c. Server instances bind to all IP addresses available in the host

   d. A network channel is automatically created using the host IP address

   e. None of the above

Coming Up

In the next chapter, we will review the details of how to create a cluster, how to configure a dynamic cluster, and what role server templates play in high availability in WebLogic Server.

CHAPTER 9

Clusters - Basics

Oracle WebLogic Server clustering is one of the most important features for which large enterprises choose WebLogic Server over other alternatives. It has a mature set of functionalities that facilitate administration of environments with stringent requirements of availability, such as those in the financial and telecommunications industries.

In the next three chapters, we discuss WebLogic Server clustering and other related high availability features. We start in this chapter with a brief overview of high availability and how clustering contributes to it.

For experienced WebLogic Server administrators, the discussion of high availability and the purposes of clustering, cluster architecture, and cluster creation in this chapter may already be well-known subjects, and may want to skip to the part covering dynamic clusters, which is new in Oracle WebLogic Server 12c. Dynamic clustering will certainly be of interest to administrators of previous WebLogic Server versions.

High Availability

With so much information available on the subjects of system availability, capacity, performance, and so forth, it is very much likely that a few lines regarding these topics could possibly raise more questions than they will answer. Knowing well we have a small opportunity, we should start looking at the fundamental notions of availability and capacity, and their relationship.

When a system is not available to users, it does not matter whether the system has had its capacity exhausted because it has been so successful, or if it is unavailable due to a malfunction or failure. When systems are not available to users, there is always a negative impact.

© Gustavo Garnica 2018
G. Garnica, *Oracle WebLogic Server 12c Administration I Exam 1Z0-133*,
https://doi.org/10.1007/978-1-4842-2562-2_9

If a system is so unique that no alternatives can be found, users will begrudgingly return, such as when a government agency is unable to provide adequate online service to its constituents. However, if they could, they would probably not come back.

In a world where we see alternatives for almost any conceivable online offer of products and services, when a system is not available, users will leave, probably for good.

One of the simplest ideas to prevent lack of availability is to increase and distribute capacity, insomuch that there will be a component to take over when a similar component fails or has its individual capacity exhausted.

Availability and capacity are thus some of the key concerns in large enterprise systems. Users must be shielded from underlying system failure. Systems must be able to handle varying workloads at sundry times, sometimes in different orders of magnitude.

As it should be apparent by now, these concerns must obviously be addressed in more areas than just the application server. The network will fail, as will disks, memory, databases, etc. Adding redundancy to each system component eliminates single points of failure. It does not matter whether your service provider is one of the largest in the planet, and commits to a very high service level agreement. It will fail, and it will do it in the least expected time. Therefore, our concern is to be prepared for when it occurs.

In Oracle WebLogic Server, this is where clustering comes into play. It can make application server environments more reliable, more capable to meet demand. It will enable several server instances to work together so that, if a part of them fails, the remaining will continue to be available serving requests. In 12c, clusters can dynamically grow beyond their initial allocated capacity in order to automatically keep up with increasing workloads.

Beyond clustering, there are many modern technologies and practices that are used to enhance system reliability, including cloud infrastructure, containers, and application architecture patterns such as microservices, all of which can be put to work together to enhance service availability. The nicest thing is that these have gone mainstream, not reserved solely for the largest multinational companies, but for every business that cares about service availability, despite its size. Very exciting times indeed.

Tiered Architectures

Clustering in Oracle WebLogic Server is most commonly used in the context of multiple-layer or n-tier architectures in which the most common implementation has three tiers: one for the presentation layer that implements the user interface, one for the business logic layer, and a third tier that houses the business data. The second tier, also called middle tier, is where the software we call middleware resides. Oracle WebLogic Server is part of Oracle Fusion Middleware and sits on this second tier.

The presentation tier commonly has web servers that deliver static content and may also consume business logic from the middle tier. The business layer will also broker access to data and other enterprise resources.

Note   Sometimes the nouns tier and layer are used distinctly, often to denote a difference between logical and physical separations between architectural components.

The benefits of a layered architecture are apparent. Functionality may be maintained, upgraded, or replaced altogether without much disruption to the adjacent tiers. To some degree, and assuming one is using standard protocols and technologies, there is also the added benefit of using different but compatible technologies in different tiers.

Figure 9-1 shows a typical three-tier architecture with optional firewalls between the tiers.

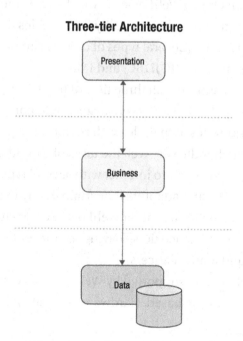

Figure 9-1. *Three-tier architecture*

This separation of duties is critical when it comes to considering the ability of a system to scale. For instance, when an application has high traffic on the front end, but such traffic is not reflected in equal load in back-end transactions, it would be an obvious waste to scale the back end equally with the front end.

Sometimes, technical requirements are not fully satisfied by these three layers alone, and they must be broken into additional layers, in order to extend these benefits to more granular types of functionality, for example, by splitting the presentation tier into a web tier and a dynamic presentation tier.

Choosing the right solution architecture requires careful consideration of several technical and business concerns, including performance, efficiency and reliability.

A more distributed architecture will allow finer-grained security and favor greater availability, including the ability to load balance calls as required. This comes at the cost of more complex administration and often greater licensing costs. The alternative is simpler and easier but comes at the cost of having a reduced capacity to remain available in a variety of circumstances.

Cluster Architecture

The basic component of an Oracle WebLogic Server cluster is the server. Server instances have built-in configurable functionality that enables them to work together as one cohesive whole. Additionally, several types of objects can be clustered, including applications and services such as EJB, JDBC, and JMS.

Oracle WebLogic Server supports all three tiers of the architecture approach described. In other words, a WebLogic Server cluster could contain a full enterprise application within its boundaries. It includes web server functionality to implement a presentation tier, and it can handle very well the tasks of a middleware Java application server, including all things necessary to interact with several types of enterprise data such as databases, messaging, and adapters for certain enterprise applications.

However, in production environments, a WebLogic Server cluster is commonly found in the business and persistence tiers, leaving the presentation tier work to specialized web servers and load balancers.

The reverse proxy architecture supported by WebLogic Server to provide the web tier can be hardware based or software based. Hardware load balancing[1] is faster and takes

---

[1]It is typical to see BigIP F5 load balancers fronting WebLogic Server clusters in large production environments.

advantage of more robust load-balancing algorithms and configuration options. WebLogic Server itself supports software load balancing. It provides this functionality through a built-in application aptly named HttpClusterServlet. However, the recommended approach to employ software load balancing to front WebLogic Server environments is to use a supported web server, and install and configure the corresponding WebLogic Server plug-in. Supported web servers are Apache HTTP Server, Oracle HTTP Server[2], and Microsoft IIS. Proxy plug-ins are limited to round-robin[3] load balancing but are able to recognize failed members to prevent further routing.

Figure 9-2 shows a high availability environment for distributed applications using Oracle WebLogic Server clusters.

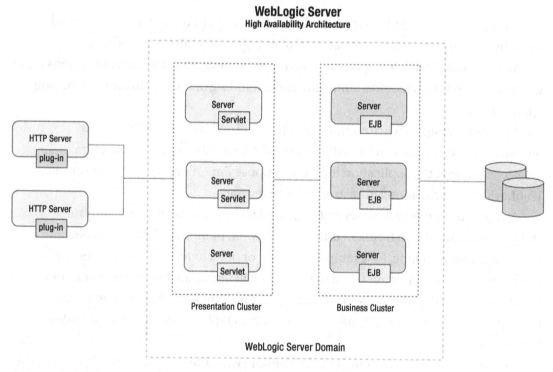

Figure 9-2. *Oracle WebLogic Server cluster*

---

[2]Oracle HTTP Server is based on Apache HTTP server and can serve static and dynamic content in a variety of programming languages.

[3]Round-robin is the simplest load-balancing algorithm. It involves sending traffic to each the cluster member without priority and in circular order.

The diagram[4] shows a pair of HTTP servers in a DMZ, each with the WebLogic Server plug-in configured to load balance incoming traffic by assigning to each member in a presentation cluster an equal share.

The diagram also shows a business cluster that will also be able to load balance incoming requests from the presentation tier to clustered EJB objects.

The sample clustered architecture supports load balancing and failover, which are the fundamental benefits of WebLogic Server clustering. The cluster size depicted in the diagram also supports zero downtime maintenance[5].

Cluster Creation

Preparing to create a WebLogic Server cluster for production environments should begin by careful requirements review and planning. The analysis should result in identifying a candidate clustering architecture that better supports the applications that will be deployed. This requires sufficient understanding of the architecture of the target applications.

A properly designed clustering architecture will enhance the ability of the application to serve customers well. However, be aware that some architectural decisions made at the application level may impose limitations on what options the WebLogic Server clustering infrastructure can leverage.

An organization may have set technical and technological and even cultural standards that must also be taken into account when planning WebLogic Server clustering. These include, for example, whether or not a hardware load balancer is available, and whether or not the load balancer will terminate SSL connections and route unencrypted traffic to the WebLogic Server presentation cluster instead. Other examples are rules defined for interaction with the DMZ, presence of firewall rules between tiers, etc.

In essence, the effort demands understanding what the applications will do; how the information will flow in a transaction, from the end user to the enterprise data stores and back, for each type of transaction that will be supported; and what types of components implement these functionalities.

---

[4]It is typical to see firewalls between each tier, especially between the DMZ and the presentation tier.

[5]In zero-downtime maintenance, one cluster member is intervened at a time, thus ensuring that at least two other members are operational at all times in order to preserve redundancy,

Depending on the size of the organization, this type of analysis could be done by individuals in the architect role instead, who would provide specifications to WebLogic Server administrators, but that is not always the case. Sometimes administrators will play this role and will need to gather this information and gain such understanding.

Once a high-level architecture has been defined, including how many clusters will be supported, their size and role, the number of hosts that will comprise the domain, the rules of how the communication will flow across clusters, from one component to another, etc., it will then be time to start working on the details of the configuration at the cluster, server, and service levels. The following is a list of sample items to consider for the next level down:

- Capacity – a starting point for defining server capacity is to allocate the correct ratio of server instances to CPU cores in a host. Experience with similar applications is useful; however, nothing beats the precision of load testing the application and similar approaches to verify assumptions.

- DNS names – when a firewall is present between the proxy and cluster tiers, server instances must bind to public DNS names. This must be specified for each server instance using the configuration property: *ExternalDNSName*

- IP addresses – it is recommended to configure static IP addresses in cluster hosts.

- Cluster address – may be defined as a single DNS name, mapping to several IP addresses or as a comma-separated list of IP addresses or hostnames and port numbers.

Once these details have been defined, the clusters can be created and configured. The tools employed to create a cluster are three:

1. The domain configuration wizard

2. The Administration Console

3. WebLogic Scripting Tool

Clusters can be created using the domain configuration wizard only when creating domains from scratch. The options to configure a cluster in the configuration wizard are limited to the fundamental, which is creating the servers, creating the cluster. and assigning cluster members. The corresponding server addresses and cluster address may also be specified using the configuration wizard. This process was reviewed as part of the domains topic in Chapter 3.

Using the Administration Console

A cluster can be created using the Administration Console in the *Clusters* option under *Environment* in the *Domain Structure* panel. The first step is creating a cluster as a simple container object. This requires specifying a cluster name and a messaging mode. When selecting unicast as messaging mode[6], which is the default and recommended option, one may optionally specify the name of an existing network channel[7] for broadcasting cluster messages. If multicast was selected, it is possible to specify a multicast address and port.

Once the cluster has been created this way and changes have been activated, many more configuration options become available from the cluster page. The following is a list of some of the most commonly configured options:

- Load algorithm – The default option is round-robin, but there are options available to balance load using a pseudo-random algorithm (random option) or by assigning a priority to cluster members (weight-based option).

- Cluster address – This is used for generating handles and failover addresses for EJB components. This may also be automatically generated, and there is a related option to specify the number of cluster members for the purpose of generating the cluster address.

- Transaction affinity – When cluster members are participating of distributed transactions, enabling this option will send requests to server instances that are already part of a transaction.

- WebLogic Plug-in – Enabling this option is for presentation-layer clusters that sit behind a web server in which the WebLogic Plug-in has been installed and configured. This will cause servers to issue a call to getRemoteAddr method on incoming requests. The method will return the value WL-Proxy-Client-IP header that contains the

---

[6]By default, cluster members will broadcast heartbeat messages every 10 seconds.

[7]Network channels were reviewed in Chapter 8, "Networking."

address of the browser that originated the request, instead of the web server from which the request was received.

- Member warmup timeout – This represents the period of time, in seconds, that a server will wait to synchronize with other servers it has discovered before timing out.

Additionally, there are options to configure properties to control the behavior of the cluster related to server membership, JTA, replication, migration, scheduling, overload, and HTTP.

The next step in cluster configuration is adding cluster members. This can be done by either adding an existing server instance to the cluster, or by creating new server instances and adding them as cluster members.

Note   Running server instances must be stopped before attempting to add them as members of a cluster.

When opting to create a new server, its name, the listen address and listen port must be provided. All other options at the server level may be subsequently configured form the individual server configuration pages.

Once the general properties of a cluster have been configured, and each cluster member has been added, the cluster is ready for use. Even though both the Administration Console and WLST offer a cluster start and cluster stop operations, these are really abstractions of the start or stop requests sent to individual servers.

At any given time, a cluster may have one or more members in either running or shutdown state. Once cluster member instances are up and running, the applications deployed on them will automatically have the load balancing and failover features discussed in this chapter available to them.

Using WebLogic Scripting Tool

Creating a cluster using WLST follows the same general process as doing it from the Administration Console. As indicated in a previous chapter, the Administration Console is really a JMX client, operating on JMX beans that represent WebLogic Server components. Therefore, since the Administration Console and WLST are both working on the same type of objects when creating and configuring a cluster, the process to create and configure clusters is equivalent in most respects.

Once a WLST edit session has been started by a user that is a member of the administrators group in a domain, a cluster object of type ClusterMBean[8] can be created and configured by invoking its methods to set the required properties.

By default, the essential cluster properties that make the object operational are set to default values. For example, the property of the cluster object that controls what protocol to use for cluster messaging is named *ClusterMessagingMode* and has a default value of *unicast*.

Objects of type ServerMBean, either new or existing, may then be added to the cluster object. This is actually accomplished by invoking the setCluster method on the ServerMBean object, rather than the other way around. Once changes are saved and activated, the cluster is ready for immediate use.

Listing 9-1 is an example WLST edit session[9] in a domain named *sample*. In the session, a cluster named *testCluster* is created, a server named *testServer* is created and configured, assigned to an existing Unix machine named *machine*, the changes are activated and the cluster is started.

Listing 9-1. Creating a cluster using WLST

```
wls:/offline> connect('weblogic','samplepass','127.0.0.1:7001')
Connecting to t3://127.0.0.1:7001 with userid weblogic ...
Successfully connected to Admin Server "AdminServer" that belongs to domain
"sample".

wls:/sample/serverConfig> edit()
Location changed to edit tree. This is a writable tree with
DomainMBean as the root. To make changes you will need to start
an edit session via startEdit().

wls:/sample/edit> startEdit()
Starting an edit session ...
Started edit session, please be sure to save and activate your
changes once you are done.

wls:/sample/edit !> cluster = cmo.createCluster('testCluster')
```

---

[8]The actual type of a cluster object is weblogic.management.configuration.ClusterMBean.
[9]As usual, an edit session may be initiated after invoking the wlst.* script, which will load and use the required classpath.

```
wls:/sample/edit !> print cluster
[MBeanServerInvocationHandler]com.bea:Name=testCluster,Type=Cluster

wls:/sample/edit !> server = cmo.createServer('testServer')
wls:/sample/edit !> print server
[MBeanServerInvocationHandler]com.bea:Name=testServer,Type=Server

wls:/sample/edit !> cd('/Machines/machine')
wls:/sample/edit/Machines/machine !> machine = cmo
wls:/sample/edit/Machines/machine !> print machine
[MBeanServerInvocationHandler]com.bea:Name=machine,Type=UnixMachine

wls:/sample/edit/Machines/machine !> cd('/Servers/testServer')
wls:/sample/edit/Servers/testServer !> cmo.setListenAddress('127.0.0.1')
wls:/sample/edit/Servers/testServer !> cmo.setListenPort(10000)
wls:/sample/edit/Servers/testServer !> cmo.setMachine(machine)
wls:/sample/edit/Servers/testServer !> cmo.setCluster(cluster)

wls:/sample/edit/Servers/testServer !> save()
Saving all your changes ...
Saved all your changes successfully.

wls:/sample/edit/Servers/testServer !> activate()
Activating all your changes, this may take a while ...
The edit lock associated with this edit session is released
once the activation is completed.
Activation completed

wls:/sample/edit/Servers/testServer> cd('/')
wls:/sample/edit> start('testCluster','Cluster')

Starting the following servers in Cluster, testCluster : testServer
................
All servers in the cluster testCluster are started successfully.
```

The code above shows that it is a relatively simple task to automate cluster creation using the Oracle WebLogic Server JMX API and WebLogic Scripting Tool.

Dynamic Clusters

Dynamic clusters are a great new feature in Oracle WebLogic Server 12c, which enhances the existing clustering functionality, by allowing clusters to grow automatically, on demand, based on a set of configuration values.

Dynamic clusters contain dynamic server instances as members. Dynamic servers are based on a single server template that contains configuration information.

Note Dynamic servers are regular server instances that get created on-the-fly by WebLogic Server.

Administrators specify the number of cluster members anticipated to be required in order to handle peak workload in their environments, and WebLogic Server will then create the servers dynamically and configure them using the parameters provided in a server template.

The functionality to create a dynamic cluster is also available from the Administration Console and WLST, but the process differs slightly as additional information is required to be able to instantiate server instances dynamically.

Server Templates

Server templates define the set of attributes that are necessary to make the configuration of dynamic servers unique, and therefore runnable alongside other server instances in a domain. These attributes include:

- Server name
- Listen port and SSL port
- Machine name

At runtime, WebLogic Server calculates the actual values to be used in dynamic servers. It uses the server name provided as prefix and appends an incremental numeric value for each dynamic server.

The value of machine name is used similarly. It controls whether servers are assigned to a machine, and what algorithm to use when assigning dynamic server instances to machines. The options include assigning all dynamic server instances to a single machine or assigning them to any machine available in the domain, or to a subset of them. This last option requires an expression that will be evaluated when selecting a candidate machine.

Listen ports are specified as a numeric literal for the first dynamic server, and WebLogic Server will then increment the supplied value by one for each dynamic server created.

Server templates may be created from the administration console and WLST, either explicitly, using the option provided in the Domain Structure panel, or implicitly, by creating a dynamic cluster from the Clusters page.

The following considerations should be followed when creating dynamic clusters:

- Controlling dynamic clusters using Node Manager requires that each dynamic server instance is assigned to a WebLogic Server machine.

- WebLogic Server plug-ins include a property named *DynamicServerList* to support dynamic updates to the list of registered target servers in the web tier.

- Dynamic clusters require cluster-wide application deployments, as opposed to regular clusters that support deploying applications to selected cluster members.

Listing 9-2 shows how to create a dynamic cluster using WLST. In this scenario, two additional objects are involved: one that represents the server template and another that represents the configuration of the set of dynamic servers in a dynamic cluster.

Listing 9-2. Creating a server template using WLST

```
wls:/offline> connect('weblogic','samplepass','127.0.0.1:7001')
Connecting to t3://127.0.0.1:7001 with userid weblogic ...
Successfully connected to Admin Server "AdminServer" that belongs to domain
"sample".
```

```
wls:/sample/serverConfig> edit()
Location changed to edit tree. This is a writable tree with
DomainMBean as the root. To make changes you will need to start
an edit session via startEdit().

wls:/sample/edit> startEdit()
Starting an edit session ...
Started edit session, please be sure to save and activate your
changes once you are done.

wls:/sample/edit !> serverTemplate = cmo.createServerTemplate('testServer
Template');
wls:/sample/edit !> print serverTemplate
[MBeanServerInvocationHandler]com.bea:Name=testServerTemplate,Type=Server
Template

wls:/sample/edit !> dynamicCluster = cmo.createCluster('testDynamicCluster')
wls:/sample/edit !> print dynamicCluster
[MBeanServerInvocationHandler]com.bea:Name=testDynamicCluster,Type=Cluster

wls:/sample/edit !> dynamicServers = dynamicCluster.getDynamicServers()
wls:/sample/edit !> print dynamicServers
[MBeanServerInvocationHandler]com.
bea:Name=testDynamicCluster,Type=DynamicServers,Cluster=testDynamicCluster

wls:/sample/edit !> dynamicServers.setServerTemplate(serverTemplate)
wls:/sample/edit !> dynamicServers.setMaximumDynamicServerCount(5)

wls:/sample/edit/Servers/testServer !> save()
Saving all your changes ...
Saved all your changes successfully.

wls:/sample/edit/Servers/testServer !> activate()
Activating all your changes, this may take a while ...
The edit lock associated with this edit session is released
once the activation is completed.
Activation completed
```

Dynamic clusters are one step forward in assisting administrators to support automatic horizontal scaling of WebLogic Server environments.

Recommended Exercises

1. Customize the sample code to create a regular cluster that comprises two managed servers on two different machines.

2. Create a dynamic cluster with a maximum capacity of two server instances using the Administration console.

3. Implement a WLST script to create a three-tier WebLogic Server clustered environment consolidated to run on a single host.

Certification Questions

1. Select the web servers supported by WebLogic Server to provide the web tier:

   a. Apache HTTP Server

   b. Oracle HTTP Server

   c. Microsoft IIS

   d. All of the above

2. What is the name of a proprietary header in the WebLogic Server plug-in?

   a. True-Client-IP

   b. WL-Proxy-Client-IP

   c. WL-Client-Proxy

   d. None of the above

3. Name the two fundamental benefits of WebLogic Server clusters:

   a. Reliability and robustness

   b. Scalability and resilience

   c. Load balancing and failover

   d. Capacity and performance

4. What is the main benefit of having the Oracle WebLogic Server plug-in in the web tier?

   a. Ability to recognize failed members

   b. Licensing

   c. Compatibility

   d. Flexibility

5. Select all features of dynamic servers:

   a. Require OS virtualization

   b. Enable a domain to scale out

   c. Enable server instances to scale up

   d. All of the above

Coming Up

In our next chapter, the discussion will review the internal communication between WebLogic Server cluster members, and what options are available to automatically recover from failed server instances.

CHAPTER 10

Clusters - Advanced

In this chapter, we review certain concepts about Oracle WebLogic Server cluster communications and its underlying, foundational technologies. This knowledge is requisite for senior middleware administrators. It covers lower-level details about how clustering communication works in WebLogic Server, and is followed by a short description of monitoring clusters using the Administration Console.

Enabling Technologies

Oracle WebLogic Server administrators need to be able to understand cluster configuration well beyond the options available in the configuration wizard. They need to understand the purpose of available configuration settings, as well as how to troubleshoot their effects when necessary. This is particularly true with cluster communication. A good understanding of computer networking topics is especially helpful for Oracle WebLogic Server administrators working on large production systems.

The fundamental technologies used in Oracle WebLogic Server cluster communications are network sockets, unicast, and multicast. Because of their importance, and that of their underlying network protocols, a basic refresher is in order.

TCP/IP

The dominant communication protocol suite in the world is informally referred to as TCP/IP, which stands for Transmission Control Protocol, Internet Protocol. Oracle WebLogic Server leverages the TCP/IP stack present in supported operating systems to communicate over the network.

© Gustavo Garnica 2018
G. Garnica, *Oracle WebLogic Server 12c Administration I Exam 1Z0-133*,
https://doi.org/10.1007/978-1-4842-2562-2_10

Protocols in TCP/IP specify how data in a network is prepared for transmission, transmitted, routed, and received. These responsibilities are distributed across a layered architecture, in which one layer provides services to its adjacent layer. Oracle WebLogic Server administrators should be familiar with three of these layers: network, transport, and application, as well as with three network protocols: IP, TCP, and UDP.

IP

IP is a connection-less, unreliable[1] protocol that works at the network layer. It has the fundamental task of delivering data in packets named datagrams, from source to destination hosts. Peers in IP networks are identified by IP addresses, either IPv4 or IPv6.

An IP address identifies a network interface configured on a host, and a host may have more than one network interface configured.

Thus, in order for a WebLogic Server instance to be able to communicate over the network, it must always have associated at least one IP address. WebLogic Server will ensure that every instance will use one: either one configured by an administrator, or one assigned as per default configuration options. For instance, when administrators create servers using the Oracle WebLogic Server configuration wizard, they can explicitly configure an IP address by typing it, or by selecting it from a list, or they may choose one of the options that implicitly configure the IP address, either to bind to all configured IP addresses, or to localhost[2].

TCP

TCP is a connection-oriented, reliable protocol that works at the transport layer, adjacent to the network layer. That is, data sent using TCP gets converted into datagrams that are sent over the network using IP.

At this layer, one side listens for connection requests to be initiated by another end. Once a connection has been established, data can be streamed both ways until the connection is closed. TCP ensures that messages delivered are identical to messages sent, thus guaranteeing reliability. Again, TCP uses IP for actual data delivery over the network to the target host.

---

[1]Unreliable as in not providing features to recover from data loss.

[2]The localhost name resolves to address 127.0.0.1 in IPv4 or 0:0:0:0:0:0:0:1 in IPv6, which corresponds to the loopback interface. These IP addresses are not routable.

TCP specifies that each end of a connection must define source and destination identifiers, known as port numbers[3]. Thus, whereas IP addresses are used to identify hosts in a network, port numbers are used to identify processes in a host. The notion of a port number is closely associated with that of a network socket.

Sockets

Sockets are network communication endpoints, and are used in much the same way applications use files to interact with drive storage. When data must be written out over the network, it is written to a socket, and when data must be read from the network, it is read from a socket.

Processes refer to sockets by their address, which are composed of an IP address and a port number, separated by a colon.

At startup, each Oracle WebLogic Server instance binds to at least one network socket[4] in order to be able to listen for incoming connection requests.

Note   The effect of choosing *All Local Addresses* while creating a server instance, is to have the instance create as many sockets as IP addresses are configured in the host, in both IPv4 and IPv6.

UDP

UDP stands for User Datagram Protocol and like TCP uses port numbers and runs at the transport layer, on top of IP. Unlike TCP though, UDP does not have reliability features and is not connection oriented.

UDP is a preferred choice over TCP, especially in cases where data payloads are small enough to fit in a single packet, or when occasional packet loss is not critical, such as with voice and video streaming.

Oracle WebLogic Server can use UDP for certain types of communications.

---

[3]Port numbers are 16-bit signed integers, classified in three ranges: system (0-1023), user (1024-49151), and dynamic or private (49152-65535).

[4]When no values are explicitly provided, WebLogic Server uses default values to build a socket address: for example, 7001 is the default port number for an administration server.

Multicast

Multicast is a mechanism that enables one-to-many communications using UDP. In multicast, a single host sends messages to a specific IP address[5] and port number, and the network automatically relays them to all associated hosts, typically an entire subnet, making it effectively a type of group communication.

Administrators must be aware that multicast presents certain challenges for which some network administrators prefer not to allow multicast traffic on their networks. One such issue is known as multicast storms, in which networks are stressed due to repeated packet relay.

When Oracle WebLogic Server instances in a cluster use IP multicast, in order to defeat UDP unreliability to a degree, they use modified multicast messages that are able to detect and retransmit lost messages.

Unicast

Unicast is point-to-point network communication. It occurs between a unique sender and a unique receiver, using sockets, leveraging the reliability features of TCP.

In the TCP/IP world, unicast works well notwithstanding the network topology implemented. This is perhaps the chief reason why unicast is the default communication mode in quite a few networked computing environments. This is also true with clustering in Oracle WebLogic Server.

Application Layer

In the TCP/IP network architecture, applications work at the top layer of the stack. The application layer is adjacent to the transport layer where TCP and UDP work. A Java Virtual Machine process that represents an Oracle WebLogic Server instance is located at this layer.

It is quite common to see other application processes running alongside WebLogic Server processes in production systems. Two common examples are log collectors and hardware monitoring tools. These other processes will bind to, and use their own network sockets, or message their own multicast addresses. Even though they could be

---

[5]WebLogic Server uses 239.192.0.0 as multicast address by default.

using different application protocols[6], the communication down the stack, through the underlying protocols, remains the same.

Cluster Communication

A fundamental requirement for clustering anywhere is that each cluster member must be able to respond to requests for service in the same way every other cluster member would do. Therefore, a core cluster feature is having cluster members replicate information among them, so that all of them are able to respond as if they were one and the same instance.

The fundamental types of information that Oracle WebLogic Server cluster members share are of three types:

- Health status

- JNDI state

- HTTP session information

Note   HTTP session replication will be reviewed in the next chapter that deals with proxies.

Health Status

Cluster members by default will send a heartbeat every 10 seconds. If the advertisement is not received by other cluster members at the right frequency, according to the protocol chosen, the server instance will be considered failed and removed from the cluster.

When a cluster is configured to use multicast communication, the default behavior is to consider a server failed after three consecutive missed heartbeats. When using unicast, since it uses a reliable protocol, only one heartbeat will be enough to consider an instance failed. Once servers cross the applicable health notification threshold, they are removed from the cluster.

---

[6]Common application protocols include Telnet, SSH, HTTP, FTP, SMTP, DNS, NTP, RTP, etc.

JNDI Replication

As briefly mentioned in the introductory chapters, JNDI is a naming service. It maintains a tree-structured registry of objects and assigns names to them. Clients may then use JNDI to locate objects by these names, similar to the way DNS maps names to IP addresses[7].

Every Oracle WebLogic Server instance maintains its own JNDI tree. Server instances that are members of a cluster maintain a tree that also contains objects that are bound to all other cluster members, effectively providing a view of all objects available across the cluster[8].

Server instances continuously monitor messages from other cluster members advertising the state of their JNDI trees, and will update their references to clustered objects in their local trees accordingly.

Because of JNDI replication, a client can connect to a cluster and consume its services as if they were hosted on a single Oracle WebLogic Server instance.

RMI[9] is the enabling technology that Oracle WebLogic Server uses for JNDI replication. RMI stubs of the clustered objects get distributed to cluster members across the network. Each RMI stub used in JNDI replication in Oracle WebLogic Server is aware of the multiple locations of the referenced clustered object.

Selecting Protocols

As stated, a critical aspect of a cluster is its ability to replicate information among cluster members. Therefore, a key responsibility of an Oracle WebLogic Server administrator is to select the right protocol for cluster communication, configure the cluster accordingly, and monitor communication performance throughout the life of the cluster.

Oracle WebLogic Server clusters can be configured to communicate using either *multicast* or *unicast*. As discussed, this implies using either UDP or sockets, with their respective nuances.

---

[7]Java EE developers are familiar with this mechanism as they use a context object to locate objects by their JNDI names.

[8]Clustered objects are only bound to the local JNDI tree only if no naming conflicts exist.

[9]RMI stands for Remote Method Invocation. It is using RMI that a client in one JVM can invoke methods from an object in a remote JVM.

Sometimes, the choice will be as simple as being informed by network administrators in the organization that multicast is not supported, leaving no choice but to use unicast.

Many times, both choices will be available. When they are, choosing one protocol over the other should result from an educated analysis that considers several factors, including cluster size, network topology and latency, and so forth. The level of experience of Oracle WebLogic Server administrators and that of network administrators is definitely an important factor in making that decision as well.

Bottom line, the protocol chosen for cluster communications should facilitate that messages from cluster members reach their destinations consistently and timely throughout the life of the cluster.

Choosing Multicast

Multicast is an efficient protocol for WebLogic Server cluster messaging that works well out of the box for domains deployed on a single network.

For domains that span multiple networks, such as when servers are deployed across data centers to maximize availability, the following considerations must be observed:

- Network latency should be low, the recommended value is 10ms.

- Network routers must be configured to fully support multicast packet transmission.

- Packet time-to-live must be configured so that routers will not discard multicast packets before they reach their final destination.

- A dedicated multicast address and port number should be assigned to the WebLogic Server cluster.

In general, multicast is recommended as the right option for large clusters, provided that the target environment can be made to comply with the considerations above.

Figure 10-1 shows how Oracle WebLogic Server cluster communication flows when multicast mode has been configured on a cluster.

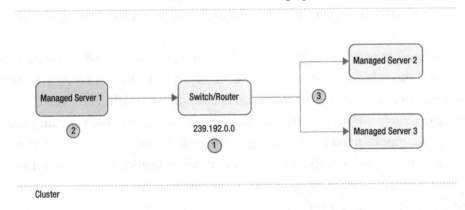

Multicast Cluster Messaging

Figure 10-1. *Cluster communication using multicast*

In the figure above, a cluster of three Oracle WebLogic Server instances have been deployed to a network whose switch or router has been configured with a multicast address of 239.192.0.0 (1). The WebLogic Server cluster has been configured accordingly.

The first managed server sends a heartbeat message targeting the multicast address (2). Since the switch or router knows which hosts have registered with the multicast address, it will make copies of the message received and relay them to the rest of these hosts (3), in our case managed servers two and three.

The process will be exactly the same regardless of which cluster member initiates the multicast communication, and the remaining cluster members will receive a copy of the original datagram for their individual use.

The following is an example of a WLST session (Listing 10-1) where cluster messaging mode is set to multicast, setting the corresponding address and port number.

Listing 10-1. Setting multicast cluster messaging

```
wls:/offline> connect('weblogic','welcome1','127.0.0.1:7001')
wls:/sample/serverConfig> edit()
wls:/sample/edit !> startEdit()

wls:/sample/edit !> cd('Clusters/cluster')
wls:/sample/edit/Clusters/cluster !> print(cmo)
[MBeanServerInvocationHandler]com.bea:Name=cluster,Type=Cluster
wls:/sample/edit/Clusters/cluster !> cmo.setClusterMessagingMode('multicast')
```

```
wls:/sample/edit/Clusters/cluster !> cmo.setMulticastPort(11001)
wls:/sample/edit/Clusters/cluster !> cmo.setMulticastAddress('239.192.0.1')

wls:/sample/edit/Clusters/cluster !> save()
wls:/sample/edit/Clusters/cluster !> validate()
wls:/sample/edit/Clusters/cluster !> activate()
...
The following non-dynamic attribute(s) have been changed on MBeans
that require server re-start:
MBean Changed : com.bea:Name=cluster,Type=Cluster
Attributes changed : MulticastAddress, MulticastPort
...
wls:/sample/edit/Clusters/cluster !> exit()
```

Note   In order to use IPv4 multicast, all WebLogic Server instances must have the preferred IP stack set to IPv4.

The preceding code invokes methods of the Cluster MBean. It is worth noting that the output of the *activate* method states that changing cluster messaging modes require a full cluster restart in order to become fully active.

Choosing Unicast

It could be argued that unicast is simpler than multicast, given the relative lower entry barrier for using unicast on TCP/IP networks of diverse topologies. It is probably fair to say that it is definitely simpler to use than multicast in many Oracle WebLogic Server environments[10].

It is not necessarily better in all cases, and indeed not more performant for high-end workloads, but certainly easier to get started with, and definitely good enough in the long run for a large share of environments.

---

[10]At the time of writing this, multicast is not supported out-of-the-box by the network stack of some virtualization technologies such as Oracle VirtualBox, or by some cloud providers such as Amazon AWS.

As explained in previous paragraphs, unicast uses network sockets, and implements a form of one-to-one communication. However, cluster communication follows a one-to-many pattern. Oracle WebLogic Server overcomes this challenge by following classifying cluster members in groups, and appoints certain cluster members as leaders of groups. Then, each cluster member sets up sockets to send and receive status messages with its group leader, and the group leader is responsible for relaying the message to the remaining cluster members in the group, and to other group leaders as well, thus limiting the number of sockets required while carrying out one-to-many communications.

WebLogic Server organizes a cluster in groups by creating an alphabetically sorted list of cluster member names and splitting them in groups of up to 10 servers. The first server instance in a group is appointed group leader. Because of this, adding a cluster member with a name in between the list will cause group membership reorganization, which will potentially affect service availability. The obvious solution to this is to use an index, or another alphabetically sensitive identifier, to name server instances in a cluster, so that WebLogic Server will add new servers to the end of the last group in a cluster.

In this context, it is very important that WebLogic Server instances playing the group leader role in a cluster have enough resources available to them, particularly the capacity to properly handle socket communications, so that they are able to both relay cluster messages timely and consistently, in addition to performing their work as cluster members themselves. It is recommended that instances use native IO[11], or in other words, the native socket reader, as opposed to the pure Java socket reader.

In general, unicast is a pretty good option for Oracle WebLogic Server cluster messaging. However, Oracle does not favor one communication mode over the other. Unicast is the default mode, but multicast is just as supported as unicast. As indicated before, the decision to choose one mode over the other should always result from an educated analysis of factors present in and around the target environments.

Figure 10-2 shows a view[12] of how Oracle WebLogic Server cluster communication flows when unicast mode has been selected.

---

[11]Native IO may be enabled from the Tuning tab in the configuration of each server instance.

[12]The diagram displays a simplified view, showing only the primary communication actors when using unicast for Oracle WebLogic Server cluster communication.

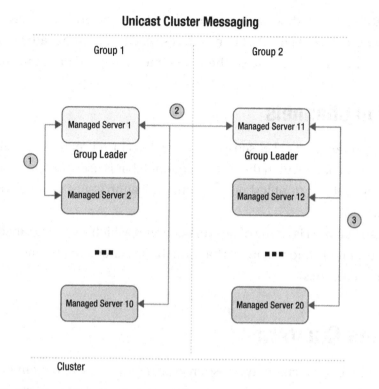

Figure 10-2. *Cluster communication using unicast*

In Figure 10-2 a cluster of 20 nodes is represented. In this scenario, WebLogic Server will create two groups of 10 cluster members and will alphabetically select the first server of each group as leader. Managed server 2 in group 1 sets up a socket with its group leader and starts sending messages (1). The leader of group 1 relays copies of the message (2) to the leader of group 2, as well as to other members of its group. The leader of group 2 will also relay copies (3) of the original message to its group members.

The following WLST method of the Cluster MBean object is used to set messaging mode to unicast (Listing 10-2).

Listing 10-2. Setting unicast cluster messaging

```
...
wls:/sample/edit/Clusters/cluster !> cd('/Clusters/cluster');
wls:/sample/edit/Clusters/cluster !> print(cmo)
[MBeanServerInvocationHandler]com.bea:Name=cluster,Type=Cluster
wls:/sample/edit/Clusters/cluster !> cmo.setClusterMessagingMode('unicast');
...
```

Invoking the above method is done precisely in the same order as in Listing 10-1, same connecting, and start editing, but no address and port number are required, only the argument to the method changes. Then the same saving and disconnecting applies.

Replication Channels

In certain environments, it makes sense to ensure that cluster replication traffic goes through a different channel than the default channel that is used for application traffic. This can be very useful in troubleshooting communication issues in large production environments.

A replication channel is a type of network channel, which were described in Chapter 8. Cluster replication channels have the same general requirements as other custom network channels[13].

Monitoring Clusters

Oracle WebLogic Server includes two resources that may be used to monitor a cluster. The simplest is the cluster *Monitoring* page in the *Administration Console*. A more robust tool is *WebLogic Diagnostics Framework* or WLDF, which is beyond the scope of this book.

The cluster *Monitoring* page has two tabs that display basic runtime data that can serve as a starting point when assessing the performance of a cluster. The first tab is labeled *Summary* and presents a series of statistics of each cluster member. Figure 10-3 shows the contents of a modified[14] cluster *Summary* tab.

---

[13]There is a known circumstance with using cluster replication channels and SSL. This will be touched on in Chapter 11, which deals with proxies and application session replication.

[14]The table must be customized to show and hide values to match this view.

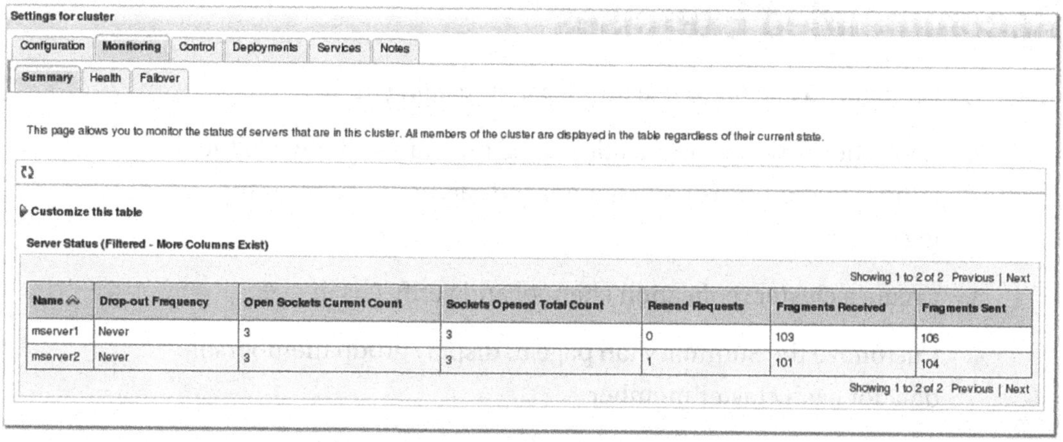

Figure 10-3. *Cluster monitoring summary of statistics*

From each cluster member, it displays the drop-out frequency, the current and total count of open sockets, the count of data fragments received and sent, and the number of resend requests.

These pieces of information present a good initial notion of how a cluster member has been communicating over time.

The second tab presents the health status of each cluster member, as well as their running status, from which we may implicitly derive cluster health. Figure 10-4 shows the contents of the *Health* tab.

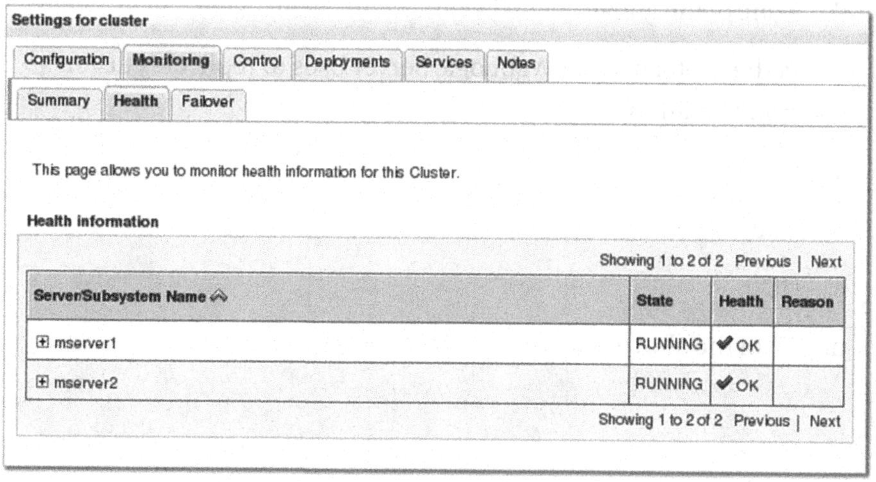

Figure 10-4. *Cluster health monitoring*

Recommended Exercises

1. Configure a cluster to use multicast messaging mode.

2. Cause network communication to be interrupted between the administration server and a managed server, check resulting log errors.

3. Create a cluster replication channel and verify it is in use.

4. Customize the Summary tab page to display group membership data for each cluster member.

5. Misconfigure multicast in a cluster and check resulting log errors.

Certification Questions

1. Cluster communication occurs at the following TCP/IP network layer:

    a. Network

    b. Transport

    c. Application

    d. None of the above

2. Select the protocols that WebLogic Server uses to replicate cluster status information:

    a. IP

    b. TCP

    c. UDP

    d. All of the above

3. What is the default cluster messaging mode in WebLogic Server 12c?

   a. Unicast

   b. Multicast

   c. None of the above

4. A cluster member will be considered failed using unicast after how many consecutive missed heartbeats?

   a. One

   b. Two

   c. Three

   d. None of the above

5. Select all prerequisites for using multicast for cluster messaging:

   a. Network support

   b. Address and port number

   c. Native IO

   d. All of the above

Coming Up

In this chapter, we reviewed the fundamentals of cluster communication in Oracle WebLogic Server. The next chapter builds on this to review cluster proxies and how a cluster performs session replication.

CHAPTER 11

Clusters - Proxies

As explained in previous chapters, clusters enable several Oracle WebLogic Server instances to work together as if they were one and the same.

WebLogic Server clusters can replicate information across instances so that cluster members are enabled to handle any incoming request, irrespective of whether the request initiates a session, or is part of an existing session, including sessions initiated in other WebLogic Server instances. This replication is required to support failover, which shields applications from failure of individual instances. In connection with this, we also discussed that clustering increases the capacity of applications to handle greater workloads using the combined resources of all cluster members.

An Oracle WebLogic Server environment requires an external agent to distribute the load of incoming requests across cluster members so that resources are used more efficiently. This agent or proxy must also be capable of detecting when a server instance is no longer available, to stop sending user requests to it.

How an Oracle WebLogic Server environment performs load balancing depends on the traffic type. In this chapter, we focus on load balancing HTTP traffic.

We start by reviewing details about HTTP sessions and how WebLogic Server handles HTTP session replication[1], and then we discuss load balancing using supported proxies, their different capabilities, and their configuration. We end the chapter by looking at how session failover occurs.

HTTP Sessions

Developers programming applications using Java EE web APIs, such as *Servlet*, require the ability to persist small amounts of data across user requests. This data is used to track what areas of an application users have visited and so forth. This is a simple yet critical

---

[1]EJB, RMI, and JMS load balancing are out of scope of Oracle certification exam 1Z0-133.

© Gustavo Garnica 2018
G. Garnica, *Oracle WebLogic Server 12c Administration I Exam 1Z0-133*,
https://doi.org/10.1007/978-1-4842-2562-2_11

feature required by most web applications. Oracle WebLogic Server uses cookies for HTTP session management, with URL rewriting as an alternative.

Even though developers are in control of the amount and type of session information that gets persisted, it is a best practice to not store more than the smallest amount of data necessary to keep track of user activity.

Oracle WebLogic Server administrators must consider the amount of information stored in sessions as an important factor that could adversely impact application performance, given that session data will get updated, stored, and transferred over the network before *each* HTTP response, for every user in the system. Therefore, it is critical to accurately estimate the amount of session data and allocate commensurate resources. This must account for the number of users, how large sessions are expected to grow, and how long they are expected to last.

Session Replication

Oracle WebLogic Server handles session persistence in a WebLogic Server cluster by replicating *HTTPSession* objects that contain this data.

WebLogic Server implements hooks on the *setAttribute* and *removeAttribute* methods of HTTPSession objects, to detect changes in session data. Therefore, programmers are required to explicitly use these methods in order to have WebLogic Server update the object accordingly across the cluster.

Also, in consideration that such data will get replicated over the network to other server instances, it is a requirement to only store objects that are serializable[2]. Oracle WebLogic Server will not replicate the session state of non-serializable objects.

Replication Groups

In order to maximize the effectiveness of session replication, and to make session replication not a single point of failure, Oracle WebLogic Server should be able to replicate sessions on servers that are hosted on different hardware. This has several connotations depending on the environment where the WebLogic Server domain has been deployed.

---

[2]Serialization is the process whereby an object is converted into a byte stream, suitable for transfer and conversion back into an object.

The default behavior is for session replicas to be created across WebLogic Server machines. WebLogic Server makes the assumption that an administrator has taken care of defining machines to run on separate hardware, which is the recommended way to proceed in production environments.

When, for specific reasons, WebLogic Server is required to choose a particular set of servers as candidates to create session replicas, an administrator may define and use replication groups.

In a domain where both are configured, WebLogic Server machines and replication groups, WebLogic Server will rank eligible servers to determine where to create secondary session states, awarding the highest rank to those servers that both belong in a machine and are members of a replication group.

Replication groups for a server instance can be configured in the Cluster tab of the server configuration, by entering arbitrary replication group names in the *Replication Group* and *Preferred Secondary Group* fields shown below in Figure 11-1.

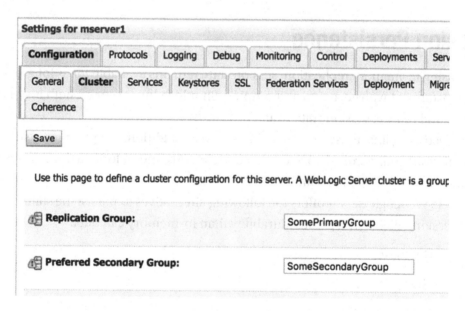

Figure 11-1. *Fields to configure replication groups in a server instance*

In-Memory Replication

In-memory replication of session state in Oracle WebLogic Server uses a primary-secondary scheme. The primary session is always created in the server that receives a user request for which no session exists. Once the request has been processed, but before the response is sent[3], session state is replicated to another server instance, following the rules described above regarding WebLogic Server machines and replication groups.

WebLogic Server ensures that the session management cookie contains a session identifier and the encoded location of the primary and secondary session states[4] formatted as follows: *sessionid!primary!secondary!.*

Note   The only way for WebLogic Server to determine session-server affinity is by using the session ID data. If this is not available in a request, it will be treated as new.

The type of agent that performs load balancing for an Oracle WebLogic Server cluster determines how session failover[5] is performed.

Session Persistence

When using in-memory replication, session state remains available for as long as the server instances involved are up and running. Should failure occur on both instances, primary and replica, session state would be lost.

Protecting against these types of failures, and for additional requirements such as replicating sessions across dispersed clusters in a WAN and so forth, a durable approach is required to handle session state.

Oracle WebLogic Server offers the following alternatives to persist the state of HTTPSession objects with greater durability than in-memory can offer.

- Database

- File

- Coherence*Web

With these options, session state would be available for recovery, even if the entire cluster fails.

---

[3]It is possible to configure WebLogic Server to use asynchronous session state replication.
[4]As a non-default option, URL rewriting is available for clients that do not support cookies.
[5]Session failover is discussed at the end of the chapter.

By reason of the operations involved in saving, updating, and retrieving session data from a database or from a file system, these session persistence methods are less performant than in-memory.

When used in production environments, these options must run on highly available infrastructure that is accessible by all cluster members.

As indicated, a typical use case for persisting session state in a database is an environment that is distributed across multiple, geographically dispersed domains.

*Coherence*Web* is a good alternative when applications require handling large HTTPSession objects[6].

When selecting a method of session data persistence, unless an Oracle WebLogic Server administrator is addressing a particular durability or capacity requirement, it is recommended to start with the default, in-memory option, which has proven to work well for applications with high user concurrency.

Session replication and persistence is configured per application in the Oracle WebLogic Server descriptor file *weblogic.xml*, which must be included in the web application file system structure from which a deployable package is created.

The *weblogic.xml* file contains a root element named *weblogic-web-app*, which contains a *session-descriptor* element. This is where session configuration is specified. Listing 11-1 shows an abbreviated *weblogic.xml* descriptor using in-memory persistence.

Listing 11-1. Sample session-descriptor in weblogic.xml

```
<?xml version = '1.0' encoding = 'UTF-8'?>
<weblogic-web-app xmlns:xsi="http://www.w3.org/2001/XMLSchema-instance"
xsi:schemaLocation="http://xmlns.oracle.com/weblogic/weblogic-web-app
http://xmlns.oracle.com/weblogic/weblogic-web-app/1.7/weblogic-web-app.xsd"
                xmlns="http://xmlns.oracle.com/weblogic/weblogic-web-app">
...

  <session-descriptor>
    <persistent-store-type>REPLICATED</persistent-store-type>
  </session-descriptor>
...

</weblogic-web-app>
```

---

[6]Oracle Coherence is out of scope of Oracle certification exam 1Z0-133.

The *session-descriptor* element is the container for all arguments relative to how sessions are identified, replicated, and persisted. The acceptable data is specified by the *weblogic-web-app* XML schema.

JDBC Persistence

JDBC persistence stores session data in a database. It requires all cluster members to be able to access the target database reliably and swiftly[7]. The steps required to configure session persistence on a database are the following:

1. Create the target database table.

2. Configure a connection pool to the target database.

3. Configure deployment descriptors to use database session persistence.

The database schema required for database persistence is available in the Oracle Fusion Middleware documentation[8], and may be adapted for several database management systems for which there is a supported JDBC driver. Listing 11-2 shows the schema, customized for Oracle DB.

Listing 11-2. Oracle DB schema for JDBC session persistence

```
create table wl_servlet_sessions (
 wl_id VARCHAR2(100) NOT NULL,
 wl_context_path VARCHAR2(100) NOT NULL, wl_is_new CHAR(1),
 wl_create_time NUMBER(20),
 wl_is_valid CHAR(1),
 wl_session_values LONG RAW,
 wl_access_time NUMBER(20),
 wl_max_inactive_interval INTEGER,
 PRIMARY KEY (wl_id, wl_context_path)
);
```

---

[7]Accessing databases using JDBC is the subject of an upcoming chapter.

[8]The code is available in chapter 10 of the Developing Web Applications for WebLogic Server book.

The database schema defines a table named *wl_servlet_sessions* with eight columns. The first two conform to the primary key, and indexes must be created from them. The actual session data is stored in a binary column named *wl_session_values*.

The connection pool to the target database must be configured with read-write access to the corresponding table, and its name must be referenced in the *session-descriptor* element in the *weblogic.xml* deployment descriptor.

Listing 11-3 shows a sample *session-descriptor* element configured for JDBC persistence.

Listing 11-3. JDBC session persistence configuration in weblogic.xml

```
<session-descriptor>
    <persistent-store-type>JDBC</persistent-store-type>
    <persistent-store-pool>HTTPSESSIONS</persistent-store-pool>
</session-descriptor>
```

The above configuration requires a data source[9] named HTTPSESSIONS made available to all cluster members.

File Persistence

File persistence stores session data in a file system. The fundamental requirement for production systems is that the target file system resides on highly available storage. It is also necessary to ensure that the target directory grants the WebLogic Server processes read and write privileges, as well as configuring the *weblogic.xml* deployment descriptor accordingly. Listing 11-4 shows a sample session-descriptor element configured for file persistence.

Listing 11-4. File session persistence configuration in weblogic.xml

```
<session-descriptor>
    <persistent-store-type>FILE</persistent-store-type>
    <persistent-store-dir>/opt/weblogic/sessions</persistent-store-dir>
</session-descriptor>
```

---

[9]A data source in WebLogic Server is a domain configuration item that specifies a target database, the URL where it may be reached, and credentials to access the data.

The above configuration requires a highly available storage device mounted on path: */opt/weblogic/sessions*. The same mount point must be made available to all servers in which cluster members run.

Session Cache

Since persisting session state durably is I/O expensive, in order to enhance performance, both JDBC and file session persistence can cache in memory a configurable number of sessions[10]. Listing 11-5 shows a sample session-descriptor element configured to cache sessions.

Listing 11-5. Session caching configuration in weblogic.xml

```
<session-descriptor>
    <cache-size>2056</cache-size>
</session-descriptor>
```

This configuration would enable a session cache that is twice greater than the default value.

When the maximum number of cached sessions is reached, the least used sessions are removed from memory, in order to accommodate new sessions.

Session cache is enabled in the *weblogic.xml* deployment descriptor by setting a positive integer value to the *cache-size* element. This element is also a child element of the *session-descriptor* element.

The documented default cache size is 1028. Setting this to a value of 0 will explicitly disable session cache.

Proxies

Proxies are the first level of interaction with an Oracle WebLogic Server cluster. They sit between clients and WebLogic Server clusters. They receive resource requests from clients, pass them to cluster members for processing, receive their responses, and forward them back to the clients that originated them. Proxies also perform load balancing of client requests to cluster members. Proxies may be software or hardware based. Oracle WebLogic Server supports both types.

---

[10]This session caching mechanism is only available to JDBC and File session persistence.

Hardware Proxies

Support in Oracle WebLogic Server for hardware load balancers is broader than for software-based load balancers. Most hardware load balancers that comply with the following requirements will work well with WebLogic Server:

1. Supports TLS persistence

2. Supports passive cookie persistence

3. Supports active cookie persistence using their own cookie

When using hardware load balancers, administrators can leverage advanced load balancing algorithms, as well as other extended capabilities such as selection of targets based on request inspection and so forth.

This is also applicable to load balancers that offer the same functionality of their hardware devices, deployable on hypervisors, or as cloud appliances, such as the well-known F5 series by BIG-IP Networks.

The general process to configure a hardware load balancer will commonly require creating a server pool with WebLogic Server cluster members as targets, selecting a load balancing algorithm, creating applicable traffic rules, and ensuring that sticky sessions are working, based on the WebLogic Server session cookie.

Software Proxies

Load balancing an Oracle WebLogic Server cluster using a software-based load balancer is generally more limited than when using hardware-based alternatives. Typically, the sole load balancing algorithm available is round-robin.

Nevertheless, where software-based load balancers excel, is in their ability to learn about failed cluster members proactively, as opposed to learning that instances have failed solely as a result of not receiving responses after requests have been sent to them.

Failed instances detection capability is a capability of a module or plug-in provided by Oracle WebLogic Server for certain HTTP servers. Because of this, third-party software-based proxies are only supported when the WebLogic Server proxy plug-in module has been installed and configured.

The WebLogic Server proxy plug-in maintains a list of cluster members; because of this, it is also able to locate session replicas.

Supported Oracle WebLogic Server software load balancers include[11]:

- Oracle WebLogic Server with *HTTPClusterServlet*

- *Oracle HTTP Server*

- *Apache HTTP Server*

The general process to configure a software-based load balancer with WebLogic Server is similar to the one described for hardware-based load balancers, that is, a server pool that includes at least a single cluster member must be configured, along with the required URL mappings to be proxied.

HTTPClusterServlet

This option requires setting up a WebLogic Server managed instance that is separate from the target WebLogic Server cluster. On this instance, a simple servlet application named *HTTPClusterServlet*[12] is configured as the root context.

Configuring this option requires editing the deployment descriptors *weblogic.xml* and *web.xml*. The configuration essentially defines that the main servlet class *weblogic. servlet.proxy.HttpClusterServlet* will respond to certain URL patterns, and will bind to the root context of the server instance.

Setting up load balancing using *HTTPClusterServlet* is comparatively more complex and also less robust than other software-based options.

Oracle HTTP Server

Oracle HTTP Server bundles a customized version of Apache HTTP server and a WebLogic Server proxy plug-in.

Oracle HTTP Server is installed using Oracle Universal Installer, which is also used to install Oracle WebLogic Server. The general process looks familiar therefore. Figure 11-2 shows the *Installation Type* screen.

---

[11]Oracle Traffic Director is another excellent choice for load balancing a WebLogic Server cluster, available for Oracle Exalogic engineered systems. Internet Information Server 8.0 and 8.5 with the proxy plug-in is also an alternative for Microsoft Windows systems.

[12]The HTTPClusterServlet application is provided as part of Oracle WebLogic Server.

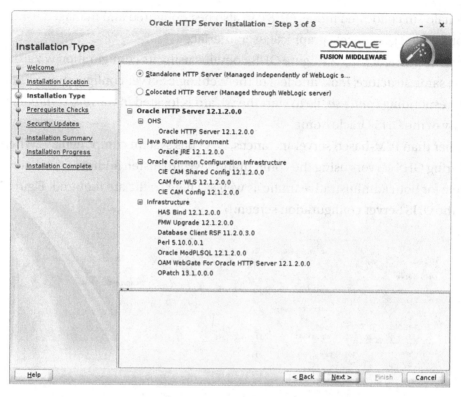

Figure 11-2. *Oracle HTTP Server Installation Type screen*

The image above shows that Oracle HTTP Server, or OHS as it is commonly referred to, may be installed in one of two modes, either *standalone* or *collocated*. In standalone mode, OHS is managed in an OHS domain, whereas in collocated mode, OHS is managed as part of an existing WebLogic Server domain.

Note   Oracle HTTP Server domains are different than WebLogic Server domains. OHS servers in an OHS domain are Apache HTTP servers. However, both domain types work with the Java-based Node Manager.

Because of component dependencies, installing OHS in collocated mode requires an existing Oracle Fusion Middleware *Infrastructure* home[13]. In both modes, Oracle HTTP Server may be managed through product-provided scripts and WLST commands.

---

[13]As opposed to installing on a WebLogic Server-only Oracle home. Refer to Chapter 2 for details about using a Fusion Middleware Infrastructure distribution to install WebLogic Server.

Additionally, in collocated mode, OHS can also be configured and managed using the Enterprise Manager console graphical user interface.

An administrator may configure OHS domains using its configuration wizard, which uses the same structure, look, and feel of the WebLogic Server configuration wizard. The corresponding *config.sh* file to start the wizard is located in the *ohs/common/bin* directory of the OHS Oracle home.

Rather than JVM-based server instances, OHS has system components[14]. When configuring OHS servers using the configuration wizard, listen addresses and port numbers for both administrative traffic as well as client traffic are required. Figure 11-3 shows the OHS Server configuration screen.

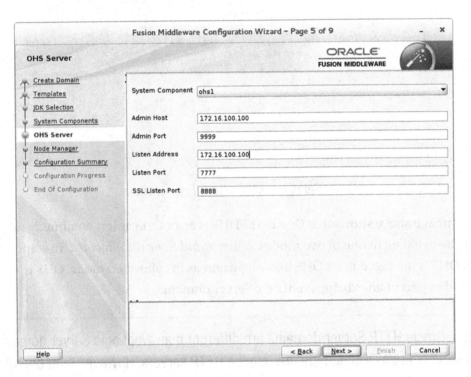

Figure 11-3. *OHS server configuration screen*

The image shows an OHS server named *ohs1*, which is listening for administrative traffic on port 9999, and for HTTP client traffic on port 7777 and TLS-enabled traffic on port 8888, all on private IP *172.16.100.100*. Most commonly, however, the configured ports for client traffic in a production environment would be 80 for HTTP and 443 for HTTPS.

---

[14]Additional system component types in Oracle Web Tier are beyond the scope of our analysis.

As with WebLogic Server JVMs, once an OHS instance is started, it creates network sockets, and binds to them to start listening for user requests.

Once OHS is installed, the actual WebLogic Server plug-in that enables load balancing requests for a cluster must be configured. The configuration can be manually performed by editing the directives in a *mod_wl_ohs.conf* file located at *DOMAIN_ NAME/config/fmwconfig/components/OHS/instances/OHS_NAME* where *DOMAIN_ NAME* is the domain directory, and OHS_NAME is the name of the OHS component.

Apache HTTP Server users will be glad to know that the *mod_wl_ohs.conf* file follows the Apache configuration format.

An *IfModule* section for a *weblogic_module* that contains the required directives to load balance requests for an Oracle WebLogic Server target, server, or cluster must be defined. The URL bindings and their targets are defined in a *Location* directive within IfModule, as shown in Listing 11-6.

Listing 11-6. Oracle WebLogic Server plug-in configuration in OHS

```
<IfModule weblogic_module>
 <Location /hello>
  WLSRequest On
  WebLogicCluster 172.16.100.101:8001,172.16.100.102:8001
 </Location>
</IfModule>
```

The above configuration would load balance requests for */hello*, across members of a WebLogic Server cluster, listening on port 8001, in private IP addresses *172.16.100.101* and *102*.

Note   It is possible to configure TLS termination in OHS by adding directives *WLProxySSL* and *WLProxySSL* to the *Location* section.

The final configuration step requires enabling, in the target WebLogic Server domain, a parameter named *WebLogic Plug-In Enabled*. This can be performed either at the server level for each cluster member, or at the cluster level itself. When set, this parameter will cause WebLogic Server instances to employ a custom HTTP header named *WL-Proxy-Client-IP*. This header will store the IP address of the actual client that originated the request, rather than the OHS address.

Once the plug-in has been configured, OHS may be started by invoking the *startComponent* script in the *bin* directory of the OHS domain, passing an OHS server name, as shown in Listing 11-7.

Listing 11-7. Command to start an OHS system component in Linux

```
# DOMAIN_NAME/bin/startComponent.sh ohs1
```

The above command would contact the underlying Node Manager process and request from it to start an OHS instance named *ohs1*.

Apache HTTP Server

Apache HTTP Server is a very mature product from Apache Software Foundation. It enjoys a pretty solid reputation as a very stable and reliable product for serving HTTP loads.

Oracle supports versions 2.2. and 2.4 of Apache HTTP Server as a proxy for WebLogic Server clusters. The version to use depends on the version of WebLogic Server to proxy for. For WebLogic Server 12c, the required version is Apache 2.4.

Installing Apache HTTP Server is beyond the scope of our analysis, but it is certainly a simple task given that it can be installed using package managers in Linux distributions, as well as from binary distributions for other operating systems such as Microsoft Windows.

Once Apache has been installed, the Oracle WebLogic Server plug-in must be downloaded from Oracle, and extracted to a file system. The configuration process is longer than with OHS because, in essence, we must manually perform the integration steps that Oracle has done in OHS, as well as checking the option WebLogic Plug-In Enabled either at the domain or server level, as done when configuring OHS. The configuration process comes down to this:

1. Adding the *lib* directory from the plug-in distribution to the value of the *LD_LIBRARY_PATH* system variable on Unix/Linux, or to the value of the *PATH* system variable on Microsoft Windows.

2. Verifying that the *mod_so.c* Apache module is enabled by executing *apachectl -l*

3. Adding a *LoadModule* directive to Apache HTTP Server
    configuration (*httpd.conf*) to enable support for the WebLogic
    Server plug-in.

4. Adding *IfModule* and *Location* directives to Apache HTTP Server
    configuration (*httpd.conf*) to configure the plug-in.

5. Verifying the syntax of the edited configuration file (*httpd.conf*) by
    executing *apachectl -t*

The code in Listing 11-8 below illustrates the required additions to an Apache
HTTP Server main configuration file, in order to configure it to load balance an Oracle
WebLogic Server cluster.

Listing 11-8. Additions to Apache httpd.conf file

```
...
LoadModule weblogic_module /opt/weblogic-plugins-12.1.3/lib/mod_wl.so
...
<IfModule mod_weblogic.c>
 <Location /hello>
  WLSRequest On
  WebLogicCluster 172.16.100.101:8001,172.16.100.102:8001
 </Location>
</IfModule>
```

The code above would configure an Apache HTTP server to load the WebLogic
Server plug-in that was extracted to path /opt/weblogic-plugins-12.1.3. It would load
balance requests just like in the OHS example before.

Deployment Architectures

There are several deployment options available to load balance traffic incoming to an
Oracle WebLogic Server cluster.

In the simplest deployment approach, an HTTP server configured with the WebLogic
Server Proxy plug-in is placed in front of a WebLogic Server cluster. It can be any of the
software-based options discussed.

As stated, this is considered a basic alternative given that load balancing using these products is restricted to round-robin only. This restriction is only natural due to the fact that HTTP servers were really not built to perform load balancing and other related tasks. Load balancing was added later, as a useful convenience.

A variation of this approach is using a hardware-based load-balancing device or its cloud appliance counterpart. One could argue that a software-based version of a hardware load balancer is better than an HTTP server with the WebLogic Server plug-in[15], and the reason should be apparent. When working with a physical hardware load-balancing device, one gets to work with specialized hardware and software.

When working with cloud appliances from hardware-based load-balancing manufacturers, one still gets the specialized software, and because of the nature of the cloud, there is freedom to run the instance in as powerful hardware as desired; therefore, no performance penalties need be suffered.

According to this, using an HTTP server with the WebLogic Server plug-in may not be the right solution in cases where an administrator must satisfy advanced requirements such as performing request mangling, or employing complex load-balancing algorithms.

Another, more robust deployment approach is available. It involves taking advantage of the features offered by both alternatives, software-based and hardware-based proxies, in a single deployment. In other words, this involves placing a hardware-load balancer in front of a cluster of HTTP Servers with the WebLogic Server plug-in configured, which in turn fronts a cluster of Oracle WebLogic Servers.

This approach provides an Oracle WebLogic Server environment with the specialized features of a hardware load balancer, and the proactive health monitoring capability of the WebLogic Server plug-in, as well as room for security and performance enhancements.

Figure 11-4 shows a view of the fully distributed proxy deployment architecture.

---

[15]Though often confirmed, this assertion should be considered a general guideline, not meant to replace due requirements analysis efforts.

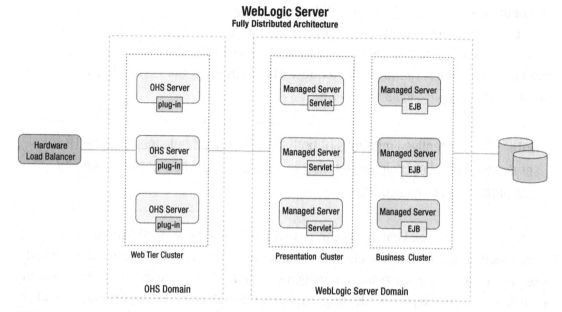

Figure 11-4. *Fully distributed proxy deployment architecture*

The image shows that by offloading static content to the web tier, one may gain in performance. It is easy from this view to conceive that firewalls may be placed between the hardware load balancer and the web tier, and between the web tier and the WebLogic Server cluster, as well as between the WebLogic Server cluster and the data tier or other system back ends.

Session Failover

We have reviewed that Oracle WebLogic Server has built-in session replication capabilities, which out of the box are operative and sufficient for basic clustering requirements, and that many HTTP session durability and size requirements can be easily addressed by configuration.

We have also reviewed the types and features of agents or proxies that sit between actual clients and the Oracle WebLogic Server cluster members.

Despite the fact that hardware load balancers have been referred to as a preferred choice for advanced load balancing requirements, when it comes to Oracle WebLogic Server session failover, they are somewhat limited. Specifically, once a hardware load balancer has determined the target instance to which it will forward a request, based on its configured load-balancing algorithm and associated rules, it won't matter whether or not the instance has failed, it will still send the request nonetheless. It is until the load balancer notices that there was no response from the target, that it will adjust and forward the request to another target, and so on, until one of the target instances in its pool processes and responds to the request. This is precisely the circumstance that the WebLogic Server plug-in aims to avoid.

Note   The respective limitations of both, hardware load balancers and HTTP servers with the WebLogic Server plug-in, are resolved when deployed side by side, forming a composed front tier.

Since hardware load balancers can send requests to Oracle WebLogic Server instances that may not be actively maintaining the required session state, the target will use the information in the session management cookie[16] to locate the secondary session replica and be able to process the request. From this point on, this target instance will become the primary session maintainer and will update the session management data before sending a response.

The key aspect when working with the WebLogic Server plug-in is its ability to maintain a dynamic list of cluster members. Plug-ins have a *DynamicServerList* property set to *ON* by default. This controls whether the plug-in will automatically adapt to changes in cluster membership[17].

Oracle WebLogic Server will return to the plug-in, as part of a server response, an updated list of cluster instances whenever changes in membership occur. This is the process whereby WebLogic Server seeks to go a bit further in anticipating failure.

If the WebLogic Server plug-in encounters a scenario where the instance maintaining the primary session state does not respond, it will not send the request to just the next instance according to the load balancing algorithm it uses; instead, since it is able to use the information in the session management cookie, it will directly forward the request to the WebLogic Server instance hosting the session replica, and the rest of the process occurs in a similar fashion as described before[18].

---

[16]The session management information is comprised of the session ID, and the location of the primary and secondary WebLogic Server instances maintaining the session state.

[17]The servers in the plug-in configuration are just a starting point for load balancing and failover.

[18]Additional HTTP session replication and failover scenarios exist, most of which involve replicating and failing over and across disparate WebLogic Server clusters. These scenarios are not covered in exam 1Z0-133.

Recommended Exercises

1. Install and configure an OHS system component in Oracle HTTP Server 12c.

2. Install and configure the WebLogic Server plug-in in Apache HTTP Server 2.4.

3. Enable instances in a cluster to use the WebLogic Server plug-in at the server level.

4. Configure an application to use JDBC session persistence.

Certification Questions

1. WebLogic Server replicates session information stored in: ...

   a. Database

   b. File system

   c. HTTPSession objects

   d. Coherence*Web

2. Durable session persistence mechanism:

   a. In-memory

   b. Replicated

   c. JDBC

   d. File

3. Load balancing algorithms supported by the WebLogic Server plug-in:

   a. Round-robin

   b. Weighted

   c. Sticky

   d. All of the above

   e. None of the above

4. Methods to improve session replication performance:

    a. Database

    b. Asynchronous replication

    c. File system

    d. Session cache

5. HTTP session configuration data is stored in:

    a. weblogic.xml

    b. web.xml

    c. wl_servlet_sessions

    d. None of the above

Coming Up

In the next chapter, we will review the fundamentals of database access: how data sources are configured and made available to selected server instances in an Oracle WebLogic Server domain.

CHAPTER 12

JDBC

It is probably fair to say that an overwhelming majority of today's applications generate, consume, and persist data during the course of user sessions and system interactions. For this purpose, applications interact with all sorts of data storage systems, depending on the nature and format of the data involved. This chapter is about the technology that Oracle WebLogic Server employs to interact with a particular type of data storage, namely, database management systems.

Data stored in a DBMS is referred to as *structured data* because, in order to be acceptable to the data store, it must conform to a predefined schema design. If data does not conform to the schema, it may not be acceptable to the underlying DBMS at all. Oftentimes, even if it gets stored, it may represent corrupt information that will diminish the use and value of the data. Designing structured data schemata and managing structured data stores is a discipline on its own, the field of *DBAs*.

Obviously, applications also generate, consume, and persist data that is *unstructured*, such as images, documents, and so forth. This type of data is equally important to businesses; it is just managed and stored differently. Managing unstructured data is also a discipline on its own, commonly dealt with in the field of *big data*.

Despite the relatively recent explosion of data generation of all types in the digital world, structured data still maintains an important spot in the realm of data management. Structured data is very frequently used in *OLTP* or transactional systems such as enterprise applications that have a web UI.

In this chapter, the architecture of Java Database Connectivity or JDBC is touched, followed by a review of its main concepts, as well as how Oracle WebLogic Server uses the corresponding objects to process the interaction between applications and databases in a DBMS[1].

---

[1]Examples in this chapter use Oracle Database Express Edition version 11g Release 2, which is lightweight and free.

© Gustavo Garnica 2018
G. Garnica, *Oracle WebLogic Server 12c Administration I Exam 1Z0-133*,
https://doi.org/10.1007/978-1-4842-2562-2_12

Architecture

As with other Java APIs, JDBC is a standard specification that is platform and vendor neutral. It defines the details required for an application to access and work with data stored in a DBMS.

A fundamental component of the specification is the JDBC *driver*. DBMS vendors provide a driver that enables their products to be accessible using Java technology. The driver is the actual interface for Java to interact with the DBMS using *structured query language* or SQL[2]. According to this, applications running on a JVM are capable of accessing any data store, on any platform, for which there is a JDBC driver.

Fundamental as they are, applications do not directly use JDBC drivers though. In order to access data stores, applications interact directly with a higher-level JDBC concept, the *data source*, and with its related objects. Data sources then use the underlying driver to translate JDBC calls into native data store calls. Figure 12-1 shows these JDBC architecture components in the context of an Oracle WebLogic Server domain.

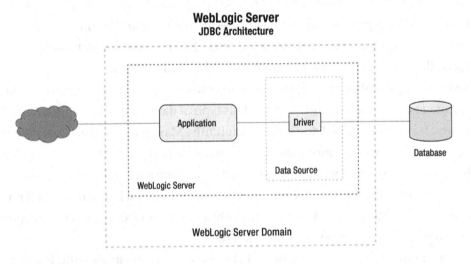

Figure 12-1. *JDBC architecture*

Figure 12-1 shows that a data source exists in the context of a server instance, on which both applications and drivers are installed and deployed.

---

[2]Even though some database management systems implement and provide Java drivers to their systems, not all of them are JDBC drivers. This is especially true with non-relational systems.

Generally speaking, administrators must be aware of fundamentally two types of JDBC drivers: those which require no client configuration and those which do. The former type is referred to as pure Java or a type 4 driver. The latter is named type 2 and requires some client configuration, such as properly installing native libraries it depends on[3].

Oracle WebLogic Server ships with several JDBC type 4 drivers. These are already included in the server CLASSPATH and thus loaded on server startup, ready for applications to use. These drivers enable access to Oracle Database, as well as to certain versions of the following database management systems:

- DB2

- Informix

- Sybase

- SQL Server

- MySQL

As stated before, because of JDBC, WebLogic Server instances are also able to interact with other database management systems beyond those listed above; in fact, WebLogic Server can work with virtually any DBMS for which a suitable JDBC driver is available.

The configuration to enable WebLogic Server to interoperate with other database management systems is a simple two-step process. First, the corresponding driver must be installed in a location in filesystem that is accessible to the server process. Second, a reference to the driver library must be added to the server CLASSPATH.

Data Sources

From the perspective of an application server, data sources are a method to manage connectivity to data stores. This implies also the ability to centralize configuration for all deployed applications to use.

From the perspective of an application, data sources are some of the actual objects that are used to interact with a data store.

Creating a data source in Oracle WebLogic Server means defining its configuration, which must include at least the target data store location, credentials, and database name.

---

[3]JDBC type 2 drivers are generally out of use.

In an Oracle WebLogic Server domain, data sources configuration is referenced in the main server configuration file but persisted separately, in individual XML files. These files are referred to as JDBC modules.

JDBC modules are of two types, system or application modules. System modules are created by administrators using either the WebLogic Server Console or programmatically using WLST. System modules are persisted in the config/jdbc domain directory[4].

Each data source contains a pool of connections to target databases. Connection objects represent physical connections to target data stores and are used by applications to issue SQL commands.

Connection pools can grow or shrink on demand. It is possible to configure minimum and maximum numbers of connections in the pool, as well as a specific number of connections to increment over time up to the maximum capacity.

Figure 12-2 displays the relationship of components in a data source.

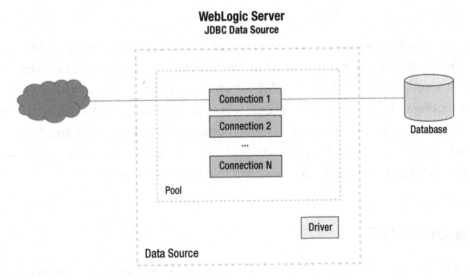

Figure 12-2. *JDBC data source components*

Figure 12-2 shows that an application uses a connection object to directly access a data store. A connection object is one of several in a pool, and it is only available in the context of a data source object.

---

[4]Application JDBC modules are included within application deployable packages and are prepared by developers.

Data sources and their connection pools are created either at server startup or, in the case of an already running server, when they are deployed.

Configuration

Even though data sources have a rich set of properties that define their behavior, creating one is possible with just a small subset of essential properties, including:

- Name and JNDI name

- DBMS and driver

- Database name

- Hostname and port number

- Username and password

When using the Administration Console to create a data source, and once an administrator has filled these properties in, a new screen appears that enables testing connectivity to the target data store. Testing is not mandatory before creating the data source module. Immediately after this, WebLogic Server presents the server instances in the domain on which the data source can be deployed. This step is also optional, but when no server is selected for deployment, the data source module is created but no actual data source objects will be instantiated.

When administrating production systems, several important and more advanced properties should be configured. The most relevant properties in this context are those related to capacity and connection testing.

With regard to capacity, as mentioned before, it is possible to specify the minimum and maximum number of connections that the pool will contain. When the minimum is smaller than the maximum, one may also define the number of connections to add every time the existing connections are used up. Connection capacity is an important aspect to keep in mind when connections to the database are restricted by aspects such as licensing or compute resources availability. When configuring the number of connections available to a data source, one must account for these settings times for each server where the data source is deployed. For instance, in the two figures shown before, a single data source deployed to a cluster of two managed servers will require twice as many connections as the maximum capacity configured.

The configuration to test connections is a very important aspect of production performance since without this, or without additional help from the database management system, WebLogic Server would serve connection objects that point to a stale or broken connection. Configuring connection testing will force WebLogic Server to test the connection before passing it to the requesting application. Connection testing may be enabled or disabled for each data source. When enabled, one may also configure testing frequency.

Once created, data sources are bound to the JNDI tree of a server instance. When applications require access to a data store, they look them up by their JNDI name in the JNDI tree, and obtain a reference through which they perform their work on the data store. Once they are done using it, they *close* the connection object.

Note   The *close()* method of the connection object does not actually close the connection to the data store. WebLogic Server returns the connection to the pool, for other clients to use.

Administrators can view data sources that have been configured in a domain by using the WebLogic Server Administration Console, under the Services option on the left-side *Domain Structure* navigation panel. The page lists all data sources configured in the domain, irrespective of whether they have actually been instantiated or even targeted to any server. Figure 12-3 displays the Summary of the JDBC Data Sources page.

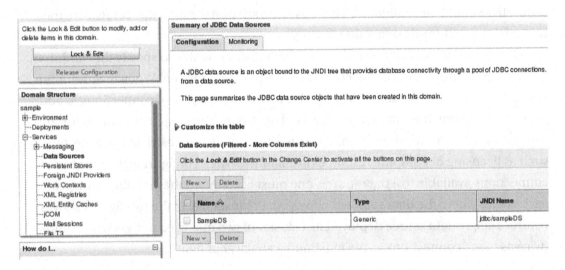

Figure 12-3. *JDBC Data Sources page in the Administration Console*

Figure 12-3 shows a single data source. It also shows the data source type and its JNDI name. Data source types will be discussed later in this chapter. JNDI name is one of the required properties when creating or configuring a data source, and is the property that developers need to use to look up the data source in order to connect to the data store it represents.

Administrators may also need to see what data sources in a given server exist at runtime and that are available for applications to use. This is possible by accessing the main configuration page of each server instance; near the top of the page under the *Configuration* and *General* tabs, there is a link to the JNDI Tree that lists all objects that have been registered. Data sources are shown under the JDBC node on the left. Figure 12-4 displays what a JNDI tree from a running server looks like.

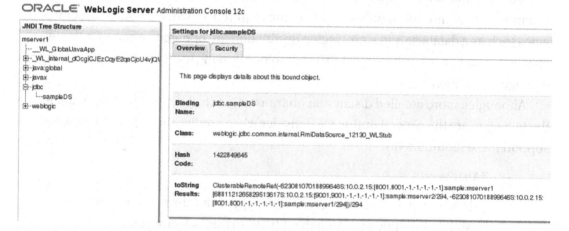

Figure 12-4. *JNDI Tree of a Managed Server*

Figure 12-4 shows the JNDI tree of a managed server named mserver1, and just like the previous figure displays a single data source. It shows details of the actual data source object[5] including its class name and additional information about its deployment configuration.

Once data sources are created, the application server is responsible to manage the pooled connection objects in each data source, according to the properties defined in its configuration. This includes verifying the health of the connections that objects represent. When connection objects fail to reach the target data store, they are closed

---

[5]Objects listed in the JNDI tree are actual runtime system resources deployed on a server.

and released, connections are reestablished and new connection objects pointing to them are instantiated.

Connection objects can be used with both one-time, ad-hoc SQL queries, or with prepared or callable statements, which as their names imply, represent commands or queries that are expected to be run more than once, often only differing in argument values. Prepared or callable statements are in general more efficient than ad hoc queries as they may also be prepared, optimized, and cached at the data store itself. Each connection object gets a manageable cache of prepared statements.

Transactionality

Sometimes applications require distributed transactionality. Typical scenarios include situations where multiple database updates are required, or when resources of different types such as a database and a messaging destination are updated as part of a single, logical transaction, as well as when EJB technology is being used in WebLogic Server to manage transactions.

Although a more detailed discussion on transactions is deferred to a later chapter, the following are the general options to consider when configuring a JDBC data source to support these requirements.

- XA Drivers

  A data source may be configured with support for the XA protocol[6] by simply selecting an XA-enabled JDBC driver. Selecting an XA driver will automatically enable and use Two-Phase Commit as a global transaction protocol.

- Non-XA Drivers

  When a non-XA JDBC driver is used in a data source, transactions are treated as local by default unless support for global transactions is explicitly enabled. When enabled, a specific option to support global transactions must be selected too. The options are Logging Last Resource, emulate two-phase commit, or use single-phase commit. In general, logging last resource is preferred

---

[6]The XA specification was created by Open Group, and it is supported in most major database management systems.

over emulate two-phase commit for performance and data safety. Single-phase commit may be used when the data source is the only participant in a global transaction.

Monitoring and Control

The Oracle WebLogic Server administration console provides a configurable page that displays runtime statistics of a data source. Accessing the main page of any data source displays several tabs, including one labeled *Monitoring*. This displays two additional tabs, one labeled *Statistics* and the other *Testing*.

Accessing the testing tab displays a page listing the deployed instances of the data source, and allows testing connectivity from the server where the data source was deployed to the targeted data store.

The statistics tab displays a table, and on top of that table a link with text "Customize this table." From there, a number of statistics can be added to the table below. Some of the most relevant in day-to-day administration of JDBC connections are these:

- Active connections current count

- Active connections average count

- Current capacity

- Highest number available

- Waiting for connection high count

Statistics labels are mostly self-explanatory. Those labeled average and high or highest are aggregations from the time the corresponding data source was created. Of particular interest for administrators working on production systems may be correlating the waiting for connection counts with the statistics indicating capacity and active connections.

The tab labeled *Control* is very important in day-to-day WebLogic Server administration as it enables performing suspend and resume, as well as start and shutdown operations on the data source, which is required in preparation for graceful application shutdown.

From the control tab, it is also possible to shrink or reset data source connections, as well as to clear the prepared statement cache.

Debugging

There are three methods available to configure debug mode on a data source, namely, WLST, the administration console, and JVM arguments[7]. Listing 12-1 is an example how JDBC debug is enabled on a data source.

Listing 12-1. Enabling JDBC debug using WLST

```
wls:/offline> connect('weblogic','...','...');

wls:/sample/serverConfig> edit()
wls:/sample/edit !> startEdit()

wls:/sample/edit !> cd('/Servers/mserver1/ServerDebug/mserver1')
wls:/sample/edit/Servers/mserver1/ServerDebug/mserver1 !>
set('DebugJDBCSQL',true);

wls:/sample/edit/Servers/mserver1/ServerDebug/mserver1 !> save()
wls:/sample/edit/Servers/mserver1/ServerDebug/mserver1 !> activate()
wls:/sample/edit/Servers/mserver1/ServerDebug/mserver1> exit()
```

The sample changes in server *mserver1* take effect immediately, without requiring a server restart. Listing 12-2 shows two log entries from the same server after the changes were activated.

Listing 12-2. JDBC debug entries on server log file

```
####<20-Sep-2017 12:43:24 o'clock PM CDT> <Debug> <JDBCSQL> <apress.
garnica.mx> <mserver1> <[ACTIVE] ExecuteThread: '1' for queue: 'weblogic.
kernel.Default (self-tuning)'> <<WLS Kernel>> <> <> <1505929404329>
<BEA-000000> <[[oracle.jdbc.driver.T4CXAConnection@6af53acb, owner=null,
rmConn=oracle.jdbc.driver.LogicalConnection@9e71c49]] isValid()>
####<20-Sep-2017 12:43:24 o'clock PM CDT> <Debug> <JDBCSQL> <apress.
garnica.mx> <mserver1> <[ACTIVE] ExecuteThread: '1' for queue: 'weblogic.
kernel.Default (self-tuning)'> <<WLS Kernel>> <> <> <1505929404329>
<BEA-000000> <[[oracle.jdbc.driver.T4CXAConnection@6af53acb, owner=null,
rmConn=oracle.jdbc.driver.LogicalConnection@9e71c49]] isValid returns true>
```

---

[7]Activating the ServerDebug option is persisted in the main domain configuration file.

Log entries shown above display how WebLogic Server is internally verifying the validity of a connection. The JVM arguments required to enable the same are `weblogic.debug.DebugJDBCSQL` with a value of *true*, and `weblogic.log.StdOutSeverity` with a value of *Debug*.

Enabling JDBC debug mode from the administration console is performed by accessing the debug tab of the main configuration page of the selected server. Here, a number of scopes where debug mode is available are listed. The JDBC scopes are available under nodes WebLogic then JDBC. Interesting JDBC scopes include:

- DebugJDBCSQL - JDBC methods invoked

- DebugJDBCConn - connection reserve and release

- DebugJDBCRMI - Similar to SQL, at RMI level

- DebugJTAJDBC - trace transactions

The connection scope also shows messages regarding applications getting and closing connections.

Multi Data Sources

When we covered Oracle WebLogic Server clustering in a previous chapter, we commented on the basic need to implement redundancy in order to increase availability in the middleware infrastructure. The exact same thing is obviously required at every tier in enterprise computing. This poses a requirement on JDBC implementations. Since JDBC connections target a single data store, how should redundant data stores, such as Oracle RAC, be handled at the JDBC level? The answer in Oracle WebLogic Server is through multi data sources, which are abstractions over multiple generic data sources.

Figure 12-5 shows the architecture of a multi data source in Oracle WebLogic Server.

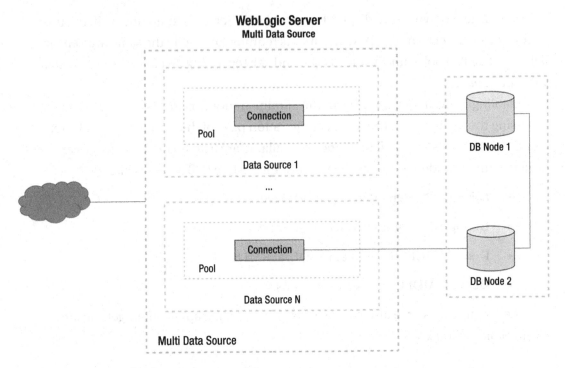

Figure 12-5. *Multi data source architecture*

Figure 12-5 shows that a multi data source comprises multiple generic data sources, each with their own connection pool, targeting a single data store node.

The list of generic data sources behind a multi data source is dynamic. Administrators may add or remove member data sources without taking the multi data source offline[8].

Multi data sources are locatable by applications just as regular data sources, but include the functionality required and configurable to manage a set of data sources. Perhaps the most relevant feature of a multi data source is its ability to internally determine which data source to use when requested a connection, use either load balancing or failover, thus increasing the reliability of the data source for the requesting application.

When a multi data source is configured to perform connection failover, it serves requests based on an ordered list of generic data sources, serving a connection from the first data source before serving one from the second, and so forth. Multi data sources

---

[8]Member data source removal involves suspension and shutdown of the generic data source.

perform load balancing by serving connections from any data source in the list of members, in round-robin fashion.

In order to perform either failover or load balancing, multi data sources require configuring *TestConnectionsOnReserve* through which Oracle WebLogic Server tests a connection before handing it to a requesting application. When a connection has become stale or otherwise non-responsive, the connection will be closed and recreated. If that also fails, the multi data source will perform failover or load balancing as configured.

Active GridLink

The previous paragraphs regarding support to clustered data stores in WebLogic Server JDBC show that despite the nice improvement made in having multi data sources test reserved connections before passing them to applications, the architectural approach still has room for improvement. Specifically, would it not be better to somehow be notified by the database management systems concerning failures in clustered nodes, so that WebLogic Server could discard connections pointing to dead data store targets, and re-create them ahead of the time when applications will request them?

Such a mechanism actually exists in Oracle RAC, and WebLogic Server supports it in the form of a data source type named Active GridLink.

Active GridLink data sources are made specifically for use with Oracle RAC[9]. It ensures that the pool always contains valid connections without the need for polling and testing, covering what a WebLogic Server multi data source would do but with greater accuracy and speed[10]. This also implies that WebLogic Server is decoupled from Oracle Database in such a way that dynamic changes to database cluster topology are permitted with no downtime.

---

[9]Oracle actually discourages the use of generic data sources to connect to Oracle RAC.

[10]Two Oracle proprietary technologies are at play for this to happen: Fast Connection Failover and Oracle Notification Service.

Recommended Exercises

1. Install and configure a third-party JDBC driver that is not included out of the box with WebLogic Server.

2. Configure a generic data source and deploy it to a cluster.

3. Configure a multi data source, deploy it to part of a cluster, and verify the total number of connections opened.

4. At runtime, add and remove data sources to a multi data source that is deployed to a cluster.

5. Enable JDBC debug mode on a server using JVM arguments, verify the results in the server log file.

Certification Questions

1. JDBC drivers translate SQL sentences to native data store calls.

    a. True

    b. False

2. Type of a pure Java JDBC driver:

    a. Type 2

    b. Type 4

    c. None of the above

    d. All of the above

3. Language or notation in which data source configuration is stored in WebLogic Server:

    a. Java

    b. JSON

    c. XML

    d. Any of the above

4. Load balancing in multi data sources is restricted to round-robin.

    a. True

    b. False

Coming Up

The next chapter is about Java Transaction API or JTA; in it we will continue the brief conversation started in this chapter regarding transactions beyond JDBC.

CHAPTER 13

Transactions

It is highly uncommon for companies to keep their enterprise data in just one database or to maintain information in a single format. Most of the time business data is scattered across several data stores, perhaps in heterogeneous repositories.

Likewise, businesses commonly have more than just a single application to process their data in day-to-day operations. Accessing enterprise data from multiple applications requires concurrent access. Concurrency brings the question of data integrity, preserving it which is a fundamental objective of transactional systems. Guarding data integrity is then a primary imperative in securing the value and usefulness of enterprise data.

Generally speaking, data integrity is preserved by ensuring that any operations that change the state of information are either committed as a whole, or discarded altogether. Also, in case of errors or other unexpected conditions, the state of incumbent data can be restored to a valid, consistent state.

Oracle WebLogic Server implements the necessary logic and exposes the required services to manage or participate in distributed transactions, entirely fulfilling its responsibility to preserve data integrity, as explained above.

In this chapter, we discuss the distributed transaction model on which WebLogic Server support for global transactions is based, followed by a review of the main aspects that administrators need to consider when configuring, monitoring, and debugging transactions in a WebLogic Server domain.

Note   Transactional support in Oracle WebLogic Server goes beyond the realm of middleware infrastructure administration, spanning into enterprise applications development, particularly when using EJB technology. In this chapter, in order to provide just enough context for our analysis, we only briefly touch on EJB, or JMS, as they are out of scope of the 1Z0-133 certification exam.

© Gustavo Garnica 2018
G. Garnica, *Oracle WebLogic Server 12c Administration I Exam 1Z0-133*,
https://doi.org/10.1007/978-1-4842-2562-2_13

Properties

The following are some key characteristics that a system that supports distributed transaction processing is required to feature.

- Transactions have clear boundaries – Conceptually, the start and end of a transaction are clearly demarcated, even though transactions may occur in the context of a more comprehensive business process, with distinct non-transactional business tasks occurring before or after.

- Transactions are atomic, complete units of work – Whatever actions considered part of a transaction must be performed as a whole, and a transaction must always result in either committing or aborting all operations involved.

- Transactions are consistent – It is expected that transactions guarantee consistency, that whether or not transactions succeed, the system remains in a valid state. Thus, transactions must take a system from a previous valid state, to a new valid state.

- Transactions are isolated – Since transactions are expected to occur in the presence of other concurrent operations, the state that is internal to transactions must not be visible to processes outside of a transaction.

- Transactions are durable – The effect of all operations in a committed transaction must be permanently persisted, with special care to ensure that the new state can be persisted even after system failure.

The latter four properties are well-known transactional features, also known as *ACID* properties.

Extended Architecture

In 1991, *X/Open*, which a few years later became *The Open Group*[1], issued the specification of a systems interface named XA, which is part of their *Distributed*

---

[1]The Open Group is a global consortium dedicated to IT standards.

Transaction Processing architecture. The current version of the same specification was released in 1994 as version 2 and is named XA+.

XA stands for eXtented Architecture, and is described as the interface between a transaction manager, a resource manager, and a communication resource manager[2].

Figure 13-1 shows the components and interfaces of the XA interface specification, as they pertain to our analysis of transactions in Oracle WebLogic Server.

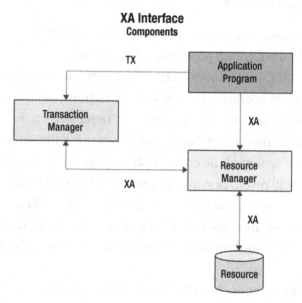

Figure 13-1. *Components of the XA interface*

The figure above shows an application program that interacts with both a transaction manager and a resource manager. The transaction manager also interacts with the resource manager, and the resource manager interacts with target resources.

According to the XA specification, the application program has the responsibility to define the actual transactional work, where it starts and where it ends, and what operations need to be carried out on target data and other resources.

The role of the transaction manager is to organize work across multiple resource managers in distributed transactions. It communicates transaction identifiers or *XIDs* to resource managers, of their assigned work, and coordinates the decision to commit or roll back changes, as well as recovery from failure.

---

[2]The XA+ specification also includes a *Communication Resource Manager* component.

Resource managers are responsible for providing and controlling access to the target resources, and to do so in a manner that is compliant with the transaction properties discussed above. The work resource managers perform on target resources is in this context referred to as a transaction branch.

Two-Phase Commit

As per the XA specification, transaction managers and resource managers perform their work by using *Two-Phase Commit* protocol or *2PC* for short.

The first phase in 2PC is commonly termed the *prepare* phase, because the transaction manager will ask resource managers of all transaction branches to prepare to commit. Resource managers will perform the work requested on the specified resources, and will report back whether or not they are able to commit the work requested.

The second phase is named the *commit* phase because in this, the transaction manager will request all resource managers to either commit or roll back work in transaction branches. The transaction manager will request all resource managers to roll back if at least one of the resource managers voted to abort. Resource managers will proceed as requested and report their final statuses. After this phase, the transaction ends.

Throughout the transaction, both the transaction manager, as well as any resource managers involved, log the state of their actions. These logs are an absolute requirement for a system to recover in-flight transactions after failure. Figure 13-2 shows a simplified sequence diagram of a distributed transaction committed using XA and 2PC.

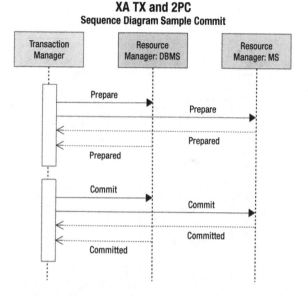

Figure 13-2. *Sequence diagram of a committed transaction using XA and 2PC*

The figure above shows a transaction manager and two resource managers in a single distributed transaction. The arrows signify bidirectional XA calls between these components.

In the first phase, the transaction manager asks both resource managers to prepare to commit, and both reply affirmatively. With that consensus, the transaction manager starts the second phase and requests both resource managers to commit their operations, and they both confirm that they have completed their commitments.

This is a rather simplistic scenario, but illustrates well that heterogeneous target resources may be part of the same transaction and that despite their types, both are afforded the same transactional guarantees.

Figure 13-3 shows a contrasting sequence diagram. It displays a similar distributed transaction rolled back.

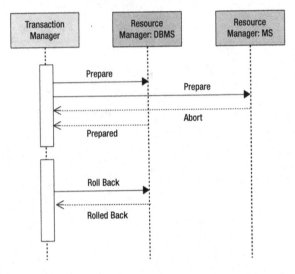

Figure 13-3. *Sequence diagram of an aborted transaction using XA and 2PC*

The transaction pictured in the figure above shows the same actors as in the previous figure. This time, the DBMS resource manager votes abort during the prepare phase. Since there is no full commit consensus among resource managers, in the second phase the transaction manager requests the JMS resource manager to roll back changes on the target resource.

It is evident from the figure that the DBMS resource manager is not part of the second phase. This is so because once a resource manager responds with a non-commit confirmation, it will not wait for the second phase, for the transaction manager to request a rollback. The resource manager itself will roll back its changes and end its participation in the transaction.

Java Transaction API

As indicated early in the book, Oracle WebLogic Server 12c release 1, the target version of the 1Z0-133 WebLogic Server certification exam, is a Java EE 6 compliant application server implementation. As such, it is required to support *Java Transaction API* version 1.1.

The Java EE specification states that Java Transaction API or *JTA* covers two aspects. First, an application-level interface that is to be used by both, application server[3] and applications, to demarcate transaction boundaries. Second is an interface between the transaction manager and a resource manager.

The Java Transaction API specification itself defines that the container must also be able to support distributed transactions, and must do so through a mapping of the XA standard.

Thus, a container that implements JTA must define interfaces for applications to start and end transactions, either directly or through enterprise beans. The container must also implement system-level interfaces for components to interact with the transaction manager, and for the transaction manager to interact with resource managers.

Oracle WebLogic Server 12c fully supports distributed transactions. It does so by virtue of implementing the JTA specification, as part of being Java EE compliant.

An understanding of the principles outlined earlier in this chapter, regarding the transactional model, architecture and execution protocols, prepares administrators to further review JTA implementation details in Oracle WebLogic Server.

WebLogic Server Transactions

It should be easy by now to map actors in an Oracle WebLogic Server environment to components in XA architecture. An *application program* is an actual user application, for example, an EJB client. The *transaction manager* is internal to WebLogic Server and is accessible to application programs using the corresponding JTA interfaces. For EJB and RMI technology, the transaction manager is presented as a transaction service. An example of a *resource manager*, that is most contextual in our book, is a database management system.

Note   The transaction service in WebLogic Server is not compliant with distributed transaction standards such as OSI TP, IBM LU, or ODMG 93.

---

[3]This is a direct reference to the EJB container rather than to Oracle WebLogic Server at large.

Demarcation and Control

As explained before, JTA supports applications that are explicitly demarcated and started by client code, or those in which the demarcation control resides in the container. This is a fundamental concept of EJB application development. EJB developers refer to them as bean-managed transactions, or container-managed transactions, respectively.

Container-managed transactions are simpler to use for enterprise application developers but they lack finer-grained control afforded by bean-managed transactions.

In container-managed transactions, developers annotate bean methods as transactional, and the EJB server manages transaction demarcation by method invocations. This generally means a ratio of one method to one transaction[4]. It also means that developers do not have direct access to controlling the transaction. For instance, rolling back a container-managed transaction takes place automatically when a system exception occurs.

Bean-managed transactions have full control of the transaction scope. EJB application code explicitly makes calls to begin, commit, or roll back methods in the *UserTransaction* interface object.

Configuration

Certain aspects of transactional support in Oracle WebLogic Server are available through either container-managed or bean-managed transactions. One such aspect is transaction timeout, expressed in seconds. This value may be set by invoking the *setTransactionTimeout* method of the *UserTransaction* interface object, or by using the Administration Console.

Thus, it is possible for an administrator to influence the way the transaction manager behaves by setting custom values to JTA configuration, either at the domain or cluster levels[5].

JTA configuration pages for both domain and cluster allow setting values to exactly the same properties. Both are available at the main configuration page of the respective scope, under a tab labeled *JTA*.

---

[4]The transaction service in WebLogic Server does not support nested transactions.
[5]Setting a JTA configuration value at cluster level takes precedence over the same values defined at domain level.

Figure 13-4 shows the upper part of the JTA configuration page at cluster level in the Administration Console.

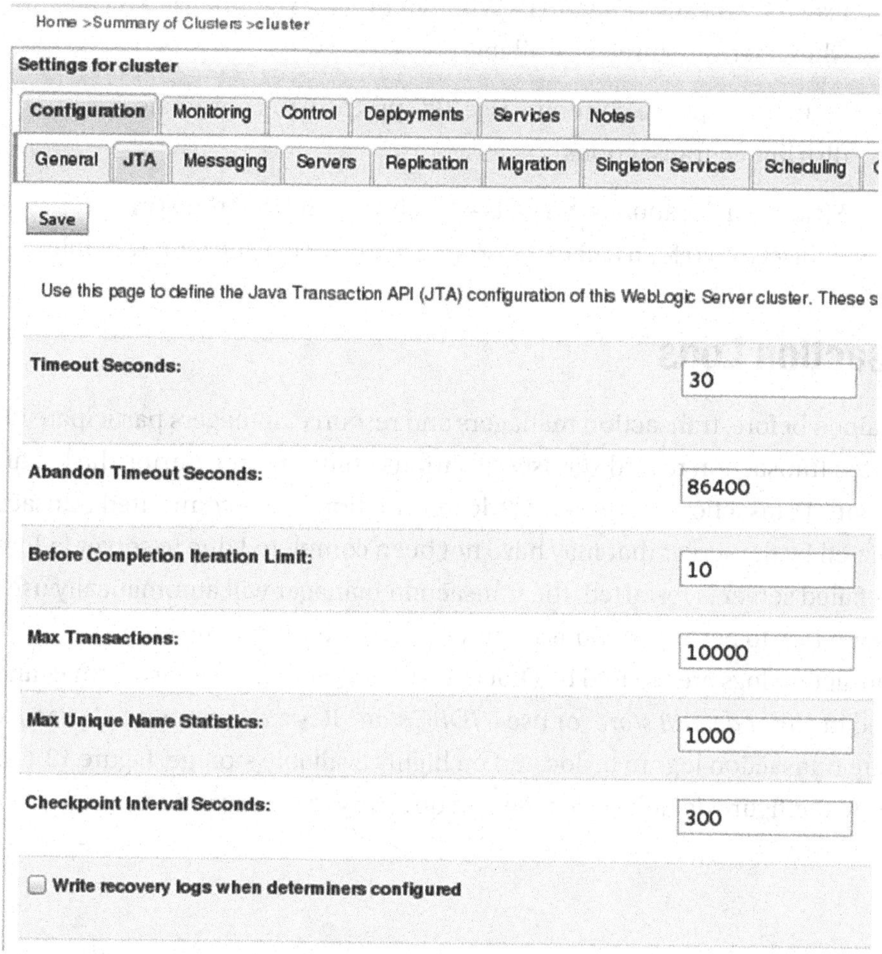

Figure 13-4. *JTA configuration page*

The JTA configuration page has a good number of settable properties. The following is a list of those considered very relevant for almost every use case.

- Timeout seconds – Maximum time a distributed transaction is allowed to remain in *prepare* or first phase

- Abandon timeout seconds – Maximum time a distributed transaction is allowed to remain in *commit* or second phase

- Max transactions – Maximum number of concurrent transactions to exist on a server instance

- Execute XA calls in parallel – Whether or not to parallelize XA calls when there are threads available

- Enable two-phase commit – Use 2PC protocol to coordinate distributed transactions

- Maximum duration of XA calls – Maximum allowed time (in milliseconds) for a call to a resource before declaring it unavailable

Transaction Logs

As explained before, transaction managers and resource managers participate in distributed transaction record statuses at various points in time during the life of a transaction. Transaction logs also include information about committed transactions coordinated by the server that may have not been completed due to server failure. When a failed server is restarted, the transaction manager will automatically use the transaction logs to perform actions required to restore consistency.

Transaction logs are created by Oracle WebLogic Server in binary format, and can be stored in either *default store*[6] or use a *JDBC store*. It is a recommended practice to configure transaction logs to be located on highly available storage. Figure 13-5 shows the how to configure default store type and directory on a server instance.

---

[6]The location of default store is data/store/default, in the corresponding managed server directory.

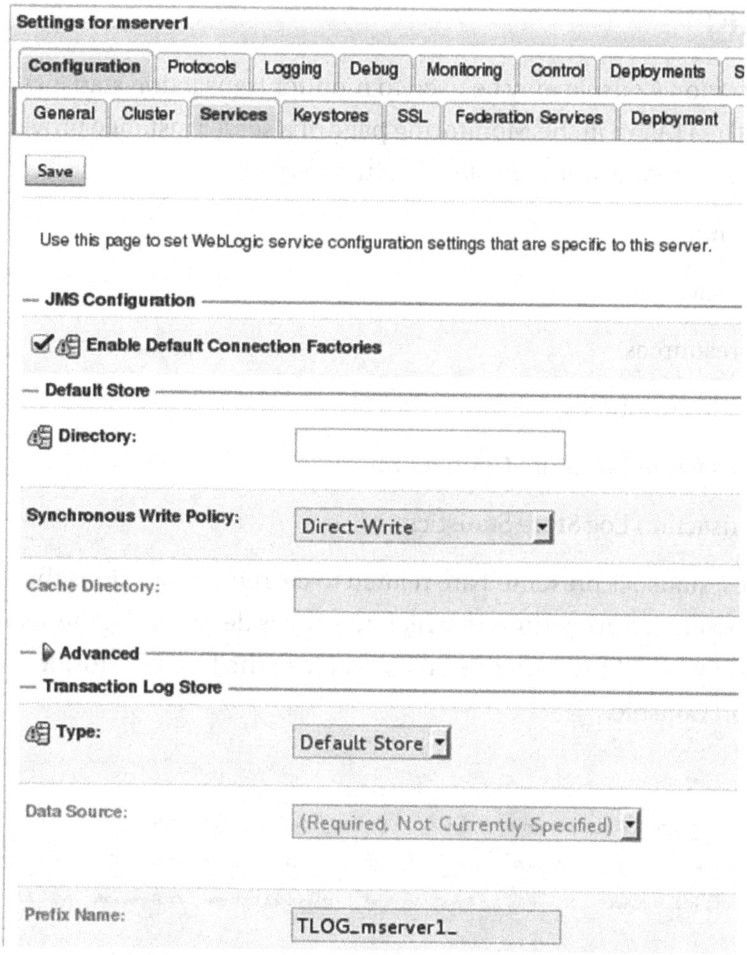

Figure 13-5. *Default store configuration page of a server instance*

The figure above shows the Services tab of the main configuration page of a server instance. Here, the transaction log store is configured by specifying either the path to a highly available directory when in Default Store type[7], or specifying a data source to use when selecting JDBC type.

---

[7]Performance of the default store is affected by the OS write-to-disk policies. Configuring these policies is out of the scope of exam 1Z0-133.

Monitoring

The Administration Console may be used to monitor transaction statistics on a per-server basis. The JTA tab in the Monitoring page of a server instance provides access to several information categories, displayed as tabs as well:

- Summary

- Transactions

- XA resources

- Non-XA resources

- Transaction Log Store Connections

- Transaction Log Store Statistics

In all cases, statistics presented are related to current transactions that the server coordinates, or about transactions in which resources deployed on the server participate. Figure 13-6 shows the XA resources statistics table of the JTA monitoring page in the Administration Console.

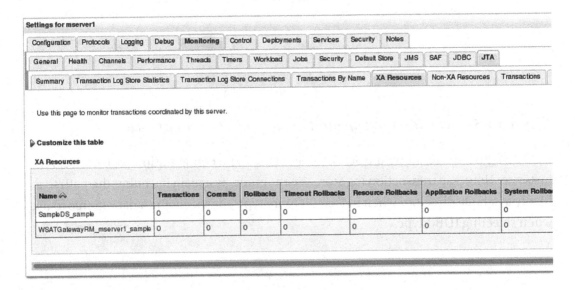

Figure 13-6. *XA Resources Statistics in JTA monitoring page*

The figure above displays a sample JTA monitoring tab. This particular view shows that it is possible to view details about the number of transactions, and the specific state they are in, for each transaction aware resource deployed on a server instance. The image shows statistics for an XA data source.

Recommended Exercises

1. Describe a case in which XA is not an appropriate distributed transaction architecture.

2. Establish a transaction with a database, kill the server JVM process while the transaction is in-flight, restart the server, and verify that the state is made consistent.

Certification Questions

1. WebLogic Server supports XA+ protocol version 2.

    a. True

    b. False

2. Resource managers may take part in prepare phase and be absent in commit phase of a distributed transaction.

    a. True

    b. False

3. XA interfaces implemented in JTA are high-level interfaces, available to applications:

    a. All of them are

    b. None of them are

    c. Some of them are

4. Property that limits the maximum time allowed for a transaction to remain in commit phase:

   a. Timeout seconds

   b. Abandon timeout seconds

   c. Maximum duration of XA calls

Coming Up

The next chapter is about application deployment and how to remotely start, stop, or restart applications deployed on a cluster.

CHAPTER 14

Application Deployment

Application deployment is yet another subject where the duties of Oracle WebLogic
Server administrators and enterprise application developers often come close together.
Traditionally, where developers ended their work, system administrators used to take
over, deploy applications, and manage them in production. In our days, new roles,
processes, and culture aim to bring software development and system administration
together, in an effort to enable application code to reach production at a faster pace,
without sacrificing security and stability.

In this chapter, we review the tools, as well as the process to make application code
available to the Oracle WebLogic Server runtime in production environments.

Note   Our review focuses on tools and practices for application deployment from
the perspective of middleware administrators.

Deployment activities are not just about releasing brand new applications.
Sometimes the code being deployed fixes or updates existing functionality. Sometimes
deployment sessions are meant to remove deployed applications altogether.

According to this, our analysis aims to cover production applications deployment and
undeployment, as well as certain related actions such as starting and stopping applications,
performing basic tests of application availability, and application redeployment.

Oracle WebLogic Server enables administrators to perform deployment activities
using the *Administration Console*, *WLST*, the *weblogic.Deployer* tool, an *Ant* task named
deploy, and a *Maven* plug-in. The deploy Ant task and the Maven plug-n are meant for
environments where those are the build tools of choice. The weblogic.Deployer tool is
very robust and is suitable for use in scripting all kinds of deployment automations.

Our analysis covers the most common application deployment scenarios primarily
using *weblogic.Deployer*.

© Gustavo Garnica 2018
G. Garnica, *Oracle WebLogic Server 12c Administration I Exam 1Z0-133,*
https://doi.org/10.1007/978-1-4842-2562-2_14

Deployment Scenarios

Even though methods and dynamics vary from company to company, the fundamental activities performed to deploy applications are roughly the same, despite company size or even organization maturity.

In small startups, for example, these activities may be performed in quick, single actions, whereas in larger organizations, they may be aggregated to other processes, supported by specialized software[1], or be performed by multiple individuals.

Most application deployment activities that Oracle WebLogic Server administrators are required to perform are comprised in the following three scenarios:

- Deploy new applications

- Deploy fixes or updates to applications

- Undeploy applications

When deploying code, which occurs in the first two scenarios, a code and configuration preparatory phase is required, after which the actual deployment, redeployment, or undeployment occurs, followed by a validation phase that aims to determine whether or not the changes made work as expected and should remain, or if they should be rolled back.

Preparatory Phase

Several considerations must be made regarding code that is considered production ready, including:

- Where code should be stored to facilitate deployment activities

- How code should be stored, in terms of application packaging

- How to prepare the application configuration so that it matches the configuration of target environments

---

[1]For instance, financial and health care organizations are required to perform security and compliance checks in their build processes.

Storage Location

Applications developed targeting Oracle WebLogic Server are far better organized using version control software. When in place, users and systems can easily get production code from a dedicated branch in a dedicated repository.

Note   Important as it is, the recommendation to store production code using version control software is ultimately a convenience recommendation only.

Application code should be placed in a dedicated location in a file system that is outside a WebLogic Server domain. Oracle recommends creating a three-level directory structure for each application. The name of the first-level directory should resemble the application name. The second-level directory is named as per the application versions it will contain. The third-level directory should be named *app*, to reflect that it stores the actual application code. For example, version 1.0 of a web application named HelloWorld could be stored in `/apress/apps/HelloWorld/1.0/app/HelloWorld.war`.

Storage Format

Enterprise application developers organize their application code also using a specific directory structure, according to the type of application they work on. Frequently, they organize their code assisted by an integrated development environment or *IDE*[2], which lets them build and test their applications in an iterative process. As part of their build process, IDEs create archives of the application directory structure[3], resulting in deployable files sometimes referred to as deployment units. Both the directory structure and the types of deployment units that can be created are defined in the Java EE specification.

Oracle WebLogic Server can deploy code that is packaged as a deployment unit, or as the directory structure that results from exploding or extracting a deployment unit. Perhaps the only sensible difference between both modes is that deploying code using exploded archives allows for partial updates after deployment, especially static files. Oracle recommends deploying applications using deployment units.

---

[2]Common IDEs that support working on applications that target Oracle Fusion Middleware are Oracle JDeveloper, Oracle NetBeans, and Eclipse, configured with the Oracle Enterprise Pack for Eclipse (OEPE) plug-in.

[3]IDEs use the jar tool available in the underlying JDK in order to create deployment units.

Deployment units differ among each other in their internal directory structure and also in their file extensions. The most common types of deployment units that can be deployed on Oracle WebLogic Server are as follows:

- EJB applications (.jar)

- Web applications and web services (.war)

- Resource adapters (.rar)[4]

- Enterprise applications (.ear)

Each of the application types listed above can include a Java EE deployment descriptor[5], as well as a WebLogic Server proprietary deployment descriptor. In general, where there is a Java EE deployment descriptor named *file*.xml, there is a corresponding WebLogic Server-only descriptor named *file*-weblogic.xml. All application deployment units are really just *jar* files with a different extension.

Configuration Plans

As explained before, application developers build and deploy their applications to a target development environment, most of the time, to a local middleware environment. Their applications are configured to work well in their development environment but because of external dependencies, they would most likely break when deployed on a subsequent environment, such as test, integration, and so forth.

Since these dependencies are meant to be externalized from code, the logical approach as developers move their code to the next environment would be to edit the corresponding deployment descriptor to match the configuration of the new environment. Oracle recommends against this practice, and advises to use WebLogic Server configuration plans instead.

---

[4]Resource adapters implement the Connector Architecture and enable Java EE applications to Access enterprise information systems such as ERPs.

[5]Deployment descriptors are XML documents that describe the configuration and runtime behavior of a Java EE application.

A deployment plan is an XML document that contains variables for the deployment properties and resource dependencies already defined in the corresponding deployment descriptors.

Configuration plans may be created from within an application project in Oracle JDeveloper, or by changing a configurable attribute value of an already deployed application using the Administration Console, or also by using the *weblogic. PlanGenerator* tool.

For example, a developer may have been working on a *HelloWorld* web application. Once she has completed her development, she distributes the application as a deployment unit named HelloWorld.war.

When deployed to an Oracle WebLogic Server environment, the application is reachable using the application context /HelloWorld. This context name is derived from the deployment unit file name, minus the file extension[6].

If a system administrator needed to deploy this application in a different environment, and have it accessible through a different context name, say the server *root* context[7] for instance, she could perform the change by using a configuration plan to override the original context name.

This is possible without having to extract and modify the original deployment descriptor included in the HelloWorld.war file.

Listing 14-1 shows how the *weblogic.PlanGenerator* tool can be used to export a configuration plan of the HelloWorld.war file.

Listing 14-1. Creating a configuration plan using weblogic.PlanGenerator

```
[gustavo@apress product]$ source wlserver/server/bin/setWLSEnv.sh
...
Your environment has been set.

[gustavo@apress product]$ cd /apress/apps/HelloWorld/1.0/
[gustavo@apress 1.0]$ java weblogic.PlanGenerator -all app/HelloWorld.war
Generating plan for application app/HelloWorld.war
Export option is: all
```

---

[6]In compliance with Java EE, a default context name is assigned to the application when one is not explicitly configured.

[7]An application is said to be configured at the root context when it is reachable using just a server name or address, such as *apress.com* or 127.0.0.1:8080.

```
Exporting properties...
Saving plan to /apress/apps/HelloWorld/1.0/plan/plan.xml...
<1-Oct-2017 2:08:34 o'clock PM CDT> <Info> <J2EE Deployment SPI> <BEA-
260072> <Saved configuration for application, HelloWorld.war>
```

The example highlighted above generates a plan containing variables for *all* configurable properties of the target web application. The command saves the plan in a file named *plan.xml.*

The resulting configuration plan is quite verbose. The developer may have decided to use the *all* option of weblogic.PlanGenerator to ensure that the configuration property she is interested in changing would be included in the plan.

Listing 14-2 shows an extract of the configuration plan created, highlighting the elements relevant to our example.

Listing 14-2. Extract of a configuration plan

```
<?xml version='1.0' encoding='UTF-8'?>
<deployment-plan xmlns="http://xmlns.oracle.com/weblogic/deployment-plan"
...>
  <application-name>HelloWorld.war</application-name>
  <variable-definition>

    ...

    <variable>
            <name>WeblogicWebApp_ContextRoots_15068849147018</name>
            <value xsi:nil="true"></value>
        </variable>

    ...

  </variable-definition>
  <module-override>
    <module-name>HelloWorld.war</module-name>
    <module-type>war</module-type>
    <module-descriptor external="false">
      <root-element>weblogic-web-app</root-element>
      <uri>WEB-INF/weblogic.xml</uri>
      ...
      <variable-assignment>
              <name>WeblogicWebApp_ContextRoots_15068849147018</name>
```

```
        <xpath>/weblogic-web-app/context-root</xpath>
        <origin>planbased</origin>
      </variable-assignment>
  ...
  </module-descriptor>
...
</module-override>
<config-root>/apress/apps/HelloWorld/1.0/plan</config-root>
</deployment-plan> </deployment-plan>
```

The important elements in this example are a *variable* element and a *variable-assignment* element, both having the exact *name* sub element.

The *variable* element is a child of a *variable-definition* element. The *variable-assignment* element is a child of a *module-descriptor* element, which has a child *uri* element with a reference to the weblogic.xml deployment descriptor. That file contains the context definition that we attempt to override. The specific element to be overridden is defined in an XPath expression contained in an *xpath* sub element.

In order to perform the required configuration change, the administrator needs to set the *value* sub element of the *variable* element to the desired application context name. It is also necessary to remove the *origin* sub element of the *variable-assignment* element and replace it with an *operation* sub element with a value of *replace*, to explicitly request WebLogic Server to perform the substitution when the application is deployed alongside the configuration plan.

It would also be useful, for the sake of clarity, to also remove the rest of elements that are not relevant to our case, particularly the extra variable and *module-override* elements.

Listing 14-3 shows the updated configuration plan. It took just two lines to modify the generated plan to match our requirements.

Listing 14-3. Updated configuration plan

```
<?xml version='1.0' encoding='UTF-8'?>
<deployment-plan xmlns="http://xmlns.oracle.com/weblogic/deployment-
plan" xmlns:xsi="http://www.w3.org/2001/XMLSchema-instance"
xsi:schemaLocation="http://xmlns.oracle.com/weblogic/deployment-plan
http://xmlns.oracle.com/weblogic/deployment-plan/1.0/deployment-plan.xsd"
global-variables="false">
```

```xml
<application-name>HelloWorld.war</application-name>
<variable-definition>
  <variable>
    <name>WeblogicWebApp_ContextRoots_15068849147018</name>
    <value>/</value>
  </variable>
</variable-definition>
<module-override>
  <module-name>HelloWorld.war</module-name>
  <module-type>war</module-type>
  <module-descriptor external="false">
    <root-element>weblogic-web-app</root-element>
    <uri>WEB-INF/weblogic.xml</uri>
    <variable-assignment>
      <name>WeblogicWebApp_ContextRoots_15068849147018</name>
      <xpath>/weblogic-web-app/context-root</xpath>
      <operation>replace</operation>
    </variable-assignment>
  </module-descriptor>
</module-override>
<config-root>/apress/apps/HelloWorld/1.0/plan</config-root>
</deployment-plan>
```

When deploying this configuration plan alongside the same HelloWorld.war deployment unit as before, WebLogic Server will ensure that the correct configuration values and resources are used at runtime.

Even though creating and using a deployment plan may appear more work compared to simply using the Administration Console for this small, one-property configuration change, it is not. It would be a bit longer to explode the deployment unit, perform the change, and re-archive the web application file, in addition to performing the module substitution using the Administration Console.

Configuration plans are a really powerful and productive approach to performing multiple configuration changes swiftly and accurately, especially in the context of production deployments. Also, this approach fosters automation, which should be the preferred way of performing middleware administration tasks whenever and wherever possible.

Deployment

Following up with our HelloWorld application example discussed in the previous section, deploying an application using also a deployment plan can be achieved using the *weblogic.Deployer* tool, in a single line. Listing 14-4 shows how to deploy our HelloWorld.war archive alongside the deployment plan that was generated and modified to substitute the default application context.

Listing 14-4. Deploying our HelloWorld application using a configuration plan

```
[gustavo@apress servers]$ java weblogic.Deployer -adminurl 127.0.0.1:7001
-username weblogic -password ### -plan /apress/apps/HelloWorld/1.0/plan/
plan.xml -deploy /apress/apps/HelloWorld/1.0/app/HelloWorld.war -targets
cluster
weblogic.Deployer invoked with options:  -adminurl 127.0.0.1:7001 -username
weblogic -plan /apress/apps/HelloWorld/1.0/plan/plan.xml -deploy /apress/
apps/HelloWorld/1.0/app/HelloWorld.war -targets cluster
<1-Oct-2017 6:53:56 o'clock PM CDT> <Info> <J2EE Deployment SPI> <BEA-
260121> <Initiating deploy operation for application, HelloWorld.war
[archive: /apress/apps/HelloWorld/1.0/app/HelloWorld.war], to cluster .>
Task 36 initiated: [Deployer:149026]deploy application HelloWorld.war
[Version=v1.0] on cluster.
Task 36 completed: [Deployer:149026]deploy application HelloWorld.war
[Version=v1.0] on cluster.
Target state: deploy completed on Cluster cluster>
```

The operation was run on the same host where the Administration Server is running. It deployed our HelloWorld application to a sample, two-node cluster. The expected result was to be able to access our application using the root context of managed servers in our cluster. Figure 14-1 shows a browser window accessing the application.

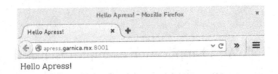

Hello Apress!

Figure 14-1. HelloWorld application deployed at root context

As expected, the configuration plan was used to modify the default behavior, and deploy our application in the target root context instead.

Staging Mode

Since deploying an application means to essentially provide new code to the WebLogic Server runtime, it is necessary to consider where that code will be available, before and after deployment.

WebLogic Server supports three staging modes:

- stage

- nostage

- external_stage

In stage mode, WebLogic Server will copy application files to a dedicated stage directory in every target before performing the actual deployment. The source of the application deployment becomes the stage directory in each target.

In nostage mode, the source of the application deployment is the path provided at deployment time. Each target must be able to access the same path in order to complete application deployment.

In our example above, if we had used nostage mode, both cluster nodes would have been required to access the directory specified as holding the HelloWorld.war file. This is commonly resolved by using a highly available file system location that is configured or mounted in the same path of each cluster node.

In external_stage mode, the source of application deployment is the same as when working in stage mode, meaning a dedicated stage directory in each target, but the responsibility to copy the files is left to an external entity.

This is an appropriate mode for scenarios where application archives are large enough that if the deployment operation were attempted in stage mode, could possibly time out while staging files for deployment. In this case, it is easier for administrators to ensure that application files are uploaded to target stage directories ahead of attempting the deployment operation.

All stage modes are available as command-line options when using weblogic. Deployer to deploy applications.

Distributing Applications

The deployment operation performed in Listing 14-4 deployed our HelloWorld application and started it in all targets. In other words, as soon as the deployment operation completed, the application was accessible without restrictions. This is not necessarily desired in every case, especially in production environments. Sometimes, final sanity checks are required before opening up access to all clients. In WebLogic Server environments, distributing an application is a deployment operation in which code is effectively distributed to all targets and validated for deployment, but one which does not conclude with automatically starting applications.

Distributing applications is particularly well suited for application deployment in production environments.

To distribute an application using weblogic.Deployer, an administrator would simply need to use the *distribute* instead of *deploy* option, as shown in Listing 14-5.

Listing 14-5. Distributing our HelloWorld application and a configuration plan

```
[gustavo@apress servers]$ java weblogic.Deployer -adminurl 127.0.0.1:7001
-username weblogic -password ### -plan /apress/apps/HelloWorld/1.0/plan/
plan.xml -distribute /apress/apps/HelloWorld/1.0/app/HelloWorld.war
-targets cluster
weblogic.Deployer invoked with options:  -adminurl 127.0.0.1:7001 -username
weblogic -plan /apress/apps/HelloWorld/1.0/plan/plan.xml -distribute /
apress/apps/HelloWorld/1.0/app/HelloWorld.war -targets cluster
<1-Oct-2017 8:45:47 o'clock PM CDT> <Info> <J2EE Deployment SPI> <BEA-
260121> <Initiating distribute operation for application, HelloWorld.war
[archive: /apress/apps/HelloWorld/1.0/app/HelloWorld.war], to cluster .>
```

```
Task 42 initiated: [Deployer:149026]distribute application HelloWorld.war
[Version=v1.0] on cluster.
Task 42 completed: [Deployer:149026]distribute application HelloWorld.war
[Version=v1.0] on cluster.
Target state: distribute completed on Cluster cluster
```

After performing the operation above, both the HelloWorld.war archive and the configuration plan were successfully copied to the stage directories of both cluster nodes, and the application was shown in status *prepared*.

Starting and Stopping Applications

Once an application has been distributed but before it is started and made available for widespread use in a production environment, administrators have an opportunity to perform final sanity checks.

In our context, this might mean verifying that all dependencies are satisfied, and that the application responds well to connection requests.

This can be accomplished by starting an application in administration mode, passing the start and adminmode options together to weblogic.Deployer. Listing 14-6 shows how an application can be started in admin mode.

Listing 14-6. Starting our HelloWorld application in admin mode

```
[gustavo@apress sample]$ java weblogic.Deployer -adminurl 127.0.0.1:7001
-username weblogic -password ### -targets cluster -start -adminmode -name
HelloWorld.war -appversion v1.0 /apress/apps/HelloWorld/1.0/app/HelloWorld.
war
weblogic.Deployer invoked with options:  -adminurl 127.0.0.1:7001
-username weblogic -targets cluster -start -adminmode -name HelloWorld.war
-appversion v1.0 /apress/apps/HelloWorld/1.0/app/HelloWorld.war
<1-Oct-2017 11:23:44 o'clock PM CDT> <Info> <J2EE Deployment SPI> <BEA-
260121> <Initiating start operation for application, HelloWorld.war
[archive: null], to cluster .>
Task 85 initiated: [Deployer:149026]start application HelloWorld.war
[Version=v1.0] on cluster.
```

```
Task 85 completed: [Deployer:149026]start application HelloWorld.war
[Version=v1.0] on cluster.
Target state: start completed on Cluster cluster
```

When in admin mode, applications are only accessible through an administration channel. Once the final checks have been done, the application can be transitioned from admin mode to full active or production mode, thereby removing access restrictions.

Stopping an application results in discontinuing access and an abrupt termination of existing sessions. In cases where existing sessions must be permitted to end, but no new sessions should be accepted, applications can be gracefully stopped. This can be done passing the *stop* and *graceful* options together to weblogic.Deployer. Listing 14-7 shows how an application can be gracefully stopped.

Listing 14-7. Gracefully stopping our HelloWorld application

```
[gustavo@apress sample]$ java weblogic.Deployer -adminurl 127.0.0.1:7001
-username weblogic -password ### -targets cluster -stop -graceful -name
HelloWorld.war -appversion v1.0
weblogic.Deployer invoked with options:  -adminurl 127.0.0.1:7001 -username
weblogic -targets cluster -stop -graceful -name HelloWorld.war -appversion
v1.0
<1-Oct-2017 11:37:27 o'clock PM CDT> <Info> <J2EE Deployment SPI> <BEA-
260121> <Initiating stop operation for application, HelloWorld.war
[archive: null], to cluster .>
Task 86 initiated: [Deployer:149026]stop application HelloWorld.war
[Version=v1.0] on cluster.
Task 86 completed: [Deployer:149026]stop application HelloWorld.war
[Version=v1.0] on cluster.
Target state: stop completed on Cluster cluster
```

Redeployment

One of the most important actions that administrators working on production environments will perform is updating applications with zero downtime. This is applicable to both, fixing issues and releasing incremental features to currently deployed applications.

This requirement may be approached from several angles. Oracle WebLogic Server attempts to resolve this by featuring an application redeployment approach that allows two versions of an application to work side by side.

In this scheme, the retiring application version[8] is permitted to complete all in-flight sessions, while new incoming application requests are sent to the new application version. This is referred to as *production redeployment*.

In case of failures or errors discovered while the retiring application is still deployed, it is possible to roll back the process by simply undeploying the new application version, which will also cause the retiring application to become the active version again. The only downside to production redeployment is that it only works for applications deployed as war and ear archives, which have HTTP clients, including web services applications, or applications that expect inbound JMS and JCA calls.

The alternative approach to production redeployment is called in-place redeployment. It causes an application to abruptly become unavailable because WebLogic Server will discard the existing class loader and replace it with a new one, based on the new code in the application. This obviously implies that there is no recovery for in-flight sessions.

Listing 14-8 shows how an application can be production redeployed using weblogic.Deployer.

Listing 14-8. Performing production redeployment of our HelloWorld application

```
[gustavo@apress sample]$ java weblogic.Deployer -adminurl 127.0.0.1:7001
-username weblogic -password ### -targets cluster -plan /apress/apps/
HelloWorld/2.0/plan/plan.xml -source /apress/apps/HelloWorld/2.0/app/
HelloWorld.war -name HelloWorld.war -redeploy
weblogic.Deployer invoked with options:  -adminurl 127.0.0.1:7001 -username
weblogic -targets cluster -plan /apress/apps/HelloWorld/2.0/plan/plan.xml
-source /apress/apps/HelloWorld/2.0/app/HelloWorld.war -name HelloWorld.war
-redeploy
<2-Oct-2017 12:14:54 o'clock AM CDT> <Info> <J2EE Deployment SPI> <BEA-
260121> <Initiating redeploy operation for application, HelloWorld.war
[archive: /apress/apps/HelloWorld/2.0/app/HelloWorld.war], to cluster .>
```

---

[8]It is recommended to specify application versioning using a standard MANIFEST.MF file.

Task 89 initiated: [Deployer:149026]deploy application HelloWorld.war
[Version=v2.0] on cluster.
Task 89 completed: [Deployer:149026]deploy application HelloWorld.war
[Version=v2.0] on cluster.
Target state: redeploy completed on Cluster cluster

The example above shows that our HelloWorld application, version 2.0 was successfully redeployed using weblogic.Deployer. Figure 14-2 shows how the deployments page in the Administration Console displays both versions of the application after the production redeployment, one in active status and the other in the retired status.

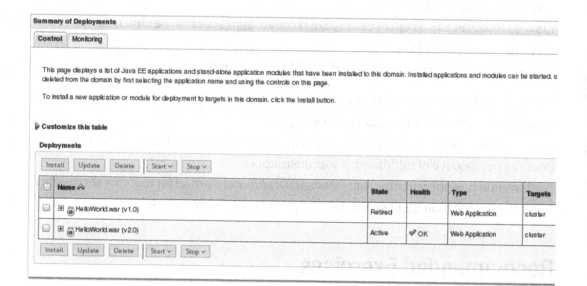

Figure 14-2. *HelloWorld application versions after a production redeployment*

Undeployment

As expected, application undeployment removes an application permanently from the Oracle WebLogic Server runtime. Listing 14-9 shows how version 1.0 of our HelloWorld application may be undeployed using weblogic.Deployer.

Listing 14-9. Undeployment of version 1.0 of our HelloWorld application

```
[gustavo@apress sample]$ java weblogic.Deployer -adminurl 127.0.0.1:7001
-username weblogic -password ### -targets cluster -name HelloWorld.war
-appversion v1.0 -undeploy
weblogic.Deployer invoked with options:  -adminurl 127.0.0.1:7001 -username
weblogic -targets cluster -name HelloWorld.war -appversion v1.0 -undeploy
<2-Oct-2017 12:29:21 o'clock AM CDT> <Info> <J2EE Deployment SPI> <BEA-
260121> <Initiating undeploy operation for application, HelloWorld.war
[archive: null], to cluster .>
Task 93 initiated: [Deployer:149026]remove application HelloWorld.war
[Version=v1.0] on cluster.
Task 93 completed: [Deployer:149026]remove application HelloWorld.war
[Version=v1.0] on cluster.
Target state: undeploy completed on Cluster cluster
```

Once an application has been undeployed, the only way to restore its functionality is by going through the deployment process again.

This concludes our review of the application deployment on Oracle WebLogic Server from the perspective of middleware administrators.

It should be apparent now that *weblogic.Deployer* is a powerful tool that thoroughly covers the application deployment landscape in Oracle WebLogic Server.

Recommended Exercises

1. Deploy an application using an exploded archive as target.

2. Modify servlet name and mappings of a deployed web application using a configuration plan.

3. Modify the targets of a web module in an enterprise application using a configuration plan.

Certification Questions

1. WebLogic Server application deployment supports scripted automations using a variety of tools.

    a. True

    b. False

2. WebLogic Server supports zero downtime redeployment of all types of applications.

    a. True

    b. False

3. Redeployment mode that replaces class loaders immediately:

    a. Production redeployment

    b. In-place redeployment

    c. Both of them

4. It is possible to undeploy an application while allowing existing sessions to complete gracefully.

    a. True

    b. False

Coming Up

The next chapter is about security providers in WebLogic Server. We will review built-in security roles and LDAP integration.

CHAPTER 15

Security

Security in Oracle WebLogic Server is a very extensive subject, both within and around middleware and enterprise applications.

As required by the objectives in certification exam 1Z0-133, in this chapter we review the fundamental concepts related to security in enterprise systems. We also cover the structural components of security in a WebLogic Server domain, as well as how to extend the configuration for one of the most commonly required security scenarios, namely, integrating with an LDAP directory for authentication.

Oracle WebLogic Server implements a security architecture that is compliant with multiple security specifications and standards. Its implementation is robust and satisfies the security requirements of most enterprise middleware environments.

Since it supports open standards and has a modular architecture that promotes configuration composability, it integrates well with many enterprise grade, security, and identity management solutions.

Concepts

Enterprise security systems are built around the notions of an entity that is subject to authentication and authorization in order to gain access to protected resources. The scope of authentication and authorization processes in security systems varies greatly, from the simple to the robust and complex, from those based on a limited set of rules, to those that comply with multiple security protocols. Our review of the WebLogic Server security implementation covers the following concepts:

- Subject

- Authentication

- Authorization

© Gustavo Garnica 2018
G. Garnica, *Oracle WebLogic Server 12c Administration I Exam 1Z0-133*,
https://doi.org/10.1007/978-1-4842-2562-2_15

- Principal

- Policy

In our current context, a *subject* is an entity, human, or system that establishes interest in accessing resources protected by a security system. After being prompted by the subject, the security system starts an authentication process. Commonly, the authentication process occurs in a conversational style where both parties exchange messages.

As part of this dialog, the subject will present the system credentials as proof of its identity. The system is expected to be able to assert the validity of credentials. When they are valid, the system trusts that the subject represents the identity it presumes.

As a result of positive authentication, a set of principals are assigned. This effectively translates the authenticated subject to its corresponding identity in the context of the target resource, and the authentication process ends[1].

The authorization process uses policies to determine whether or not access should be granted to requesting principals.

Policies have different levels of granularity, both in terms of the principals to which they apply, and also in terms of the level of access control they exercise over the resources.

Every time access to a resource is requested, the security system will determine what set of policies are applicable, and will go through each of the rules in them, to make a final decision of whether to grant or deny the request.

Security Realms

Oracle WebLogic Server organizes the main components of the security service in a *realm*. Every WebLogic Server domain contains a security realm named *myrealm*, which comes preconfigured with the minimum set of components to support a functional security service.

Administrators are free to create their own, custom-configured security realms[2], but they must ensure that all default security artifacts associated with domain resources are correctly configured.

---

[1]Some systems consider that assigning a principal to an authenticated identity is the beginning of the authorization process, instead of the end of the authentication process.

[2]At any time one and only one security realm can be active.

Figure 15-1 shows an architecture diagram of the basic components of a security realm.

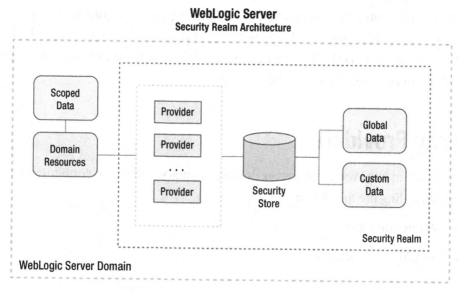

Figure 15-1. *Architecture of a security realm*

The diagram shows that a security realm consists of fundamentally two parts: a set of security providers and a security store. The security store can be either *DBMS*-based or *LDAP*-based, and is used to persist the working data of security providers.

The diagram also conveys that WebLogic Server resources interact with security providers and consume their services, and that enterprise applications and other domain resources may define security policies that are also considered in the context and operation of a realm.

Security Store

The security data store maintains *global security data*, which includes default groups, roles, and policies, and it can also store *custom security data*, meaning the additional groups, roles, and policies that an administrator creates to configure the environment to the unique needs of her organization.

The security store of *myrealm* is an LDAP server, which comes embedded out of the box in Oracle WebLogic Server[3].

The security store is physically hosted in the Administration Server, and is automatically replicated to each managed server at regular configurable intervals.

For the sake of efficiency, WebLogic Server performs write operations on the master copy of the embedded LDAP server, whereas read operations may be performed by managed servers on their locally replicated copies.

Security Providers

The default realm in a WebLogic Server domain comes with a set of configured security providers including the following:

- Authentication

- XACML Authorization

- Identity Assertion

- Credential Mapping

- XACML Role Mapping

- Adjudication

- CertPath

The first two providers may be easily recognized from our review of the fundamental concepts. The remaining providers are either called indirectly, or may be included as dependencies of other providers.

A WebLogic Server realm supports other security providers not included in the default realm configuration, such as *auditing* providers and providers that enable configuration of certificate revocation lists when accepting *x509* certificates as credentials for authentication.

WebLogic Server security providers that integrate with other systems may be also purchased from third parties, or for very particular needs, they can be implemented from scratch.

---

[3]The embedded LDAP server in WebLogic Server supports workloads of up to around 10 thousand objects, with production-like performance.

In the following paragraphs, we review the purpose of the base set of security providers configured in *myrealm*.

Authentication Provider

Processes verification of the identity of a subject, given a set of credentials provided. The default implementation supports authentication using username and password, as well as certificate authentication directly with WebLogic Server instances or with a supported reverse proxy.

An authentication provider contains exactly one *LoginModule*. In an environment where multiple kinds of authentication are required, multiple login modules will be required.

System administrators can organize multiple authentication providers to be called in a specified order.

A WebLogic Server domain always requires the configuration of at least one authentication provider.

XACML Authorization Provider

Controls access to protected resources, making access decisions based on a set of XACML-compliant policies[4]. In order for authorization providers to use a policy when controlling access to a resource, it must have been associated with a resource type[5], or with a specific instance of a resource. Likewise, WebLogic Server resources are not covered by an authorization provider until after a security policy is assigned to them.

A WebLogic Server domain always requires the configuration of at least one authorization provider.

Note   Administrators implicitly create a security policy by associating a WebLogic Server resource with a user, group, or role.

---

[4]XACML stands for eXtensible Access Control Markup Language. It defines a declarative access control policy language that promotes loose coupling between access policies and resources.
[5]Policies defined to protect all instances of a resource type are called *root-level* policies, whereas policies applied directly to resources are called *scoped* policies.

Security Policies

Policies contain one or more conditions that are evaluated by an authorization provider, in order to determine whether to grant or deny access.

Single-condition policies are not uncommon. However, when multiple conditions are defined in a policy, they can be combined using AND & OR operators, and they may also be negated.

The default security providers in WebLogic Server support composing policies using three types of conditions.

The first kind is a basic condition that includes just the name of a role or a principal. The second kind of condition defines a time constraint, based on definitions of *after*, *before* or *between*, in terms of both time and date.

The third kind of condition is application context based. These conditions use information that must be available in requests to applications. Servlet requests, servlet session attributes, as well as EJB method parameters are supported.

Identity Assertion Provider

An identity assertion provider is a specialized form of authentication provider. It validates the identity of a subject using a token. Success in validating a token also involves mapping the token to a username, which may also be assigned principals. Identity assertion providers support for single sign-on using for example SAML tokens and Kerberos.

A WebLogic Server domain does not require the configuration of an identity assertion provider, although configuring more than one is supported.

Credential Mapping Provider

A credential mapping provider performs the association or map of local WebLogic Server credentials, with credentials in a remote system. This association intends that a subject that has been authenticated locally may also be authenticated with a legacy or remote system.

A WebLogic Server domain always requires the configuration of at least one credential mapping provider.

XACML Role Mapping Provider

A XACML role mapping provider supplies an XACML authorization provider with role information that is granted to subjects whose identity has been verified. This information is obtained dynamically from application deployment descriptors or calculated using existing policies and parameters of the current request.

A WebLogic Server domain always requires the configuration of at least one role mapping provider.

Adjudication Provider

An adjudication provider settles a contended access decision, caused by multiple authorization providers disagreeing on whether or not access should be granted to a requesting subject.

Adjudication providers are required in WebLogic Server security realms only when multiple authorization providers have been configured, and only one may be configured.

CertPath Provider

CertPath providers complete certificate paths and validate *x509* certificates[6]. CertPath providers are of two types: CertPath Builders and CertPath Validators. The former perform lookup and validation of a chain of certificates, and the latter perform certificate revocation verification.

Providers in Action

Oracle WebLogic Server administrators experience first hand the security service in action all the time, even when working in a new, apparently empty, domain. When creating a domain, the configuration wizard requires defining credentials for a user that will become a domain administrator by virtue of being granted membership in the administrators group. This username is a subject, and the password defined for it is its credentials, both of which are stored in the embedded LDAP.

Out of the box, a domain includes built-in policies and security providers already configured to authenticate and authorize this first subject as a domain administrator.

---

[6]x509 is the designated name of a standard of public key cryptography.

The Administration Console is also associated by default to security policies in the default realm.

Once an administrator enters a username and password at the login page, the authentication and authorization providers, assisted by a role mapping provider, perform their functions. If the credentials provided are correct, the subject will be authenticated and granted the *admin* role.

The Administration Console is not the only place where the security providers are at work. Every time a user, administrator or not, starts a session, the same general security process is performed.

Custom Security Configuration

The default security realm configuration may be sufficient to protect server resources in many different scenarios. Typically, system administrators will just need to extend the security configuration of the default realm, rather than replace it[7].

Extending the configuration means that an administrator must define additional users, groups, and security roles, as well as create and assign security policies to protect custom domain resources.

A few typical yet useful ways to extend the security configuration of a WebLogic Server domain include:

1. Configure additional security providers, for example to support authentication of subjects in an external LDAP-based identity management infrastructure.

2. Upgrade the security provider store to persist security data in a database management system.

3. Configure an auditing provider to provide a documented trail of administrative actions performed by administrators in a domain.

4. Implement single sign-on with an identity assertion provider, SAML, and Kerberos.

---

[7]WebLogic Server supports creating additional realms, although only one of them may be active. It is a best practice to create a new realm based on the configuration of *myrealm*.

LDAP Integration

The requirement to integrate Oracle WebLogic Server security with a third-party directory service for authentication is quite common, simple to perform, and a good example that demonstrates how the security configuration of a domain can be easily extended to support fairly advanced requirements.

The review in this section will present the general guidelines that must be followed to integrate any WebLogic Server domain with external LDAP directories for authentication purposes.

WebLogic Server includes support for LDAP protocol versions 2 and 3, thus it should be possible to integrate with any directory that conforms to those protocol versions.

Several product-specific LDAP authentication providers are available in all WebLogic Server domains, supporting products such as Oracle Internet Directory, Microsoft Active Directory, and OpenLDAP, among others.

Note   When integrating with an external LDAP directory for authentication, user and group information is still primarily stored in the embedded LDAP.

Configuring an LDAP authentication provider in a WebLogic Server security realm can be performed using the Administration Console or using WLST. Both methods require the following information:

- Defining the order of execution[8] in relation to other providers, and whether authentication with this provider will be optional, required, or sufficient.

- Connection settings, including destination host and port, principal DN[9], and credentials to connect.

- User and group filters including base DNs as well as attributes that identify user and group objects, including whether or not the retrieved user name is used as principal in WebLogic Server.

Despite the fact that LDAP is a standard protocol, most of the information we use when configuring an authentication provider is product specific. To illustrate the

---

[8]Required when the LDAP authentication provider will be configured alongside other providers.
[9]A DN stands for distinguished name, and in the context of LDAP it represents a full search path to a particular LDAP object.

integration, our WebLogic Server sample domain has been integrated with a simple deployment of OpenLDAP version 2.4[10]. Once the provider was selected and given an identifier, the key configuration properties and values were entered as follows:

- Principal: cn=admin,dc=garnica,dc=mx

- User base DN: ou=People,dc=garnica,dc=mx

- User name attribute: cn

- User object class: person

- User filter: (&(cn=%u)(objectclass=person))

- Group base DN: ou=Groups,dc=garnica,dc=mx

- Group object class: groupOfNames

- Group filter: (&(cn=%g)(objectclass=groupOfNames))

This configuration expects that our LDAP schema contains two organizational units, named Users and Groups. These in turn are expected to contain all interesting objects of types *person* and *groupOfNames*. These filters are specified as LDAP search starting points for our lookups.

Our sample LDAP schema comprises two groups and two users. One group is named Administrators with a user named Jane Doe, and another group is named Users containing a user named John Doe.

After entering these details, the authentication provider configuration is complete[11]. By accessing the *Users and Groups* tab in *myrealm* we find that users and groups from OpenLDAP are now available for WebLogic Server as subjects for authentication and authorization.

Figure 15-2 shows user and group identities in our sample implementation, propagated from OpenLDAP to *myrealm* in WebLogic Server.

---

[10]OpenLDAP is a free, open source implementation of the LDAP protocol.

[11]Configuring an LDAP authentication provider is not a dynamic change and therefore requires restarting the Administration Server.

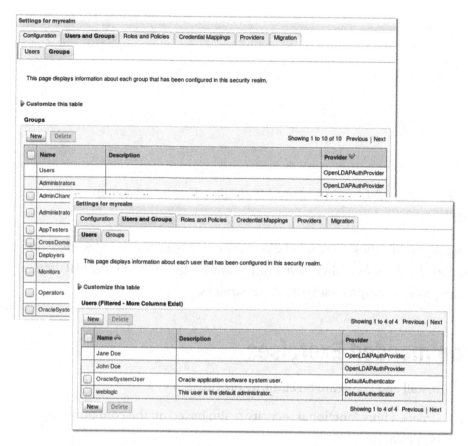

Figure 15-2. *LDAP users and groups in a WebLogic Server security realm*

At this point, the propagated identities are eligible for additional interaction with other security providers. In fact, we created an *Administrator* group in our OpenLDAP schema precisely to illustrate that interaction.

Since a built-in policy states that the system role *admin* is granted to members of a group named *Administrators*, user Jane Doe, who is a member of this group in OpenLDAP, may now log in to the Administration Console and be granted full *admin* privileges.

Figure 15-3 shows our OpenLDAP identity Jane Doe, authorized as a WebLogic Server administrator.

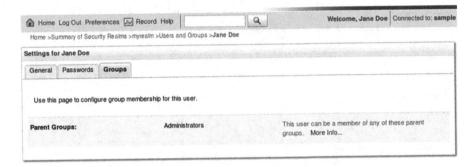

Figure 15-3. *LDAP identity granted WebLogic Server administration privileges*

In scenarios like these, it would be easier for an organization to leverage the propagated identities from their own administrators group in their LDAP directory, rather than maintaining two sets of administrators.

Recommended Exercises

1. Install and configure an auditing provider.

2. Create a fully functional security realm based on the configuration of *myrealm*.

3. Configure a DBM.S-based security store for a security realm

Certification Questions

1. Authorization providers are optional in a security realm.

   a. True

   b. False

2. It is possible to restrict access to an application at certain hours of the day using XACML policies.

   a. True

   b. False

3. Security provider that supports single sign-on using Kerberos:

   a. CertPath provider

   b. Identity assertion provider

   c. Adjudication provider

4. Built-in role in *myrealm* with read-only access to the Administration Console:

   a. Operator

   b. Deployer

   c. Monitor

   d. None of the above

5. Supported repositories for security data:

   a. File system

   b. LDAP

   c. DBMS

   d. All of the above

Coming Up

The next chapter is about upgrading Oracle WebLogic Server domains from the 11g version series to 12c Release 1. It also touches on the requirements and practices to back up a production domain.

CHAPTER 16

Backup and Upgrade

Performing backups and recovering Oracle WebLogic Server environments are really not that different from doing so in other enterprise software environments. If anything, the one critical difference is knowing what to back up precisely. The rest of backup considerations and practices can be borrowed from experience administrating other systems. The same is mostly true about restoring and recovering from backup.

Things are completely specific in upgrading from previous WebLogic Server versions. In the context of WebLogic Server, Oracle specifies exactly what can be upgraded and how. Furthermore, the upgrade process we will cover in this chapter, from WebLogic Server 11g version series to 12c release 1, might be different and incompatible with the process to upgrade to future 12c releases and beyond.

Backup and Recovery

The scope of activities related to backup and recovery that administrators must perform varies greatly, depending on the type and size of organization they are in. Some system administrators may have responsibility to back up all components of an entire solution, including operating system configurations, structured and unstructured data, identity management directories, network services configuration, networking configurations, and so forth. For obvious reasons, this perspective is out of scope of this book.

Our review focuses on the scope of work that administrators are responsible to perform regarding WebLogic Server environments. This is the perspective covered in exam 1Z0-133 and the focus of our review.

Because of their nature, backup and recovery operations are optimally performed when they are automated. Human error is all too frequent, more so when taking backups, which may result in data that is useless to properly restore and recover a system. In large organizations, automating backups may simply mean including

WebLogic Server domains in backup processes that are already set up and performed regularly by enterprise backup systems. In smaller companies, startups perhaps, it may just mean scripting backup operations so that they are performed without user intervention. In any case, automating backups should be a priority.

In addition to automation, there are four fundamental considerations regarding backup and recovery that we will review, these are frequency, integrity, mode, and scope.

Frequency

Backup operations must be performed at regular intervals. However, every organization should determine what the right frequency is for them to perform backup operations, according to their unique needs.

For example, organizations that have addressed all single points of failure in their systems have different needs and options for performing backups than those who are just starting down the road to implement high availability.

The right frequency is always related to risk calculation. The higher the risk, the greater is the need to perform backups more frequently. In transactional systems, for example, restoring today from a backup archive that is a month old will not be enough to recover the system to the required state. Backing up systems frequently is an absolute requirement for production systems.

Integrity

Backup operations bring to mind the question of integrity of backup data. Every time a backup is performed, regardless of the frequency, the resulting backup artifacts must be tested for integrity. Sometimes this may be as simple as calculating hashes of both, source and backup files. Other times it may involve having a third party to pseudo-randomly verify individual files for integrity. In certain scenarios, verifying integrity of backups may be a much more complex process.

Perhaps the ultimate test of integrity is to actually restore from backup, to confirm that the system can be brought back to the desired point in time. It is advisable to perform this level of verification at regular intervals too.

Mode

Backup operations can be performed on a system that is up and running. We call these online backup operations. Obviously, backup operations performed when a system is stopped are referred to as offline backups.

Online backups may result in less consistent backup data than offline backups. This is due to the fact that between the times a backup operation is started and before it is completed, target files may change. One way to overcome this situation is to implement a backup system that logs changes to files as they occur, very similar to the role that t-logs[1] play in WebLogic Server transactions. This would also require a process by which the differences are reconciled. Logs themselves must obviously be included in the backup.

The upside to online backups is that they may be performed without incurring system downtime. If the degree of consistency obtained from an online backup is sufficient, online backups are an excellent choice to preserve system uptime.

Offline backups are found in the opposite extreme. They are consistent but they demand the target system to be taken offline. This can be prohibitive in cases where backup operations take considerable time to execute.

Scope

There are fundamentally two scopes that can be defined to back up a system, full and incremental. Obviously, incremental backups are more efficient but they have a dependency on the integrity and availability of previous backup data. Even in the presence of an incremental backup system, full backups are still needed everywhere though. They should be taken around certain critical events in the life of a system, for example, after a major system upgrade or before a system migration.

WebLogic Server Backups

All four aspects of backup operations just reviewed apply to backups of Oracle WebLogic Server domains but there is no right or wrong approach to any of them. They should all be taken into account when planning and performing backup operations of a WebLogic Server domain.

---

[1]The role of T-logs in WebLogic Server transactions was reviewed in Chapter 13.

Now, in reviewing what specific artifacts should be covered by a WebLogic Server environment backup process, the short answer, definitely expected, is that you must back up every component and configuration that your environment state depends on. This means everything that cannot be replaced by an out-of-the-box component and that is required to restore a system to its desired state.

The long, general answer is that a full WebLogic Server domain backup must include certain parts of *MIDDLEWARE_HOME*[2], all of *DOMAIN_HOME*, as well as application archives and other artifacts, such as deployment plans, which are not kept in the file system structure at either of those paths.

The same is true about other custom configurations that have been made to a domain, for example, the location of file stores and transaction logs. They must be included in a domain backup.

There are important differences between backing up managed servers and backing up the administration server. As explained in previous chapters, managed servers maintain copies of certain information that are centrally kept in the administration server, such as the main domain configuration repository[3] and the contents of the embedded LDAP. Upon starting, managed servers will contact the administration server to obtain a fresh copy of those artifacts. Therefore, it is sufficient to back up managed servers by exporting their configuration using the *pack* command with the *managed* option. One such domain template is required from each remote machine that hosts managed servers.

This approach works better for domains whose servers are configured with DNS names instead of IP addresses in their respective *listen-address* properties. Otherwise, after using the *unpack* command to restore the domain template in a managed host, but before it is started, the original IP address definitions *must* be updated to match the target host.

Oracle WebLogic Server includes an optional, automated option to back up a domain configuration. Figure 16-1 shows this option in the Administration Console.

---

[2]It is not uncommon that organizations choose to back up the entire MIDDLEWARE_HOME as it contains the full product installation directory.

[3]Since the configuration repository is file system based, this means the *config* directory is at the domain root level.

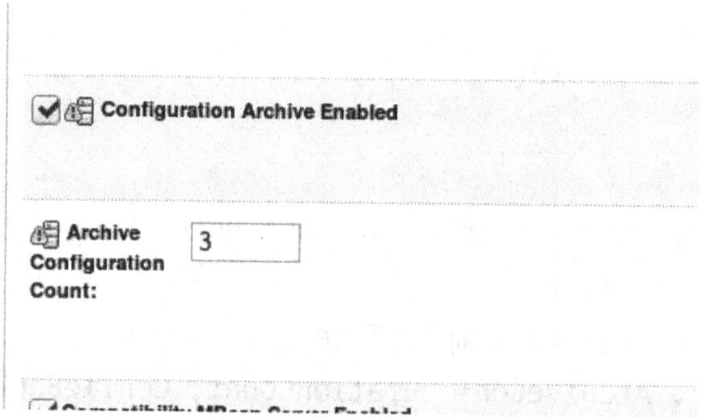

Figure 16-1. *WebLogic Server domain configuration auto-backup option*

The *Configuration Archive Enabled* option is accessible from the domain configuration page, in the *General* tab, under the *Advanced* section. Once enabled, as shown above, it is also possible to define the number of configuration archives to keep.

These two values are also configurable using other methods, by updating the *ConfigBackupEnabled* and *ArchiveConfigurationCount* properties of the *DomainMBean* object. Listing 16-1 shows how to apply this configuration using a WLST online session.

Listing 16-1. Updating WebLogic Server domain configuration backup using WLST

```
wls:/offline> connect('weblogic',###,'127.0.0.1:7001')
Connecting to t3://127.0.0.1:7001 with userid weblogic ...
...
wls:/sample/serverConfig> edit()
...
wls:/sample/edit !> startEdit()
...

wls:/sample/edit !> set('ConfigBackupEnabled',true)
wls:/sample/edit !> set('ArchiveConfigurationCount',3)

wls:/sample/edit !> save()
...
wls:/sample/edit !> validate()
```

```
...
wls:/sample/edit !> activate()
...
```

```
The following non-dynamic attribute(s) have been changed on MBeans
that require server re-start:
MBean Changed : com.bea:Name=sample,Type=Domain
Attributes changed : ArchiveConfigurationCount, ConfigBackupEnabled
Activation completed
```

As shown in this code, the change requires restarting the administration server. When this option is enabled for the first time, every time it starts, the administration server will create two archives, one named *config-original.jar* and another named *config-booted.jar*. As per their names, one will contain the previous or original domain configuration, and the second will contain the configuration that was used to boot the administration server.

Additionally, for each change in domain configuration thereafter, the administration server will create an archive named *config-N.jar* where *N* represents an index, counting up to the number specified by the *ArchiveConfigurationCount* property.

These configuration archives back up the contents of the config directory located at the domain root level, including the master configuration file *config.xml*, applications that were deployed in stage mode, Node Manager encrypted credentials, and system configuration modules such as JDBC data sources. Once generated, the configuration archives are an important asset to include when performing domain backups.

Managed Server Independence

As explained before, backing up the administration server is a very important aspect of WebLogic Server domain backup. Picking up the notion of backup modes discussed in this chapter, stating that in terms of consistency it is better to perform backups in offline mode, Oracle WebLogic Server includes a feature that enables backing up an administration server in offline mode, while all managed servers remain online and unaffected. This feature is called *Managed Server Independence*, and is enabled by default in all managed servers. Figure 16-2 shows this option in the Administration Console.

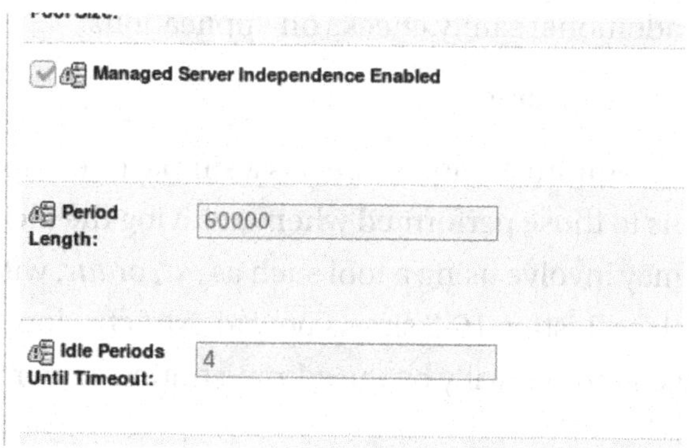

Figure 16-2. *WebLogic Server Managed Server Independence option*

The *Managed Server Independence Enabled* option is accessible in the Administration Console, for each server instance, in the *Configuration* page, under the *Tuning* tab, in the *Advanced* section.

The two additional options, shown in the figure above, define when a managed server instance enters independence mode. The *Period Length* property configures the heartbeat period in milliseconds, which is set at one minute by default. The *Idle Periods Until Timeout* property specifies how many missed heartbeats until the administration server is considered unreachable. This means that by default, managed servers enter independence mode after four minutes.

Once backup operations in offline mode on an administration server are completed, it may be restarted. Once it completes booting, it will contact managed servers and cause them to abandon independence mode.

Recovery

Recovering an Oracle WebLogic Server environment requires several operations. A typical workflow would include the following tasks:

1. Restoring a backup archive

2. Performing sanity checks on the recovered files

3. Starting servers

4. Starting applications in administration mode

5.   Performing additional sanity checks on applications

6.   Enabling access to clients

Restoring archives of administration servers is a simple operation. Often it involves using similar operations to those performed when archiving the files in the first place. For instance, it may involve using a tool such as *jar*, or *tar*, with the appropriate extraction options in place. Listing 16-2 shows how to extract a domain configuration archive that was created automatically by the administration server of our sample domain.

Listing 16-2. Extracting a domain configuration archive

```
[gustavo@apress configArchive]$ pwd
/home/gustavo/apress/lab/domains/sample/configArchive
[gustavo@apress configArchive]$ jar xvf config-1.jar
...
  created: deployments/
 inflated: deployments/readme.txt
  created: deployments/HelloWorld-Web.war/
  created: deployments/HelloWorld.war/
  created: jdbc/
 inflated: jdbc/readme.txt
 inflated: jdbc/SampleDS-9369-jdbc.xml
...
 inflated: config.xml
```

As shown in this code, the jar tool is used with options *xvf*, which mean *extract* a *file* in *verbose* mode. Restoring managed servers involves using the *unpack* tool.

Note   Administrators are responsible to ensure that files are restored to compatible locations in target hosts, and that references in *config.xml* to DNS names or IP addresses are correct.

Initial sanity checks could verify constraints such as whether or not files have the correct user and group ownership, and the correct access rights applied.

Additional sanity checks before opening up applications for client access may involve verifying if connectivity to databases or other remote resources has also been restored.

Upgrade

Upgrading an Oracle WebLogic Server 11g environment *version 10.3.6*[4], to 12c release 1 *version 12.1.x*, fundamentally aims to have newer product binaries run a domain created using a prior version of product binaries.

The process starts by checking that all components required by the target environment are compatible with WebLogic Server 12c. This includes operating system support, JDK version, JDBC access, and so forth, and resolving any conflicts.

Next, administrators install Oracle WebLogic Server 12c release 1 on all target hosts, as they would on a new environment. The rest of this section is focused on upgrading the domain[5], and it involves:

- Using the *Domain Reconfiguration Wizard* to perform the actual upgrade

- Distribute the domain to each managed host in the domain using *pack* and *unpack*

The reconfiguration wizard file *reconfig.sh* in WebLogic Server 12c is available in the same location as the regular configuration wizard, meaning at *MIDDLEWARE_HOME/oracle_common/common/bin*.

The first screen of the reconfiguration process allows selecting the target domain. Advancing to the next step in the process performs the actual domain migration by:

- Reading the domain

- Selecting and applying domain templates

- Validating the upgraded domain

---

[4]Oracle WebLogic Server 11g versions prior to 10.3.6 are not eligible for direct upgrade to 12c. The process for these versions requires patching the *MIDDLEWARE_HOME* to 10.3.6, and running the Domain Upgrade Wizard. The process to upgrade an Oracle WebLogic Server environment to 10.3.6 is out of the scope of this book.

[5]Oracle recommends upgrading non-production environments before attempting to upgrade a production environment.

Figure 16-3 shows the domain migration results screen after running the *Reconfiguration Wizard* on a sample WebLogic Server 11g domain.

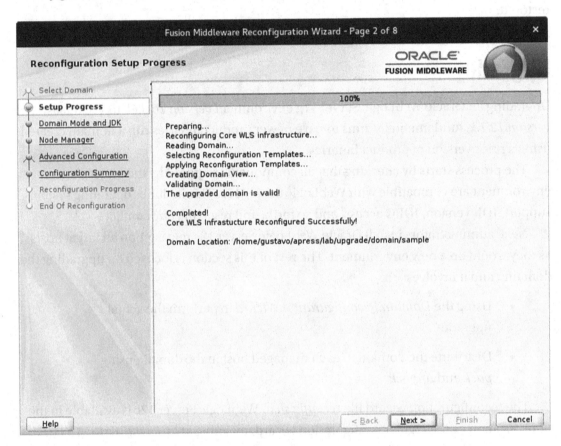

Figure 16-3. *Domain migration results screen in Domain Reconfiguration Wizard*

A subsequent screen, shown in Figure 16-4, enables an administrator to reconfigure Node Manager according to 12c modes and settings.

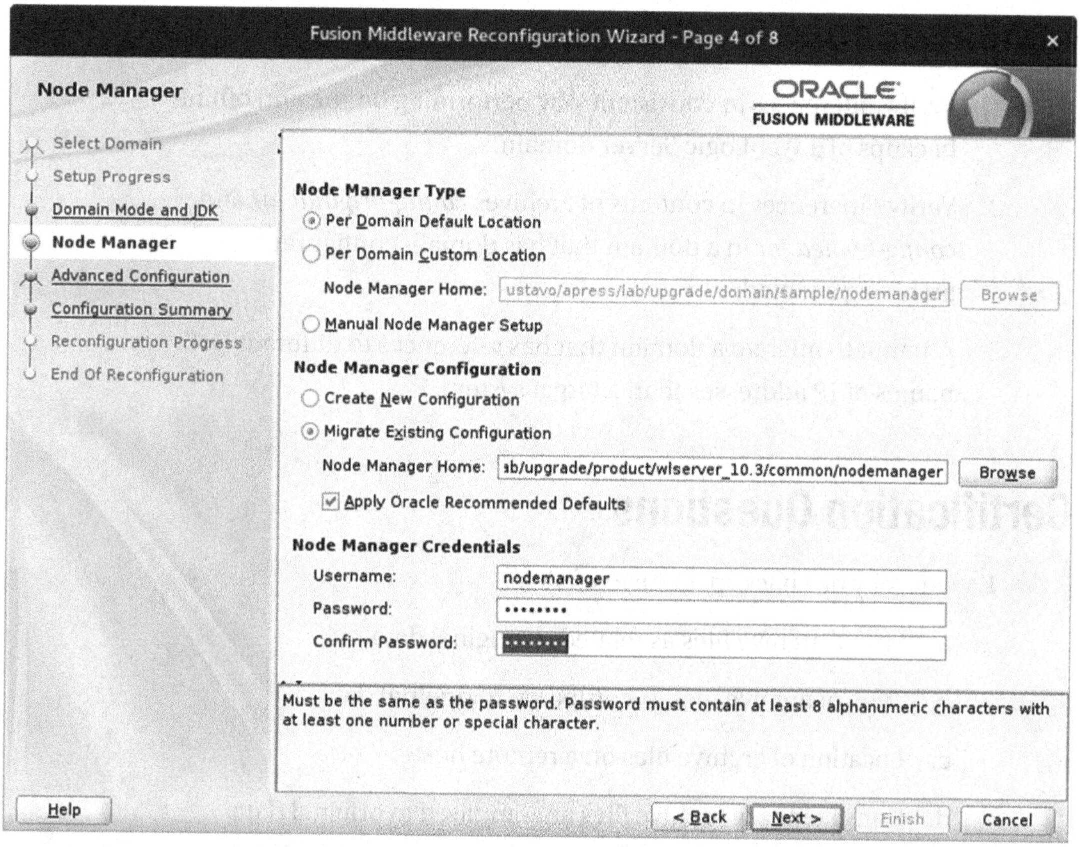

Figure 16-4. *Node Manager configuration in Domain Reconfiguration Wizard*

The screens shown in the previous figures are the core of a migration process when using the *Reconfiguration Wizard*. The remaining screens are entirely optional. They allow an administrator to change configuration settings on domain components, just like when a domain is created for the first time.

At this point, server instances in the domain are ready to be started for final sanity checking, after which the migration process would be complete.

Recommended Exercises

1. Verify differences in consistency by performing online and offline backups of a WebLogic Server domain.

2. Verify differences in contents of archives *config-original.jar* and *config-booted.jar* in a domain that has domain configuration archiving enabled.

3. Attempt to migrate a domain that has references to different DNS names or IP addresses than a target system.

Certification Questions

1. Integrity of a backup archive refers to:

    a. Size of archive files as related to original data

    b. Type of archive files as compared to original data

    c. Location of archive files on a remote host

    d. Consistency of archive files as compared to original data

2. A domain may be recovered from a managed server domain template.

    a. True

    b. False

3. Versions of WebLogic Server 11g eligible for upgrade to WebLogic Server 12c Release 1:

    a. 10.3.5

    b. 10.3.0

    c. All of the above

    d. None of the above

APPENDIX A

Answers to Sample Questions

In this appendix, we list all sample certification questions presented and introduced at the end of each chapter in our book, together with their correct answers.

The sample certification questions are meant to provide first-time test takers with insight into the type and variety of questions in the actual certification exam. These questions are not intended to represent the depth nor breadth of content of the 1Z0-133 certification exam.

Overview

1. Enterprise applications may run directly on top of the Java SE platform.

   a. True

   b. **False**

2. What are the certified Java SE versions to run Oracle WebLogic Server instances?

   a. All the latest

   b. Java SE 7 only

   c. Java SE 6 only

   d. **Java SE 6 and 7**

   e. Any

© Gustavo Garnica 2018
G. Garnica, *Oracle WebLogic Server 12c Administration I Exam 1Z0-133*,
https://doi.org/10.1007/978-1-4842-2562-2_17

3. What fundamental component of the Java EE architecture is provided by an application server?

    a. The virtual machine

    b. **The runtime environment**

    c. The database drivers

    d. The Management Console

    e. None of the above

4. Provides support for creating Web Service clients and endpoints using a REST architectural style:

    a. JAXP

    b. JAX-WS

    c. JMX

    d. All of the above

    e. **None of the above**

5. What edition of WebLogic Server should I license if I intend to use the Oracle JVM profiling tools?

    a. WebLogic Server Standard Edition

    b. **WebLogic Server Enterprise Edition**

    c. **WebLogic Server Suite**

    d. All of the above

    e. None of the above

Installation and Updates

1. Select the operating systems certified to run WebLogic Server 12c in production environments:

    a. **Red Hat Linux 7**

    b. Ubuntu Linux 14.04

c.   Microsoft Windows 7

d.   **Mac OS 10.5**

e.   Oracle Solaris 11

2.   Select the product distribution types supported to run WebLogic
     Server in production environments:

a.   Physical media

b.   **WebLogic Server JAR file**

c.   **Middleware Infrastructure JAR file**

d.   ZIP distributions

e.   All of the above

3.   Select the option that lists the correct components of the standard
     installation topology:

a.   One administration server, one managed server, one machine,
     one domain

b.   Two administration servers, two managed servers, two
     machines, one domain

c.   One administration server, one cluster, two managed servers,
     one machine, one domain

d.   **None of the above**

e.   All of the above

4.   Select all of the supported installation methods:

a.   **Graphic**

b.   Console

c.   **Silent**

d.   Remote

e.   Local

5. Select the required command to apply a security patch:

    a. bsu -install

    b. bsu -apply

    c. opatch install

    d. **opatch apply**

    e. opatch secure

Domains

1. How many servers can be designated as administration servers in a domain?

    a. **One and only one**

    b. More than one

    c. Two

    d. Any

2. Each managed server in a domain requires its own product installation to run.

    a. True

    b. **False**

3. Is it possible to run more than one domain in a single host?

    a. **True**

    b. False

4. What format is used to persist the domain configuration?

    a. A database schema

    b. **A set of XML files**

    c. In-memory

5. Select the tools that enable domain configuration and customization:

    a. **The configuration wizard**

    b. **The administration console**

    c. **WLST**

    d. The pack and unpack commands

    e. All of the above

Node Manager

1. What are the two Node Manager implementations available on WebLogic Server 12c?

    a. **Java-based and script-based**

    b. Java-based and Windows-based

    c. Windows-based and UNIX/Linux-based

    d. Java-based and Bash-based

2. WebLogic Server Node Manager can control server instances in more than one domain.

    a. **True**

    b. False

3. Select the supported options to secure Node Manager traffic:

    a. **One-way SSL**

    b. **Two-way SSL**

    c. Passphrase

    d. SSH

    e. All of the above

4. Node Manager is capable of automatically restarting any WebLogic Server instance.

    a. **True**

    b. False

5. What is the WLST command to configure Node Manager on multiple WebLogic Server machines?

    a. configure()

    b. createConfig()

    c. nmAuthorize()

    d. **nmEnroll()**

Servers

1. A server instance may be started using several commands.

    a. **True**

    b. False

2. What is the name of the standard script to start a managed server instance?

    a. startServer

    b. startWebLogic

    c. **startManagedServer**

    d. startManagedWebLogic

3. Which script sources the setUserOverrides script to apply configuration customizations?

    a. **setDomainEnv**

    b. startWebLogic

    c. startServer

    d. None of the above

4. Oracle WebLogic Server provides standard server start scripts for each supported platform.

   a. **True**

   b. False

5. What is the correct method to add a library to a server instance configuration?

   a. The PATH

   b. **The CLASSPATH**

   c. A system property

   d. All of the above

Configuration Management

1. The edit lock on acquired on a WLST session is released automatically when closing the session.

   a. True

   b. **False**

2. What is the group in the WebLogic Server security realm that effectively has read-only access to the Administration Console?

   a. Readers

   b. **Monitors**

   c. Watchers

   d. All of the above

3. What types of configuration changes may be reverted in a WebLogic Server domain?

   a. **Saved**

   b. Activated

   c. None

   d. All

4. What are the arguments to the encrypt() method to create encrypted byte arrays in WLST?

    a. String to encrypt

    b. String to encrypt, encryption algorithm

    c. String to encrypt, property to update

    d. **String to encrypt, domain path**

    e. None of the above

5. It is possible to automate all types of domain configuration changes using WLST.

    a. **True**

    b. False

Logging and Monitoring

1. It is possible to define a custom log message severity.

    a. **True**

    b. False

2. What type of Java object distributes log messages to a destination?

    a. Logger

    b. Log4J

    c. **Handler**

    d. All of the above

3. It is possible for applications to send custom log messages to the server log file.

    a. **True**

    b. False

4. WebLogic Server can report information about operating system users logged in the system.

   a. **True**

   b. False

5. Contains statistical information about the number of threads allocated:

   a. Channels

   b. Performance

   c. **Workload**

   d. None of the above

Networking

1. Select all protocols supported by the default secure channel:

   a. **HTTPS**

   b. **T3S**

   c. SNMP

   d. Cluster-broadcast-secure

   e. All of the above

2. What objects store the default network channels configuration?

   a. NetworkAccessPointMBean

   b. **ServerMBean**

   c. ConfigurationMBean

   d. SocketMBean

   e. None of the above

3. Select all required properties to configure a cluster replication channel:

   a. Tunneling

   b. HTTP Enabled

   c. **Outbound**

   d. External listen address

   e. External port

4. It is possible to configure two network channels using the same listen address and port number as long as:

   a. They both support secure protocols

   b. **They both support different protocols**

   c. They both support the same protocols

   d. It is not possible

   e. All of the above

5. When no listen address has been specified in any network channel, the following occurs:

   a. Server instances fail to start

   b. Server instances bind to localhost and loopback

   c. **Server instances bind to all IP addresses available in the host**

   d. A network channel is automatically created using the host IP address

   e. None of the above

Cluster Basics

1. Select the web servers supported by WebLogic Server to provide the web tier:

   a. Apache HTTP Server

   b. Oracle HTTP Server

   c. Microsoft IIS

   d. **All of the above**

2. What is the name of a proprietary header in the WebLogic Server plug-in?

   a. True-Client-IP

   b. **WL-Proxy-Client-IP**

   c. WL-Client-Proxy

   d. None of the above

3. Name the two fundamental benefits of WebLogic Server clusters:

   a. Reliability and robustness

   b. Scalability and resilience

   c. **Load balancing and failover**

   d. Capacity and performance

4. What is the main benefit of having the Oracle WebLogic Server plug-in in the web tier?

   a. **Ability to recognize failed members**

   b. Licensing

   c. Compatibility

   d. Flexibility

5. Select all features of dynamic servers:

    a. Require OS virtualization

    b. **Enable a domain to scale out**

    c. Enable server instances to scale up

    d. All of the above

Clusters Advanced

1. Cluster communication occurs at the following TCP/IP network layer:

    a. Network

    b. **Transport**

    c. Application

    d. None of the above

2. Select the protocols that WebLogic Server uses to replicate cluster status information:

    a. IP

    b. **TCP**

    c. **UDP**

    d. All of the above

3. What is the default cluster messaging mode in WebLogic Server 12c?

    a. **Unicast**

    b. Multicast

    c. None of the above

4. A cluster member will be considered failed using unicast after how many consecutive missed heartbeats:

   a. One

   b. Two

   c. Three

   d. **None of the above**

5. Select all prerequisites for using multicast for cluster messaging:

   a. **Network support**

   b. **Address and port number**

   c. Native IO

   d. All of the above

Clusters Proxies

1. WebLogic Server replicates session information stored in:

   a. Database

   b. File system

   c. **HTTPSession objects**

   d. Coherence*Web

2. Durable session persistence mechanism:

   a. In-memory

   b. Replicated

   c. **JDBC**

   d. **File**

3. Load-balancing algorithms supported by the WebLogic Server plug-in:

   a. **Round-robin**

   b. Weighted

   c. Sticky

   d. All of the above

   e. None of the above

4. Methods to improve session replication performance:

   a. Database

   b. **Asynchronous replication**

   c. File system

   d. **Session cache**

5. HTTP session configuration data is stored in:

   a. **weblogic.xml**

   b. web.xml

   c. wl_servlet_sessions

   d. None of the above

JDBC

1. JDBC drivers translate SQL sentences to native data store calls.

   a. **True**

   b. False

2. Type of a pure Java JDBC driver:

   a. Type 2

   b. **Type 4**

   c. None of the above

   d. All of the above

3. Language or notation in which data source configuration is stored in WebLogic Server:

    a. Java

    b. JSON

    c. **XML**

    d. Any of the above

4. Load balancing in multi data sources is restricted to round-robin.

    a. **True**

    b. False

Transactions

1. WebLogic Server supports XA+ protocol version 2.

    a. **True**

    b. False

2. Resource managers may take part in prepare phase and be absent in commit phase of a distributed transaction.

    a. **True**

    b. False

3. XA interfaces implemented in JTA are high-level interfaces, available to applications:

    a. All of them are

    b. None of them are

    c. **Some of them are**

4. Property that limits the maximum time allowed for a transaction to remain in commit phase:

   a. Timeout seconds

   b. Abandon timeout seconds

   c. **Maximum duration of XA calls**

Application Deployment

1. WebLogic Server application deployment supports scripted automations using a variety of tools.

   a. **True**

   b. False

2. WebLogic Server supports zero downtime redeployment of all types of applications.

   a. True

   b. **False**

3. Redeployment mode that replaces class loaders immediately:

   a. Production redeployment

   b. **In-place redeployment**

   c. Both of them

4. It is possible to undeploy an application while allowing existing sessions to complete gracefully.

   a. **True**

   b. False

Security

1. Authorization providers are optional in a security realm.

   a. True

   b. **False**

2. It is possible to restrict access to an application at certain hours of the day using XACML policies.

   a. **True**

   b. False

3. Security provider that supports single sign-on using Kerberos:

   a. CertPath provider

   b. **Identity assertion provider**

   c. Adjudication provider

4. Built-in role in *myrealm* with read-only access to the Administration Console:

   a. Operator

   b. Deployer

   c. **Monitor**

   d. None of the above

5. Supported repositories for security data:

   a. File system

   b. **LDAP**

   c. **DBMS**

   d. All of the above

Backup and Upgrade

1. Integrity of a backup archive refers to:

    a. Size of archive files as related to original data

    b. Type of archive files as compared to original data

    c. Location of archive files on a remote host

    d. **Consistency of archive files as compared to original data**

2. A domain may be recovered from a managed server domain template.

    a. True

    b. **False**

3. Versions of WebLogic Server 11g eligible for upgrade to WebLogic Server 12c Release 1:

    a. 10.3.5

    b. 10.3.0

    c. All of the above

    d. **None of the above**

Index

© Gustavo Garnica 2018
G. Garnica, *Oracle WebLogic Server 12c Administration I Exam 1Z0-133*,
https://doi.org/10.1007/978-1-4842-2562-2

D

Get the eBook for only $5!

Why limit yourself?

With most of our titles available in both PDF and ePUB format, you can access your content wherever and however you wish—on your PC, phone, tablet, or reader.

Since you've purchased this print book, we are happy to offer you the eBook for just $5.

To learn more, go to http://www.apress.com/companion or contact support@apress.com.

Apress®

Printed in the United States
By Bookmasters